Afghanistan With Love

Ijeoma Ozed Williams

Copyright © 2021 **FOTT Banner Books**

All rights reserved. No part of this publication may be reproduced, distributed, or transmitted in any form or by any means, including photocopying, recording, or other electronic or mechanical methods, without the prior written permission of the publisher, except in the case of brief quotations embodied in critical reviews and certain other noncommercial uses permitted by copyright law. For permission requests, write to the publisher, addressed "Attention: Book Rights and Permission," at the address below.

Published in the United States of America
ISBN 978-1-955243-31-5 (SC)

FOTT Banner Books
P.O. Box 213,
Linthicum, MD 21090, U.S.A.
icozedwilliams@gmail.com

Order Information and Rights Permission:

Quantity sales. Special discounts might be available on quantity purchases by corporations, associations, and others. For details, contact the publisher at the address above.

For Book Rights Adaptation and other Rights Permission. Call us at toll-free 1-888-945-8513 or send us an email at admin@stellarliterary.com.

DISCLAIMER

Although the towns, cities, and countries mentioned in this book are real, and some of the catastrophe described were current affairs at the time they happened, the characters and other events are fictitious and merely from the author's imagination. Any resemblance to anyone living or dead is purely coincidental.

Ijeoma Ozed-Williams

Contents

PROLOGUE i
PART 1 6
CHAPTER 1 7
    THIRTY MONTHS 13
    EARLIER 13
CHAPTER 2 29
CHAPTER 3 38
CHAPTER 4 51
CHAPTER 5 58
CHAPTER 6 65
CHAPTER 7 73
CHAPTER 8 85
CHAPTER 9 94
PART 2 102
CHAPTER 1 103
CHAPTER 2 112
CHAPTER 3 123
CHAPTER 4 133
CHAPTER 5 145
CHAPTER 6 156
CHAPTER 7 165
CHAPTER 8 176
CHAPTER 9 187
PART 3 198
CHAPTER 1 199

CHAPTER 2	206
CHAPTER 3	212
CHAPTER 4	219
CHAPTER 5	226
CHAPTER 6	236
CHAPTER 7	248
CHAPTER 8	257
CHAPTER 9	272
CHAPTER 10	282
CHAPTER 11	289
SHORT STORIES BY IJEOMA OZED-WILLIAMS	301
CHAPTER 12	302
CHAPTER 13	309
CHAPTER 14	317
CHAPTER 15	326
CHAPTER 16	332
CHAPTER 17	341
CHAPTER 18	351
EPILOGUE	357
GLOSSARY OF UNFAMILIAR WORDS	363
SUGGESTED TOPICS FOR READING GROUPS	365
ALSO BY THE SAME AUTHOR	370

PROLOGUE

The official name of the mountain was Lor Koh. The natives called it Sharafat Koh (Honor Mountain). The natives knew it as a refuge from pursuing enemies. Their enemies knew that once they got to these mountains, not only did it become difficult to hunt them out, but they also actually went on the offensive. The mountain was like a protective mother who allowed her children hide behind her skirts.

But when the enemies became brothers fighting against brothers, who then should the Mountain Mother protect? Hiding amongst the peaks and crags, they launched offensives against one another, committed atrocities against one another, and even against the mountain herself. They endured, they survived, and they avenged. Finally, the Taliban stepped in to restore some sort of order. They tried to unite the people by something they had in common, their religion. Who could argue against God? "Let us live according to the dictates of God" they said. "Let us precisely follow the Holy Book!"

It seemed to work for some time but then things began to happen. The saviors became the oppressors. The peacemakers became the perpetrators of injustice. Other oppressive elements from all over the world came to shelter among the oppressive oppressors because all seemed lawless. They felt they could more easily hide their evil. Things escalated until the attention of outsiders was drawn again. Some American marines were sent to investigate. "Only look, observe, and see but try not to be seen yourselves" they were told. "Do nothing at all, unless it is extremely unavoidable".

And so, in 1998 four of them, young officers in their mid-twenties, found themselves among the crags of Lor Koh. The mountain did not do anything to them. Maybe the mountain knew they had no bad intentions towards her children. She was actually protective of them and hid them well while they tried to carry out their mission. From the mountain they watched beautiful sunrises, spectacular sunsets, and breathed fresh air, free from pollution. One evening, they found themselves near a hollow under some rocks. It was a natural cave with another rock standing right in front of it. It was a good hiding place. They decided it was also a good place to bivouac. They set up a scope to scout out the land, and took turns keeping watch. The night was quiet and uneventful.

Alex was on the last watch. He was handsome and tall with a noble head of blond curls, piercing blue eyes over a hawkish nose, and a heart full of adventure. He was looking forward to the beautiful wash of colors that painted the sky as the sun rose. Suddenly he felt the ground shaking with the pounding of hooves. He sat up. He felt his colleagues come alert at the same moment. On top of the mountain to their right came a figure on a horse riding very hard towards them. Just before it reached their hiding place, the horse veered to the left and kept going. By the beardless face, and the mass of reddish-brown hair flying behind like a defiant banner, they deduced that the rider was probably a woman.

About six horsemen rode in pursuit hard at her heels. Although she was very fast, they were not making real efforts to gain on her. The Americans watching from their hiding place willed her to move faster and outstrip them. Suddenly she literally flew off the horse and landed a few feet below them. She lay there immobile. She was probably stunned, unconscious, or even dead. The horse righted its gait and went a bit further before stopping. It was a well-known trick. There must have been a nearly invisible rope stretched across the path which the rider had not seen. No wonder her pursuers were not making more serious efforts to catch up with her. They knew they could pick her up easily after she fell.

As the Americans continued to watch, the horsemen came up and surrounded her. They came down from their own horses and just sat around until she groaned and started coming to. She looked very young and had defiant, flashing green eyes. She must have known what was in stock for her; but her immediate reaction was anger at her tormentors. She was probably also angry at herself for having fallen to their trick. The Americans could not understand the words the men were saying to her. However, they could well imagine what they were. She stared at them defiantly and challengingly. She was not verbally replying to their taunts and threats, but her expressions were eloquent. There was no visible display of her fears even though she was very obviously outnumbered.

The tormenting riders moved about resolutely. They tied her hands and feet together as they got ready for whatever they had in mind for her. Alex could no longer bear the injustice of it all. He took a step forward and his commander shook his head almost imperceptibly. Alex either did not see or chose not to heed this restraining gesture. He ran a short distance up the hill, towards the direction the girl and her pursuers had come from. Crooking his arm in the habit of one well practiced in playing baseball, he tossed a grenade as far as it would go. He then hurried back into the hollow a little less than a minute before the grenade exploded. The noise was magnified in the early morning quiet by the mountain echoes.

Immediately, the men tormenting the girl froze for a moment and listened. They dived for cover under the spare bushes. Cautiously, they began to crawl towards the distracting explosion, neglecting their prisoner. They were apparently also confident in the bonds which now held her hands and feet. As soon as they left, Alex was beside her in one bound. He cut her bonds with two slashes of his army issue knife, rubbing her ankles and wrists briefly to help the return of circulation. He spoke as he worked. "Now Princess, you probably don't understand a word I'm saying but this is your lucky day. I don't know who you are, but I hope for God's sake you know what to do. Try very hard not to mention anything about us in return for this favor. Now make good use of your chances and run for your life. Good luck!"

As soon as she got up, she flashed him one green-eyed look and then peered closely at his name tag. To his astonishment she said with a sweet and low musical voice, "Thanks Mr. Pearson. I understand you perfectly, and I owe you my life. I hope I shall return the favor one day."

Alex turned towards their hiding place, but his company was already moving across the mountain, ninety degrees to where the drama had just taken place. They crossed to the opposite side of their former hiding place, found another hollow behind some dwarf shrubs and set up their scope again. "What on earth…" Alex exclaimed when he looked through the scope.

The other men nudged him out of place so they too could take a look. They reacted with emotions ranging from bemusement to amusement. The girl whom Alex had just risked their cover to liberate had not bounded away as he had told her to, and as was plainly the logical thing to do. She was calmly rounding up the horses of the men who had been pursuing her. She tied them one to another. When she was good and done, she mounted the lead horse. Before she turned and canted off with all the horses, she first turned and childishly thumbed her nose at her returning pursuers.

"A very strategic planner with an astute mind" remarked the American squad leader, with genuine admiration. "She has accomplished several things including covering up your tracks, Alex. By letting her captors see her get away, they will not have to search the area closely, and accidentally discover our presence. By taking their horses, they must either pursue her on foot or go back for fresh horses. They do not know if she has accomplices, so they dare not fire at her and draw attention to their position. She will be a formidable opponent in war. Afghan women usually are. That girl is someone I would really love as an ally, and hate as an opponent in battle."

Part 1

CHAPTER 1

---∞---

The week started normally enough for Greta, Laura, and Lil. They had truncated their lessons with Ayesha because they felt they were quite proficient in their language and culture studies. Besides, they had quite a busy week ahead. They hurried through their office work on Monday morning. By the time their UNESCO driver arrived they were all packed, and ready to go. They each threw their light travelling bags into the back, and piled into the middle seat of the truck. The bed of the truck held supplies which would be dropped off at schools along the way. Laura got in and sat directly behind the driver with Lil next to her. Greta hurried to give the key to their apartment to Ayesha calling out, "See you on Thursday". She got in from the other side and slammed the door. Lil was sandwiched between Greta and Laura. This was their usual seating arrangement when all three were travelling together. The driver sat alone in front. His own travel supplies, important papers, and documents rode shotgun.

The major road in Afghanistan was Highway 1, also known as The Ring Road. This road almost encircles the country, starting from Mazar-il-Sharif in the north, through Kabul to Ghozni, coming down south, through Qandahar in the southeast and going northwest to Farah and Herat. Major extensions ran off it to major cities like Jalalabad, Lashkar Gah, Delaram, and so on. As part of their contribution towards the efforts of rebuilding war-torn Afghanistan, the Indian

Government had undertaken to rebuild the international road extending from Delaram to Zaranj. The Taliban said this was a ploy to re-establish the old silk and spice road which had in time past been used to drain the ores and other natural resources found in Afghanistan. Consequently, they kept trying to upstage the project. In truth, the road opened up the landlocked country for international trade in that region. It also created a shortcut to the Iranian town of Zabol, and to the Persian Gulf port of Chabahar. This effectively cut off the more treacherous route through Pakistan. Despite several bombings and the wanton loss of human lives, the construction went on.

Road travel in Afghanistan could be a nightmare. With decades of warfare, landmines, time, and erosion, roads which had once been tolerable were now rutted due to non-maintenance. As long as one stayed on the major highways, the trip itself could be safe and enjoyable. Once off the highways though, the roads became narrow, full of ruts, and sometimes nonexistent. A road trip then became a nightmare. The trick was to stay on the highway for as long as possible and turn in at a spot closest to where one was going. This was the formula the UNESCO drivers had always followed.

The second reason for the treachery on the highways of Afghanistan was the presence of bandits, and sometimes the militia. There were roadblocks every few miles. Some of these were manned by the International Security Assistance Force – ISAF. ISAF was a coalition in which the allied forces were training the newly revamped Afghan police force. Some roadblocks were by the allied forces themselves. Some were by the local vigilante of that particular village or hamlet. Some roadblocks were mounted by ordinary bandits, and some by the Taliban. If the men were in uniform, the likelihood would be that the roadblock was somehow legitimate, and at least relatively safe. Non-uniformed people might be the local vigilante but more often than not, were bandits or the Taliban.

So far, Greta, Laura, and Lil had come across several roadblocks but were yet to come across an unsafe one. Their various drivers usually told them things like "Three of you must have very lucky streaks. You have not come across even one unfriendly roadblock. It is also evidence that our country is getting better. Before now, it would have been a daily or at least a weekly occurrence."

The only complaint the ladies had about roadblocks was that it rather delayed their progress and messed up their time schedules. On this trip, they had in mind to visit villages within three districts in the Nimruz province. Starting from Khash Rod, they hoped to pass westwards to Chakhansur, turn southwards to Chahar Burja, and then make their leisurely way back to Lashkar Gah. Everything went well. They inspected fledgling schools, delivered packages to needy schools, held shura to persuade some villages and hamlets to let them help by setting up schools, renovating schools, or enrolling their children, especially the girls in schools. They generally felt they had made a good outing. By two o'clock on Wednesday afternoon they had visited everywhere they intended to, and done everything they had set out to do.

"You know, if we set out now, we could be home before it is too late tonight" Greta said.

"Oh yes, and then we could add another chapter to our experience to reflect night travel in Afghanistan" Lil said. "If any tragedy should befall us on the way, people will only remember and talk about how foolhardy we were."

"Do you know, from where we are now, if we hit the Zaranj-Delaram road we could actually get to Farah long before it is dark. We could get there much earlier than we would have reached Lashkar Gah" Laura commented.

"And then tomorrow we will take the long route home?" Lil asked.

"It would probably be longer in terms of distance, but the journey will be smoother and faster because we would be driving on Highway 1 practically all the way" Laura answered with a wistful look.

"I told you that girl is in love. Don't for one moment assume she has no ulterior motive for wanting to go to Farah" Greta said.

"Anyway, that is totally out of the question. We are expected at Kadesh tonight. Our hosts would worry if we don't show up on time" Lil concluded.

In the early afternoon, the air was hot and oppressive except for air current generated by the movement of the truck. They rolled down their windows partway. The desired air current proceeded to immediately whip off their scarves and scatter their hair but they did not mind it a bit. They sat back to enjoy the rest of the day with the pleasant satisfaction of great accomplishment. For some time, there was silence as they watched the scenery sliding past them. This part of Afghanistan was very easy on the eyes. They passed fields of wheat as often as they passed poppy fields, broken infrequently, and at long intervals by lone houses or hamlets.

In Afghan villages, people generally lived communally in compounds. A compound would be made up of several rooms around a central courtyard. There would be another inner courtyard at the back, secluded from visitors. Women did their cooking and other womanly chores together in this inner courtyard. A compound would house several generations of a family, related by birth or marriage, and ruled over by the oldest person alive. They remarked again on how Afghan culture resembled what they had in the west in the distant past but differed from their modern culture of individual isolation. "There are undoubtedly lots of merits in this kind of communal living" Lil said. "However, as much as I greatly admire my mother-in-law to-be, I cannot imagine her having an eye on my daily affairs or looking closely into what I do with her son. Having Bjorn move in with my family would probably be worse. It would wear all our nerves out in no time."

Greta and Laura agreed, although Laura now had no family to speak of. If she had, she would rather have them nearby, visiting occasionally like Katie's, not living right under the same roof, all the time. "I would prefer for them to be living very far away, in another city or preferably another continent" Greta said. "I know that every man eventually longs for his mother. If I ever decide to get married, I'll make sure I have no in-laws alive!"

Their driver, Aziz who was usually quite reticent, joined the discussion. He pointed out the advantages of this kind of arrangement. "Do you know how much money could be spared from such an arrangement? All the money made could come back into the family instead of going into paying rents to an outsider. Tradition, culture, and respect for elders would be transmitted directly from the older generation to the growing one. It will bypass the middle generation which is always so busy and muddled up anyway. "Think also of the security. You will know your youngsters are always safe at home, being cared for by older adults who have their best interests at heart! I could go on."

Aziz lamented the fact that urbanization had broken this system down to a large extent so that urban dwellers had lost a lot of these advantages.

The discussion was getting interesting when Aziz suddenly let out an expletive which was totally uncharacteristic of him.

"What?" asked Greta.

"What is it?" asked Laura.

"What's happening?" asked Lil.

They peered through the windshield.

The reason for the driver's distress was apparent. There, up ahead, was a roadblock. The barricade was almost total. It was formed with a tree trunk and other rubbles. The men minding the roadblock were not in any form of uniform! All the ones they could see, and they counted up to six, were toting machine guns. Their heads and faces were hidden in kaffiyeh (scarves). That alone meant trouble. On either side of the road were cultivated fields with tall plants waving in the afternoon breeze. The plants were high enough to hide any number of people. It would not be very wise to make a run for it even if they could. The last hamlet they passed was some distance back. No other vehicle seemed to be on that particular stretch of road at the moment. Maybe nemesis had finally caught up with them.

Greta tried to wind up the glass on her side but Aziz stopped her with a word as he came slowly to a stop at the barricade, engine still running. "Try not to appear menacing. This is the time to look as helpless as possible. We will throw ourselves at their mercies," he said from the corner of his mouth. And then he added "Please adjust your veils."

They had already automatically adjusted their veils even before the truck began to slow down. Two of the men approached. Aziz greeted them, "Salaam Alekheim." They did not bother to return the greeting. The taller of the two bent down and looked into the truck as if doing a head count. He straightened up, beckoned to two other men who approached the vehicle from inside the fields. Laura noted that it was a good thing they had not decided to make a run for it into the fields. Who knew how many more people were hiding there? The second set of men had their own guns slung to their backs. When they came nearer Laura saw they had some sort of black devices in their hands. They did something funny with their wrists, and Laura felt a sting at the side of her neck. As she raised her hand to rub the spot, she saw that Greta and Lil were mirroring her movements. For that matter, so was the driver. Before she could ponder this clearly, she felt her head go woozy. The front seat floated up towards her, or was she floating above the ceiling of the truck? That was the last thought she had before her vision blacked out and she became unconscious.

The tall man moved the unconscious form of the driver over to the passenger's side and slid into the driver's seat himself. He drove off down the road in the same direction the UNESCO party had been travelling. Even as he approached, other men began to totally dismantle the barricade. In a few short minutes nobody would have guessed that anything happened there. Everyone else then melted away into the fields.

The tall man drove the UNESCO truck a few miles down the road and then veered off into the first turn on the left. Two other trucks were waiting there with their drivers. Together the two men unceremoniously transferred the women to the bed of the second truck, and covered the bed with a tarp, effectively hiding them from sight. They carried poor Aziz into the poppy farm at the side of the road and dumped him in a hollow, well hidden from the road.

Getting back to the UNESCO truck again, they proceeded to strip it of anything which could be moved including the women's and the driver's personal effects, documents, the satellite radios, leftover educational packages, the car rugs, carpets, the spare tire, the tool kit, and every other movable object. They opened the bonnet, removed the battery, distribution cable, the fuse box, and a few other things. Last of all, they moved some roughly even stones under the car. Jacking it up, they removed all the tires and their rims. These men were obviously very knowledgeable about these things. They were very competent, organized, and efficient. In about twenty minutes they were done. Anyone wanting to move that vehicle again would need to do some major refitting first. They piled all the car parts into the second waiting truck. Driving after the one with the women, they drove along the byroad, circled, and came back to the major road the UNESCO team had been travelling, and headed in the opposite direction. They encountered no other vehicles.

The operation had taken about thirty minutes from start to finish. Ironically, it had taken Laura about thirty months to reach this point in time.

THIRTY MONTHS EARLIER

Laura found herself alone in the small house she had shared with her grandmother for over a decade. This was the first time in her memory that she had ever spent New Year's Eve alone. For as long as she could remember, if she was not at one boisterous party or making the round of parties, she was with friends or family. Even on this very day, if she had wanted, she could have taken advantage of a number of invitations but she had managed to evade them all, even that of her closest friend, Katie; and Katie could be persistent and tenacious when she chose to be. Laura had been adamant that she was indeed not suicidal, and that her choosing to be alone on this festive day had healthy connotations. Even Katie knew when to back off. "Okay, I will call you every once in a while, to know how you're doing. Just pick up the phone, ask me how the night is going, and respond to my questions so I'll be sure I am not dealing with your machine. If you don't, I'll have no other choice than to bring the party to you. Believe me, these people know how to do Party, Plus" she threatened.

Laura agreed, and Katie had let it drop – for then.

2005 had been a very trying year for Laura. In that year she had lost and mourned for three people, the last remaining member of her family, a potential life mate, and a best friend. She wanted to be alone to take a good hard look at her life. Was there something wrong with her or was she just plain unlucky? She counted her blessings and stacked them against her woes. She was not entirely sure she had anything left over on either side. On the blessing side, she counted the fact that she was alive and healthy; she had a good job and some financial asset, thanks to her grandmother and some shrewd personal investments. She still had some close friends like Katie who cared about how she was coping. She counted herself lucky indeed for those. Some people would also have counted her looks among her assets but Laura was not one to think often about her looks. With her big, beautiful, and expressive, green eyes set in a small oval face, and crowned with beautiful rich auburn hair, she was quite a looker. At five and a half feet, she was taller than many women but still managed to look petite and feminine enough to project an air of fragility that made men want to protect her.

On the downside was the fact that even though she had all these good things going, she could find no pleasure at all in them. She felt totally lost and cast adrift. She had received several job offers after her Master's in Business Administration but she had chosen to stay back in Memphis with her frail and aging grandmother. It was not just a sense of duty and gratitude; it was a seeking after belonging. When she was fifteen years old, her parents had died in a car crash. Laura and her grandmother found themselves totally alone in the whole world. They had formed a bond which they did not have before that event. This bond had grown stronger over the years. Beyond some terrible arthritis, a thyroid problem, and after two strokes she believed her grandmother just hung on to life so that she would not leave Laura utterly alone. At last, after Mike came into her life, she felt her grandmother finally relaxed enough to let go. She was all of ninety-four years old when she finally slipped away one night in her sleep.

The funeral was well-attended. Her Nana was loved by many people. Mike was her bulwark then, and Laura believed they would be together for the rest of their lives. A month later, Mike had gone to close a business deal in Los Angeles, promising to pick her up for dinner afterwards. Instead, state troopers came knocking on her door that evening to tell her that Mike would not be coming home. He had been in a freak accident and had not survived it.

It was like the nightmare following her parents' death all over again except that this time around, her grandmother was not there to help her get over it. She was not close enough to Mike's parents and sister for them to share their sorrows together. The only people who cared enough to dig deeper than the surface she showed to everyone were Katie and Allison. Katie lived two doors down the street. She was married with two children and had been friends with Laura since the latter had come to live at Memphis with her grandmother. Allison had been her childhood friend. They had lived close to each other at Buffalo until Laura's parents died in that terrible motor accident. They had the kind of enduring friendship which even after they had moved apart to different cities, they still got permission to visit each other for the holidays. They had kept in touch until recently when they had become too busy as they each climbed the corporate ladder of their different companies.

Laura had written to inform Allison about her grandmother's death and Allison had promised to come for the funeral. At almost the last moment, she had telephoned to say she could not make it. She was in the hospital, very ill. Overwhelmed by her own grief, Laura had not enquired into what type of illness was keeping her friend in hospital. Soon after the funeral, Allison's mother called Laura to tell her that Allison was even sicker. Could Laura come out to Buffalo to see her?

It was an odd request especially since Laura was the one grieving, and in need of comfort. However, friends are friends. Allison was even more like a sister. Laura had discussed it with Mike, and they agreed they would go out to see her "Buffalo family" together but then the tragedy of Mike's accident happened. After the accident, Allison had sent emails, but quite unlike her, she did not even so much as make a phone call. In her emails she said she was still too ill to travel. Instead, she begged Laura over and over to come to see her at Buffalo, stressing that it was really important. Laura read her first few emails dispassionately. She was past feeling angry, betrayed, or even bewildered. She felt totally numb inside.

After Mike's death Laura moved through life in a fog. She did not remember if she ate, slept, or did anything normal. She stopped showing up at the office. One day just blurred into another. If she was a drinking person, she would have taken to alcohol at this time because she had nothing to give her a buzz. She had no idea how long she continued in this way until one day Katie blustered into the house like a hurricane. Katie was like that. She was big, blond, and blustery!

"Look at you! Just take a look at yourself. When last did you have a bath? When did you last comb your hair? If you are planning to die, at least try to make a decent corpse. What will your grandma say? What will Mike think? Get up immediately and get yourself into that bathtub before I bulldoze you out with the garbage!"

Katie would brook no arguments. She ran a luxury bath, complete with the works. She had Laura up, bathing, and dressing while she cleaned the house to what she felt was an acceptable degree of decency. She sat in the kitchen, and made Laura eat a real meal for the first time in heaven-knows-how-long. But Katie had a home of her own to also run. However, before she left, she told Laura, "You know what you need? You need someone to need you; so I want you to call Allison now. Tell her you are going over to see her tomorrow."

"I cannot do that" Laura wailed. "This is not how things are done, Katie."

"What is it you cannot do?" asked Katie.

"I cannot go to see Allison on such short notice."

"Sure, you can" Katie insisted. "That is how friends are meant to visit each other. However, if you think tomorrow is too short a notice, then tell her when you will be going to see her before the end of this week; but you are going to see her, period!"

And so, before all the good Katie did could be undone, Laura found herself packed and sent off to Buffalo in two days flat. Katie would have gone with her but since she could not, she did the next best thing. She called Allison's mother with what time to expect Laura, drove Laura to the airport, and checked her into the plane to Buffalo.

Katie was right and wrong about visiting Allison being the therapy Laura needed. In her self-pity, Laura had not imagined Allison to be so sick. She was not just sick, she was dying. She had a vicious kind of leukemia. No medical knowledge was helping. The onset had been rapid, and the course unrelenting. They had put her through different forms of chemotherapy protocols, reaching maximum allowable doses that someone could take in a lifetime. She had received total body irradiation and had even gone through bone marrow transplant. Everything they had hit her with gave her only brief periods of respite but no true remission. At the end, everyone had become tired of fighting. Her parents clung to each other, grown gaunt through the worry of it all, and not knowing what they wanted anymore. Did they want their only daughter to die and be at rest; or for her to continue to fight for as long as it took? When she met Laura at the airport, Mrs. Pearson fell into her arms sobbing. Their relationship had been more like mother and daughter even before Laura's parents died, courtesy of the very close friendship between Laura and Allison.

"We wanted to spare you this after all you have been through this year. However, Allison thought you would want to say goodbye" Libby Pearson said.

And so, Laura felt that Katie was wrong. How could she cope with yet another loss so soon? And yet Katie was also right. As Laura thought about it, it was indeed good that she should have some closure with Allison at least. Her Grandma's death had been expected but even then, there had been no time for a proper goodbye. Mike's death had been sudden. She still kept expecting him to come back even though she had seen his dead body cremated. Her parents' deaths were a totally different kettle of fish. She had nightmares for years after they died.

Yes, she would prefer to say a gradual goodbye. She indulged herself for a few minutes of weeping with the older Pearsons, and then found herself taking charge. The human mind and body are elastic, and so full of surprises. Even when it seems nothing could be squeezed out anymore, hidden sources of strength that were never known to exist would suddenly come to the fore. From the moment Laura straightened herself and walked into Allison's hospital room, she was like a totally transformed person. The sweet girl she had known had all but vanished. As tall, and as slender as Laura, what was now left of her were huge watery grey eyes in a very pinched face. She had grown thin and gaunt. All her muscles were wasted, and her skin stretched tight over her bony frame. Chemotherapy had taken all her hair but when she volunteered a tired smile, Laura could still see the spirit of her friend behind that smile.

Allison watched her face closely to know her reactions. "I already wept with your parents outside" Laura told her. "My mind tells me my tears are not what you want now. Quick, time is short. What can we accomplish with these remaining days?"

And just like that, Allison seemed to get better. She rallied well enough to be discharged from the hospital yet again. The two friends insisted on staying in the same room just like at other times. They spent hours reminiscing about the old days, planning Laura's future, and finding a lot to still laugh about. Allison made Laura promise to have lots of children including at least two daughters. "You must name the first one Allison" she said. "That way, you get to scold me by proxy as much as you like".

Those were the good days when Allison could stay awake for a few hours at a time and they would talk, plan, or play. There were the bad days also when she would be in very severe pains. Laura then soothed her with medications, massages, or compresses – whatever worked best at the time. She was glad for her small financial independence and not having to worry about losing her job or staying for too long. Her presence in the house also spared the older Pearsons the trouble of having to engage a nurse or a care aide. It also helped them get out once in a while to relieve their own sorrows, knowing their daughter was with someone who loved her very dearly.

Laura learned to care for Allison in every way including administering her medications and taking care of her bodily needs. It took her mind totally off her own sadness. She phoned Katie to say she did not know when she would be back. She asked Katie to please look into her house once in a while and let her know if there was anything that needed her urgent attention. She let her utility providers and her office know she was on an indefinite vacation; and devoted her entire energy to caring for Allison.

One morning, Allison said to her, "Guess who is coming today."

"I already know your dad is going to pick Alex up from the airport this afternoon" Laura replied.

"You spoilsport!" Allison pouted playfully and then asked, "Are you still in love with him? You had this giant crush on him in tenth grade."

"Now we are all grown up and have different interests" Laura said, avoiding a direct answer.

The truth was that somewhere in the deep recesses of her heart, Laura still had feelings for Allison's big brother. He had always seen Laura as a little sister, nothing more. He treated her with affection and teased her a lot. He was in the Marine Corps and had been serving outside the country for the past ten years. He was then in between postings and was coming home to see his ailing little sister.

"I always wanted you to marry him" Allison said now. "That way you will always be family."

"I am family" Laura said with emphasis. "Show me who says otherwise, and I will handle the person."

Allison laughed. That had been her line to anyone who ever dared suggest Laura was not a Pearson. "You know what I mean but I could never have asked for a better sister. You belong with us Laura, you know that."

"I know" Laura agreed, still fully aware of the subtle differences.

"You will not leave my parents without a daughter?"

"God forbid!"

That was another thing. Maybe it was the very prospect of death but talks of God and eternity had crept more and more into their conversations. Ever religious, the older Pearsons had become even more so since Allison's ordeal. They met with their pastor frequently these days and always came away from such meetings looking more peaceful than when they went in. They seemed to be totally at peace with Allison dying, despite the occasional bouts of tears and sadness. Laura did not know what they got there but she for one had a grudge against God. Her grandmother had been religious enough. Even her parents had their own fair share of religion. Laura felt God was always handing her the short end of the stick in every deal. She saw no sense in his allowing someone as young, and as vibrant as Allison die at the prime of her life. However, since the said Allison derived some comfort from this God business, she went right along with her.

Alex came that evening, his usual boisterous self. He seemed to blow in with a refreshing wind that blew all the cobwebs away from the sickroom. He was full of stories of the strange places he had been to, and the interesting things he had been doing. He made Laura and Allison forget their present distresses and hold their sides in laughter. He broke all the sickroom rules and insisted on everyone having dinner there. Usually, Allison would have complained about how nauseating the smell of food made her but that day, her appetite seemed to have improved by the very fact that the meal was being shared by everyone else. He pulled at Laura's ponytail, and teased her about how much taller and fatter she had grown.

"Thank you. Everyone tells me about how thin and gaunt I look these days."

"Gottcha!" Alex roared with laughter. "You should think twice before accepting anything I say to you, you green-eyed cat! Haven't you learned any lessons at all?"

"Thank you, blue-eyed Blade" Laura replied demurely. "I choose to hear compliments even when they're paid differently!"

And just like that, they seemed to fall back into their bantering of the old days. Allison watched them and whooped with glee but she tired soon enough.

As soon as dinner was cleared away, she fell asleep. Everybody crept out of the room except for Laura who slept in the next bed.

Restless, she tossed and turned on the bed but could not just go to sleep. There was a tempting full moon outside. She wandered onto the patio to take some fresh air. That was when she heard some queer sounds in the small garden at the backyard. The sounds were not easy to describe. It was partway between the stalling of a car engine and a rusty saw on metal chains. Could someone be trying to break into the house? Was it a wild animal in distress? Startled, she held her breath to better discern the direction the sounds came from. As soon as she determined it was from the tree in the middle of the yard, the tree trunk moved! Laura was stuck to her chair, too petrified to even scream. It was not unknown for bears to wander this far into town, and she did not relish the idea of a tangle with a grizzly. Slowly, powers returned to her limbs. Just as she was about to spring up and run, the terrible sound came again. It was followed by a sigh, and then the shadow became the form of a man. The man came towards her. By the moonlight, she saw it was Alex. Her heart melted. All the love she had ever had for this man came pouring forth.

Alex was not aware there was anyone on the porch but as he took the first step up, Laura said softly, "Been out enjoying the cool breeze too?"

Startled, Alex came to a stop with his hands at his side as if he was going into combat mode. "Don't do that! Don't ever do that! If I had a gun then, I would have shot you first and thought later" he hissed.

"It's a good thing you didn't have a gun, then. I know your prudence would not have allowed you to bring one back home, or did you?" Laura asked, unmoved.

"I didn't."

"So come and sit down and tell me what you have been doing all by yourself in the night, frightening a poor little lady out of her wits."

Alex came up two more steps and sat at her feet. He was so close that if she reached out she could bury it in his thick blond curls but she did not. Such intimate gestures were not solicited, and she did not want to begin something she could not continue.

Ordinarily he would have teased her about calling herself a little old lady, but things were not ordinary. "It's so unfair, it's so, so unfair" he began. Laura did not ask what was so unfair. She knew what was bothering him, but she just kept quiet. "She's so young! She's not even thirty yet. She has everything made. What is the use of her dying so early, and leaving it all behind? I saw her six months ago. There was nothing wrong with her at all. Now, six months later, there is nothing right. She has always been the good one. If God is up there, why doesn't He take me and leave her, if for nothing, at least for the sake of our parents?"

With his elbows on his knees, he carried his head in his hands as if he was supporting the weight of the whole world. He began to make that queer noise again which Laura now recognized as his trying very hard not to sob aloud. Laura cast all caution to the winds. Sinking her hands into his hair, she knelt down and brought him close to her bosom. She held him and comforted him. She kissed his face over and over, murmuring words of comfort. Alex clung to her like a lifeline. She stopped talking and let him cry out the storm. After some time, which neither of them kept track of, he spoke. "You must think I am phony, after how I carried on during dinner."

"I never think of you as phony Alex, never. Don't think we didn't all have our own moments. We even still have them from time to time, including Allison herself. It's just that we have had more time to get used to the situation, and to reconcile ourselves to the facts. Your parents are leaning on God. Even Allison herself seems to have found some stability in God."

"And you? How do you cope?" Alex asked her.

"I cope the best that I can. I like to think that past circumstances have numbed me to suffering but I find myself crying a lot in private. I cope by doing what I can at the moment. I don't allow myself a lot of time to think."

"I'm sorry. I hear you have faced a lot of tragedies recently too."

"Yes, "Laura said simply. She loosened her hold on him and got out of the embrace. "That is really why I am here. A friend suggested that looking after another person would help me handle my grief."

"And has it?" Alex probed.

"Yes, it has, in many ways but I wish there are other more pleasant ways to achieve the same end. If I was younger and a bit brasher, I would have turned to alcohol, tobacco, or something stronger. However, I guess I am basically a coward."

"You are not a coward, Laura. You never have been. That is probably the most opposite of what you are. You are one of the bravest people I know."

"Thanks," she said in an abstracted tone, and got up to turn in. Alex immediately jumped to his feet. He gathered her in a tight embrace and kissed her on the forehead as they stood there rocking back and forth. "Thank you so much Laura. You are such a good tonic."

She squeezed him back and they remained standing there for some time before he let go. There was no charged electricity, no sensuous tensions. They were simply two people who were very sorrowful, deriving comfort from mere contact with another human being. "If only", Laura's heart cried in anguish, "if only…" and then she turned in to try to catch some sleep before Allison awoke to want something. Alex went to his own room too, much lightened. He meant what he said. Laura had always been like a good tonic. He greatly admired her courage, and that was it.

Alex stayed for about a week. The house always seemed so different whenever he was around. He was often in the sickroom, teasing the ladies. He also found time to potter around the house with his father fixing up things. He even helped his mother cook in the kitchen and to do laundry. He found time to drive his parents to some of their meetings and hospital appointments. Twice, he met with their pastor but did not derive the same comfort his parents did. He never had another intimate moment with Laura. Both of them understood that Allison was their primary focus. Whatever else happened, Allison had to be kept happy and cheerful.

At last, the day came for Alex to leave. He gathered Allison close to him, intravenous tubing and all. "You know this is goodbye, Big Brother," Allison said with some cheer. "I'm going to tell God how good you've been so He will let me reserve a special seat for you."

"Don't say that" Alex retorted. "I might get there before you. I will ask Him to let me pull your braids one last time."

"Goodbye, Alex" she said sombrely.

"Goodbye, Baby Sister."

"And don't forget to be good to Laura. We're all the family she has now."

"I won't forget. How can I possibly forget?"

"Good. I'm not a good schemer for nothing. Now go before I start bawling. A lady has to have some dignity."

"Where?" Alex asked looking around him. "Where is the lady?" but he left with misty eyes. He knew he would never see her alive again.

A week later Allison went rapidly downhill and slipped into a coma. Two days later, she was dead. Alex had not shipped out yet. He was given a two-day pass to attend the funeral. Everyone was very sad and very busy. He caught a glimpse of Laura but did not even get to talk to her. By the next day, before the house had fully woken up, he was gone.

Laura went back to Memphis and tried to pick up the tattered pieces of her life but was making a very poor job of it. That was why she found herself alone on New Year Eve meditating over the meaning of life rather than trying to live it up in one party or the other. After counting her assets and her liabilities in life, and asking herself where her life was headed, she had still not arrived at a satisfactory answer. She went to bed early, resolved to just plod on until something broke.

When the New Year began, she returned to work. Although her supervisors complimented her, she just did not find the kind of pleasure she used to find in it. One day, researching a financial plan project, she came across a United Nations Advertisement for women to go and serve in rebuilding Afghanistan. What was it Katie had said? Sometimes one needed to take care of another person's needs in order to snap out of one's ruts! Maybe she should go to Afghanistan and offer her services. She had heard how dangerous it was for some categories of people to live in

Afghanistan - for foreigners and women in particular. Laura was both. The killing of Aid workers was like a weekly routine. But what did she have to live for anyway? Catching a bullet in Afghanistan could be no worse than the slow burning death she called life now.

That very afternoon, she applied to the program and then forgot all about it. Surprisingly, someone phoned, and then emailed her within two hours of her sending off the application, showing a lot of interest. The United Nations contact sent her more forms to fill over the internet. Later that day, when she told Katie what she had done, Katie went ballistic. "Are you mad? Don't you know a better way of committing suicide when you get a death wish?"

"It's true Afghanistan is far from safe, but I will be going under the protection of United Nations. Did you not always say that one way of helping myself was to help another person in need?"

"Yes, sure!" Katie fired back. "There are lots of people in need right here. There are soup kitchens always looking for extra hands downtown, there are women shelters, runaways, and so on. If that is not the kind of needy people you want to help, look at me. I am in need of a babysitter so I can go out with Dave on Saturday night."

Laura smiled tightly. "You know I love babysitting for you when your mother can spare her grandchildren. I just want to get out of everything I have always known for some time. I want to distance myself a bit from this life and see if things will become clear again."

"Why do you have to go all the way to Afghanistan to do that? You can distance yourself to Florida, to Colorado, to Toronto, or even to Costa Rica. I bet you could see very clearly from those places just as well."

Katie had no sense of adventure. She had been born in Memphis, grew up in Memphis, received all her education there, and married her high school sweetheart who operated his construction firm out of Memphis within several blocks of almost all her close relatives. To all intents and purposes, she also intended to grow old in Memphis, die in Memphis, and be buried in Memphis. She saw nothing wrong with that at all. To Katie any travelling involved taking the children to Disneyland or some such resort for about two weeks at most. Even that, was not something one did every year. She was so content with her present life. She had no ambition to get out of it to seek any kind of interpretation to any other type of life. "Don't we have enough heroes going to throw away their lives at Afghanistan?" she asked Laura.

"Yes," Laura countered "but Memphis also has her own criminals. After 9-11, you cannot believe there is anywhere that is truly safe, even in this country."

"That's true but we understand our own kinds of crooks, and our army is just round the corner."

"I will have the army even closer to me there than they are here" Laura pointed out.

Katie never minced words when she had an opinion to express. Laura did not mind her airing those opinions either. Katie playing the devil's advocate helped her sort through the pros and cons in her muddled mind. At the end of the day, she felt she was making the right decision by taking up the UN position. She filled the final application forms and waited. It alleviated the seeming deadness of her life and made it more purposeful again. At least, it gave her something to look forward to. That she had sent in an application did not mean she would automatically be accepted. They would still need to do things like criminal record check on her, make sure she was medically and mentally fit, and so on. The signs were good though. If they rejected her, she would be very disappointed, but she made up her mind to accept it as an indication that maybe she was not meant to go.

But she was not rejected. She was accepted. The UN wrote her a letter inviting her to come to New York for a three-day orientation session to prepare her to go later in the year. Suddenly there were myriad things to do. She had to resign from her job. She had to attend send-off parties. She had to prepare documents and make arrangements for how her house would be cared for while she was gone, and so on. Laura's life perked up again.

CHAPTER 2

───────∞───────

The briefing took place at downtown Manhattan, New York, amidst the hustle and bustle of the city that never sleeps. At twelve o'clock midday, it was even more awake than ever. That was the time that those who stayed cooped up in schools and offices burst out to take their midday meals, stretch out their muscles, and hopefully take in a bit of the bright afternoon sunlight. Natives and tourists mingled on the busy streets. As Laura sat at the picture window of the fiftieth floor waiting to be processed by a UN official, the streets below looked like a veritable active beehive. All the sights interested her. Although a native New Yorker, she had lived at what must be regarded as the rural part of the state. In fact, she had been to the city itself only on a handful of occasions, as part of educational programs. Even this very occasion was more or less, also an educational event. The group of people gathered at the United Nations offices was for the three-day briefing, as the beginning of an education team to be sent to Afghanistan under UNESCO.

Dorothy Simmons, neat and svelte would not have fitted anyone's imagination of "Afghan Specialist" but that was how she was introduced. She took the initial opening section and was so good in her subject that her audience sat enrapt. With slides of still and moving pictures, she made her subject come alive. This was a deciding moment for every one of them, the last opportunity to get out but nobody left. "

The real war is over, or as some people would say, may have just begun. The events following 9-11 unseated the Taliban and the Al-Qaeda. The war on the surface has been won by the allied forces but the fact is that the militants just went underground. Newer, and sometimes more vicious groups, are always forming. Some of these groups remain faceless, and it is difficult to know who the leaders are. Some of them openly fight against the Taliban while others affiliate themselves to some extent with the Taliban. Inasmuch as control is concerned, there is really no central focus. Since the Taliban glories in claiming responsibility for atrocities, they never protest any crimes attributed to them whether they are connected to it or not. For the ease of administration and writing reports, the resident NATO officials let such inconsistencies in nomenclature remain.

"Driven from the cities, the militants have retreated and gone underground, or rather into mountain hideouts and to the countryside. From these places they continue to wreak a lot of havoc. The allied forces are there now, not to do battle but to maintain peace. Maintenance of peace is always a more difficult thing than fighting an outright battle. As much as possible, our forces are told not to kill or arouse aggression. The offshoot is that the allied forces, if they have the opportunity often shoot their guns as a warning; but the Taliban, when they get the chance often shoot to kill. Almost on a weekly basis the Allied forces suffer the loss of men, and the Taliban glories in these so-called victories. Any hint of any Afghan civilian shot by mistake is always blown up as a massacre by the international press. It is not at all a pleasant situation."

She paused dramatically at this point and took a drink from a small plastic bottle while looking at their faces as if to say, "Are you still sure you want to get into this?"

When nobody got up to leave, she continued.

"Most of the efforts now being made by the allied forces are geared towards training the good element in the recognized government to stand up for themselves and form a local opposition against the bad elements. Sometimes however, it is difficult to distinguish who is the good, and who is the bad. Even those who show themselves friendly towards the allied forces and seem to understand the ground rules for the proposed peace, often have their philosophies warped. Besides, they sometimes have their own hidden agendas. Many times, the allied forces are hard put to draw a line between upholding the native culture of the people, and imposing their own imported western culture. Incidentally, those who wholeheartedly embrace western culture strive very hard to deny this to the rest of the population. It sometimes ends up breeding another splinter group which is sometimes even more merciless.

"In the midst of all this fighting, the common man suffers, caught as they are, as the grass between two raging elephants. We say 'the common man' but really it is the common woman and the common child. The United Nations and many leaders of thoughts feel that a way of getting to the root of the problem is by empowering the women. It has been proven to work through the ages; through many civilizations; in many underdeveloped areas of the world, and so on. Indeed, the Taliban and the Al-Qaeda also recognize this as the basis of all things. They have set about systematically wiping out all the rights of women, even the right to think and act on their own. This is what has brought about this present initiative. Already, soldiers and United States Marines corps squads made up entirely of women have been deployed to sensitive areas. Your groups will be going to Afghanistan villages. Your projects are devoted to educating and empowering women. While living among the people, you will strive to impart literacy and do skills training. Hopefully, you will also act as role models that the native women could aspire to."

It was an ambitious plan, and theirs was to be the pilot.

"Many other subsets are going in with food and other aid programs. Your project will be alongside others including health, agriculture, water supply, home rebuilding, road construction, and other social amenity programs. The governments of some countries have also undertaken tasks of rebuilding and improving the road and rail network as well as transport systems which will open up the interior of the country to bring in vital trade. It is hoped that these measures will improve the economy of this landlocked country. These activities go on amidst the enduring opposition of the Taliban and other guerrilla groups. They do their best to foil every advancement and every overture of peace. It's so touching to see the amount of transparent gratitude the grassroots citizens show when eventually the relief materials meant for them actually reaches them. "Many of them come to the distribution centers with tales of how they had been threatened by the Taliban not to come out at all. Others come to report that the Taliban had actually encouraged them to come. As soon as they returned, the same Taliban would proceed to relieve them of the aid materials. At the height of their power, The Taliban initially banned the growth of Opium. Now their leaders encourage opium farming in order to fund their arm supplies. The people have to comply. They plant their farms with opium instead of staple crops, and so they starve.

"You will see women coming out with their babies so that Aid workers would at least have compassion on the powerless innocents. You are the manpower that will see that at least some of these relief materials actually get to those for whom they are meant. As one UN director puts it, 'We must also aim to go beyond giving them fish, and actually teach them how to fish for themselves.'"

As the first session ended with questions and answers, someone asked why the Afghan women were so "Stupidly powerless". That question set off a raw nerve in Dorothy Simmons. She dismissed those who wanted to go for break but nobody moved. She spent the next forty-five minutes talking about how the Taliban had felt that the problem with their society was that their women had too much power and freedom, much more than the Islamic religion allowed them. The Taliban had instituted a lot of religious changes but had gone to their greatest extremes in what concerned their womenfolk. The result was that women were suppressed and oppressed more than ever before. The Taliban, claiming sometimes to apply the

Muslim Sharia laws, and at other times the traditional Pashtunwali that governed the Pashtun tribes, as it suited them, subjected Afghan women to untold limitations of freedom. Women were denied western education, and on some occasions even Islamic or any other form of education. Women who hitherto had delighted in displaying their varied colors of traditional dressing with beautiful coiffures were forced to don Burqas (baggy veils that enveloped them from head to foot with the exception of their eyes). They were not allowed to move about during daytime except in the company of at least one male relative. In some places, they were denied even the company of other women who were not relatives. Punishment for daring to breach any of these laid down rules were very appalling. They ranged from public flogging, mutilations, even to death by some horrible means like beheading, hanging, or starvation.

The world screamed at the human right violations being meted out by the Taliban. They watched appalled as surreptitiously taken pictures and videos of amputations and beheadings went viral on the media. It was very commonplace to gather a whole village to the flogging of a woman caught indecently exposing an ankle or a curl of hair. A woman could be beheaded on the trumped-up charges of illicit sexual dealings. Never mind that often, the said culprit would be punished alone and whoever her lover was, was justified or just allowed to go scot-free.

But Ms. Simmons also made concessions. "If the whole truth is told though, some Afghan women took part in the atrocities committed by the Mujahedeen during their decades-long war with the Russians. In fact, many a man in the opposing army said it was better to fall into the hands of the male militants than to be captured by Afghan women. The women at that time were fiercely independent, merciless, and uncompromising. They did not just come outright and kill captured enemy soldiers but tortured them very thoroughly. They always fell short of immediately killing them. They perfected the art of leaving them half dead in a way that even those who somehow survived wished they had not. Afghan women could never be classified as

'Stupidly Powerless'. There may have been sense in trying to curb their activities then, but the Taliban carried its mistreatment of them beyond the pale.

"However, though," she told them, "a few Moslem women have been known to speak out supporting the treatment of women by the Taliban, and condemning the 'indecent' way of life of western women. We would have let the matter drop and minded our own business but many other women have begged covertly and overtly for help. In different circumstances, safely away from the long arm of the Taliban or sometimes in secret, those same women who had praised and upheld the Taliban's treatment of women tended to sing a different tune, begging for help. Afghanistan is like that. It is a land full of controversies but is the rest of the world any different?" she asked.

After a very short break, she carried on from this point since this group was going in for the women after all. "Now I want to tell you about Mut'ah. When the world raised a hue and cry over the Taliban-supported practice of Mut'ah, the Taliban had a good defense for it. They asked the West to keep its nose out of their affairs. Indeed, in Islamic laws, Mut'ah has been one of the conflicts between the orthodox Sunni and the more radical Shiite Muslims. However, they had a meeting point and agreement over it. Mut'ah is a method of contracting a temporary marriage which could last anything from an hour, a few days, weeks, or months. All agreements are verbal, not witnessed, and eminently changeable. Bridal gifts or dowry are exchanged in advance. At the end of the marriage, the woman is often not paid off so that it will not be seen as prostitution.

"Let me show you a video clip of a top Afghan Taliban Mullah, Nemabullah strenuously explaining the practice of Mut'ah." She took a break from talking to drink some water while her rapt audience listened attentively as the Mullah explained that what the Faithful were very much against was sex outside of marriage. "Sex should be practiced only within the confines of a marriage contract. Women should keep themselves fully and decently covered at all times, baring themselves only in the presence of their husbands or close relatives. The exposure of any part of a woman lures the imaginations of men and keeps them constantly occupied with sex rather than with higher and purer values. Overall, we treat our women with more dignity and decency than you treat your women in the west. You constantly parade your women like common harlots."

As the interview continued, it became clear to the listeners that the higher and purer values which the men should aspire to were the art of making war and perpetuating chaos. Nemabullah then went on to praise the values of marriage, chastity, and decency in relationships. It took strenuous effort. As Shakespeare said, it appeared the man was "protesting too much." The listeners could very easily conclude that Truth never needed so much explaining.

At the end of the clip, Dorothy resumed. "In the version of Mut'ah practiced by the Taliban in rural Afghanistan, the initial payment or gift is assumed to have been given to the woman or her guardian, often under the duress of a loaded gun or by some other means of force. The problem most times is that such "women" were often really little girls ranging in age from eight to fifteen, usually from homes that are very far away, and had lived sheltered lives more or less up till then. At the end of the temporary marriage, they are let go with nothing at all or at most a loaf of bread and a can of soda. They find themselves with no means to survive, too ashamed, and often too disoriented to go back home. They would wander the street starving slowly to death unless they find a quicker way of ending their misery. They would often be caught by the same Taliban, re-enslaved, or charged with prostitution, and then summarily executed. Once, there was even a rumor that these Taliban soldiers after overcoming the resistance of a particular village, rounded up the women and girls, married them for some nights of pleasure, and then executed them. They say their law forbids the killing of virgins."

The end of the first day's sessions gave the UN recruits lots of food for thought but no one withdrew. Everyone seemed determined to go to Afghanistan to be martyred.

Laura's particular group was constituted of about thirty people working with UNESCO. They were to work in groups of three and they were supposed to get to know one another immediately. They spent the three days of briefing shuffling from one seminar to another, briefed by experts on topics ranging from the current political state of affairs in Afghanistan to what to eat and what to avoid. They were briefed on the expectations of UNESCO and the expectations of the Afghans. They were told about monetary allowances, exchange rates, and how to convert, hold onto, or spend their money. What UNESCO was going to give them was a mere stipend compared to the earnings they would be leaving behind. Even then, that stipend was a palatial amount compared to what the natives were earning. Spending extravagantly would sometimes appear tempting and insulting to the natives. Not spending at all would deprive the natives of the advantage of hosting them. Even the use of money in Afghanistan was a very sensitive issue which took up one whole morning session.

They were briefed on religious affairs in Afghanistan including the dangers of being seen as proselytizing. They were told they must not have any outward show of religion. Any religious observances must be seen as very strictly personal otherwise their whole mission could be jeopardized. There was so much information. Their heads swam with it. On the first day, they finished early and were mandated to get to know their teammates. Laura's team was made up of Lil, a sweet slender Swede with the blonde coloring of her people. She worked as a statistician in Sweden and had never been to New York City. She had come along with her long-time boyfriend, Bjorn, and they were making a holiday of it. Bjorn was an international businessman and had been to New York many times before.

The other member of their team was Greta who was as voluptuous as Lil was slender. She was from Berlin and a stated extrovert. At Berlin, she had worked as an area school supervisor. She was a few minutes late for the first seminar but within minutes of arriving, she had made so many friends. She twinkled and shone and treated life like a joke. She said she had never been to New York, but she intended to get to know the city very well, "And let it know me well too."

Laura liked them immediately even though she still felt somewhat intimidated. Greta said she was going to Afghanistan because it felt adventurous, and she felt she had something to give. Lil was going to test what the period of separation would do to her relationship with Bjorn before she finally committed to him. Laura told them she was going because her life felt empty at the moment and she was trying to find a meaning to life again. They were well content with the reasons given by one another. When the coordinator asked if they felt they would be able to live with one another and work together for the first six months of their probation, they had no objections at all.

On the last afternoon of the briefing, a large map of Afghanistan was projected onto the screen. Against it, they saw where each team was posted. Some areas like Kabul, Qandahar, Herat, and Jalalabad had more than one team. Some provinces, especially in the northern parts of the country had no one because the UN felt it was not yet safe enough to send in workers there. Some teams were to overlook other teams and liaise with other core UN teams. Laura's team was to be based at Lashkar Gah, the capital of the Helmand province. From there they were to cover that whole province and also an area which extended to the Nimruz province to the west, and parts of Qandahar to the east. It seemed like a rather large area but the population, they were told was not that much, comparatively.

"Great" Greta said. Lil and Laura had nothing to add. Three of them exchanged phone numbers and email addresses. They agreed to be there by late August. UNESCO would contact them individually about travelling arrangements once it had concluded their accommodation arrangements. Laura returned to Memphis to put her affairs in order.

Chapter 3

∞

"Dear Ms. Jackson, a United States Marine Unit is shipping out to Qandahar on August 15 from Miami. Please confirm that you are able to join this unit as this would give you some time to settle in Afghanistan before you begin your project. Sincerely…"

Laura received the mail at a time she had already moved most of her memorabilia to storage. She had decided that she would rent out the house, furnished, and ask Katie to oversee the property while she was abroad. With all her goodbyes said, there was no reason why she could not join the unit shipping out on the 15th. She wrote to confirm that she could join the unit. Reservations were made for her at the Miami Sheraton for the 13th. Katie drove her to the airport and hugged her fiercely. "Look after yourself Girl, and don't you dare die in that place. Make sure you write me every week at least, else I'm gonna come there and fetch you back."

"Don't tempt me, Katie. I just might stop writing to see if you would really come to get me."

"Don't try me Girl, don't try me" she said huskily as she rushed off so that Laura would not see the tears in her eyes.

Laura turned to check in, her own eyes not too dry either but Miami beckoned. She was on to an adventure. She was not ready to turn back from it just yet.

The flight was uneventful. From Miami airport she got a cab to the Sheraton. As soon as she got down she saw a vision in the lobby! Alex Pearson, dressed in all his Marine glory, was there in the lobby with some of his colleagues! He saw her at about the same time as she saw him. Her stomach gave a leap. Alex extracted himself, and coming to the door, literally swept her off her feet in a bear hug. "Laura Jackson! Where on earth did you appear from? Aren't you the sight for sore eyes?"

Laura was also overwhelmed. This must be a good sign. "What on earth are you doing here?" she asked back.

"We are waiting to ship out in two days" Alex replied.

"Me too!" Laura exclaimed excitedly.

"You're shipping out?" Alex asked genuinely puzzled.

"Yes," Laura replied. "I'm going to Afghanistan."

"No! Seriously?"

"Yes! Seriously. I got my orders to come here and wait to ship out on the 15th of August. That is in two days."

"We need to talk about this" Alex said as his friends came up to see what the excitement was all about. He introduced them. "Hey you guys, this is Laura, my kid sister. I dare not say otherwise. Laura, these guys are Randy and Charlie, Guelph and Chapman. That one over there is Tim. Tim is our chaplain. These other ones are just common sinners like me."

Laura laughed heartily with them as she shook hands all round. She did not dwell on the words he chose to introduce her to his friends but one of them asked about her being his sister. "Man, are you trying to tell us 'hands off the lady?' We thought your sister…"

"Oh, but a guy is entitled to more than one sister!" Alex said with emphasis.

"This one is particularly dishy. May we…?"

"Don't you dare!" Alex growled. "But why are we standing here delaying her. Laura how about you join us for dinner after you have freshened up? Should I come for you, or will you just come on down and join us when you're ready?"

Laura agreed to the latter plan, hoping she would not sleep off. She had been feeling tired after all the last-minute arrangements of the past few days; and her early start from Memphis that morning. Nevertheless, she had not been able to sleep on the plane. She was probably all charged up on adrenaline from the anticipated trip but the unexpected meeting in the lobby added a lot to it. Alex still had that effect on her systems.

She had no time to appreciate the luxuries of her hotel suite. She just went into the bathroom, splashed some cold water on her face, arranged a few personal things for her two-day stay, and changed into one of the few formal gowns she had brought along. She surveyed herself in the mirror. The image that stared back at her was "quite fetching", to use a quaint term, even with minimal makeup. With her rich auburn hair brushed off her face, swept to one side, and left to curl at her left shoulder; combined with her clear silky skin and her sparkling green eyes, she looked very exotic and beautiful. The fact that she was totally unaware and not self-conscious about her beauty only made her more charming. There was just this hint of sadness in her eyes which made her look so vulnerable and appealing at the same time. It made everyone she met instinctively want to shield and protect her. Her eyes had not always been this sad, but they had always been very expressive with emotions that ranged from simple enjoyment, laughter, mischief, to adventure, awe, and pain at different times of her life. She sighed gently, applied gloss over her lips, grabbed her purse, and headed for the elevators that would take her down to the lobby.

To her surprise, when she arrived only Alex and the one called Tim were there of the original group. They already had a table. When they saw her, they rose gallantly to their feet, and Laura blushed daintily. Alex hugged her and kissed her cheek. Tim shook her by the hand. They seated her between them and plied her with appetizers. It was all he could do not to stare at her, but Tim took every possible polite opportunity to just drink her in with his eyes.

"I feel like a princess" she said to cover up her embarrassment. "Do they teach this kind of thing to the marines?"

"What kind of thing?" Alex asked.

"You know, how to make a woman feel like a million dollars…"

"You will be surprised at the kinds of lessons they give to the US marines" Alex informed her conspiratorially. "We learn how to treat people like a million dollars, and we also learn how to make asses out of people."

"Ah! Ah! Ah!" chided Tim. "Remember we have respectable company. I think what Alex is trying to tell you is that the company determines the manners. The present company elicits the best of our behavior. You definitely look more than a million dollars."

Laura colored up again and Alex said "You better stop paying her compliments Preach, before the lady turns beet-red."

Laura laughed but she colored more deeply still. It had been a long time since she had been in company which she enjoyed as much as the present one. "What happened to the rest of your troop?" she asked.

"Alex frightened them away, so they've gone to seek recreation elsewhere" Tim explained helpfully.

"Who did the frightening? I am the innocent party here" Alex protested. "They were frightened of the thought of Tim's preaching grazing their consciences so much that they would be denied the pleasures of their last days in civilization. I'm different. I tolerate Tim because he is good for my conscience."

"Now, that is quite a thought" Tim countered. "Tell us about your shipping out to Afghanistan, Laura. Were you joking?"

"I wasn't" Laura assured them. "I am going with a team to Lashkar Gah as a UNESCO initiative for improving the education and the status of the women of Afghanistan."

They had lots of questions for her. What exactly would she be doing? What motivated her to go? How much did she know about Afghanistan, Afghan policies, and so on? Of course, she did not know as much as she would have liked but she convinced them that nobody had coerced her into going. She was not going only out of frustration or with militant motives to do the Afghans harm. She made them understand she was willing to learn and apply safety measures so that she would not be a risk to herself and to others.

By the time they finished dessert she realized how late it was. "And I don't even know much about you guys. Where are you shipping to? What makes you tick? What exactly do you do for the marines or are they all classified information?"

"Why don't we meet again to talk some more tomorrow? Maybe we could then answer your questions" Tim suggested. "Alex what do you say?"

"I have nothing pressing to do until around 1800 hours. What do you say to lunch? Tomorrow is our last full free day. There will be no chance at all on shipping out day."

And so, it was arranged. They saw Laura to her room and then left to theirs. Laura was so overcome with a feeling she could not define. Meeting with Alex usually turned on all her nerve endings, but she also had a reaction to his friend, Tim. He exuded a kind of peace and calmness which somehow said, "Welcome home." If she had described it to Allison, her friend would have understood. Katie would have laughed at her fancy way of putting things, but she too would have liked Tim. Laura had not even begun her adventure and already she was having something to look forward to. She was to have lunch the next day in the company of two very attractive men.

They were both very attractive but O so different! They were both tall and muscular with the training which their profession demanded. Other than that, where Alex had fair hair and piercing blue eyes, Tim had dark hair and grey eyes which so far Laura had seen as calm and serene. She suspected they could also become cloudy or stormy. Where Alex had a craggy face with sharp features, Tim's features were almost blunt, broad, and rather very endearing. They both exuded strength and leadership. They were men among men. However, where Tim radiated a personality which someone would want to have as a friend, Alex radiated that of someone one would hate to have as an enemy. Yeah, Laura enjoyed their company immensely. She looked forward to having lunch with them the next day.

She dashed off a text message to Katie to let her know she had completed the first leg of her journey and had the pleasant surprise of meeting Alex in the hotel. On that thought she fell asleep and slept very deeply. By the time she was woken by the shrilling of the telephone, she was at first very disoriented. She groped about with her eyes closed until she located the offending instrument by the side of the bed.

"Hello?" she said groggily into the phone.

"Hello, Sleeping Beauty. Is this how you are going to take on Afghanistan?"

"Alex! Stop being pert! What time is it?"

"It's almost midnight. Why did you stand us up for lunch?"

"What?" screamed Laura before she caught sight of the time on her cellphone. It was not almost midnight, but it was definitely past noon. "I'm so sorry. Have you ordered lunch already?"

"Well, we might have finished it but as the gentlemen we are, we decided to be sure you were still in the land of the living before we started."

"I'm very sorry. I will be there as soon as I can."

"Take your time. We are the United States Marine. One missed meal makes no difference to us."

On that sarcastic note he hung up. Laura hurried to meet them in the lobby. It was still the two of them, Alex and Tim. Laura remarked on this. "I will soon be leaving too" Alex informed her. "We have last minute arrangements and all that. I'm afraid you will have just Tim to entertain you. The army chaplain has nothing to do. He can afford to sit around being idle all day."

"Tim is really an army chaplain?" Laura asked incredulous.

"You better believe it. You will soon find out that the men call him 'Preach'" Alex said playfully. "I'm the only one who can stand him for any length of time."

Laura was still looking at Tim with interest and could have sworn he colored. "I'm afraid most of what he said is true. I am about the only one who has no special assignment this evening. If you are not averse to my company, I will like yours very much" Tim offered.

"I will like your company very much too" Laura concurred.

"It's all settled then" Alex said. "By the way, Mum said to say hi to you, Laura. I talked with them on Skype yesterday and she commanded me to keep an eye on you."

"How are they doing?" Laura asked.

"Very well, it seems. My present posting seems to give them the jitters. I never let them know where I am in particular so they won't worry so much. I had to tell them this time though because of you."

"I think not telling them is not entirely fair" Laura objected. "If anything should happen to you it would be more of a shock if they didn't know where you were."

"What? Have you been taking lessons from Preach here? Listening to you, one would think you have known him your whole life instead of just a few hours."

"I'm not going to apologise, Alex. You need someone to put you in your place once in a while. If Tim does that then he must be a very good friend indeed."

"Yes Ma'am! No arguments Ma'am!" he said with mock humility. He then wolfed down his lunch, shouldered his backpack, and with a kiss to her cheek was gone.

Laura and Tim had a leisurely meal. Towards the end of it Tim asked, "So what would you want to do?"

"What are my options?" Laura asked.

"We could sit around inside or outside the hotel and just talk. We could go to the wharf and look at the beautiful yachts moored there. If you are culture-inclined, we could take in some of the museums or go shopping. We could also do a little bit of everything."

"We couldn't do all of that in one day. What do you suggest?" Laura countered.

At the end they opted for just walking around the city. They did not go far when they were almost irresistibly drawn to a scenic park. They sat there on a park bench in the inviting shade of the trees. They were far from alone, and yet they felt as if they were the only ones in the park. They talked and laughed like old friends. Maybe Tim, being a trained counselor was used to drawing people out of themselves. However, on this occasion he opened up about himself too. Laura was a very absorbed listener. She showed herself more curious about him than she allowed him to be about her. He admitted that Alex had told him much more about her than what she had chosen to reveal the previous night. "Tell me about yourself so we can be on equal footing at least" she asked.

"Okay" he began, "I am originally from Austin, Texas. I was an only child. My parents were divorced when I was about eight years old. My dad remarried about ten years ago and is living with his family not far from here. Through him, I now have a half-sister and a half-brother that are about five and eight years old now. My mum never remarried. She died of cancer about five years ago. I have an aunt and some cousins who still live all around Texas."

"What made you join the army?"

"It was the zeal of every young man immediately after 9-11. I had just finished college, I applied, and I was accepted."

"And you chose to be in the Marine Corps? Why did you choose to be a chaplain?"

"Actually, the marine corps chose me. It happens that way sometimes. My commanding officer felt I had what it took to be a good Marine, so he recommended me for the training. I saw action in Iraq. It was there that for the first time I was confronted with my own humanity. There are times in the army one asks, 'God, where are You?' If one listens, God really answers. Many of us would have gone mad but for that presence of God. However, many times after this kind of divine encounter there is often no one nearby to help the person understand what had just happened. I was lucky. My experience made me seek out the army chaplain. He helped me understand the meaning of life and God. Afterwards I resolved that was what I wanted to be, an army chaplain.

"Soon after that experience, my mother was diagnosed with advanced cancer. The faith I had then helped me deal with her struggles and eventual death. In simply sharing my faith with her, it helped both of us through the ordeal. I guess people who are close to death are more open to such experiences than others. I have found out there are so many other people seeking and groping in the dark. Many people do not nail down that call of God's spirit. Some others choose to follow a wrong path thereafter."

"So, have you seen that happen a lot? Have you seen people following the wrong path?" Laura asked.

"I have seen it a lot of times, and even more often these days. Christianity in the West is so very watered down nowadays, it almost makes no sense. Who is to blame for this really? Many young men feel that Islam has more to offer now in terms of giving quality to what one should believe, live for and even die for. Islam preaches, 'if you really believe, take up your arms and fight a jihad' "Many young people, when they come to that spiritual point of seeking who they are and why they are here in this life, weigh between what so-called Christianity allows and what Islam preaches. Whereas Christianity now is a lot of fables like Santa Claus and Halloween, Islam preaches arise, fight, and die for the faith. Serious-minded young people choose the one which gives them a deeper purpose in life. They choose something worth living and dying for. And yet true Christianity is really a call to 'Take up your cross daily, and follow me', for those who really want to believe. It's really a religion of 'live for Christ and die for Christ'."

"But Christians don't fight jihads."

"No, they don't but they're engaged in more warfare than you can imagine, and not just spiritually speaking. Christians all over the world today are in a position where they are constantly being persecuted. Jesus Christ was not joking when He said that men will hate his followers. In many parts of the world for instance, when you openly proclaim you are a Christian you face instant execution or blatant persecution – even here in our beloved country, and in the so-called free West. "In many Moslem countries, conversion from Christianity to Islam is allowed but not vice versa. As we get into Afghanistan for instance, you will hear stories of people who were killed or got missing because they were suspected, not even necessarily confirmed, to be Christians. The briefings must have told you of Aid workers who were killed if they were suspected of preaching to natives to convert them to Christianity. Even here in the States, it also happens but no one investigates too closely."

"So it is that dangerous?"

"Even more than I am telling you but it also has an advantage. It means that whoever says he or she is a Christian under those circumstances really is a believer, and willing to die for it. Here, being a Christian is just an assumption. It is more or less a casual admission without true meaning. Over there, it also invites reasonable people to explore and ask questions such as 'What is in this thing which we are not allowed to see?' More often than not, once they start seeking, they usually find Christ."

"And then what?"

"Well, God takes over their cause from there. Many of us are never privileged to know how those stories end. There are many secret believers in these countries and God knows them and is keeping them, even in Afghanistan."

Her imagination aroused, Laura mulled this over for some time. "What is the work of the army chaplain then? Are you there to make converts of the natives?"

"Far from it! One could actually be court-martialed by the U.S. Army for doing anything like that. It has happened before. I am there to look after the spiritual wellbeing of our troops, offer spiritual counselling when it is needed, and organize special services on occasions like Thanksgiving, Christmas, etc. Actually, most of my work is done in the hospital where I offer as much solace as I can to the wounded and dying. Sometimes, if we have prisoners, I also minister to them. Consider me the social welfare services in a very broad sense."

"Do you then never come in contact with the natives except when they are imprisoned?"

"Oh, sometimes I have to liaise with the local cleric over religious affairs as it concerns our troops, or as a public show of solidarity. I am also a fully trained marine so when there are lapses, I am pressed into duty, provided it does not involve my carrying arms."

"You don't carry arms!" Laura trembled for him. "How are you protected then?"

"When the occasion arises, the others must protect me, or I just trust God for protection."

"You brave man!" Laura exclaimed sincerely, "so you must have found yourself in very tight spots sometimes."

"Many times, many, many times. Fortunately for me those were in Iraq where they recognized my insignia as a chaplain and let me go. One of my colleagues was not so lucky. They recognized his insignia, but he was also toting the gun of the fallen soldier he was helping. They gunned him down immediately. Incidentally, the soldier he was helping survived. In Afghanistan, the Taliban seem to have a special enmity for chaplains. In fact, a recognized chaplain is sure to be executed. It happens often."

Laura trembled some more "And yet you're going?"

"And yet I'm going. I actually volunteered for this posting. Who is there to look after our men at their most vulnerable? They lay down their lives to defend our country. Any sacrifice made on their behalf is paltry by comparison." He said it so humbly and so simply that Laura was unaccountably moved to tears.

They talked on and on. Tim was talented in using words to bring stories to life. Laura enjoyed listening to him and watching his animated face. She also began to see how small her life had been besides so many of the people Tim talked about. They talked about the ethics of his profession, the obstacles he had to face and overcome almost on a daily basis, and on different fronts. They talked about Alex too. "We were at boot camp and Iraq together" Tim said. "We got separated when I went for my chaplaincy training. I was pleasantly surprised to meet up with him again for this posting. He was feeling depressed over his sister's illness and eventual death, but he is adjusting to it now. I must say that your coming seems to have done a lot of good for him."

Laura glowed and accepted it as a compliment. This man was very easy to talk to. She found herself discussing her feelings for Alex with him. "I have had a crush on him since we were younger, but he has always seen me as his bratty little sister. Now, it is even more so, since he believes he has to look after me. I am rather relieved that I shall not be all alone at Afghanistan though. I can at least list him as my next of kin."

Tim covered her hand with his. "You have me now too, Laura. In fact, you have all of us. No one dares mess with what the US marines deems precious" he said.

The look in his grey eyes was quite intense. Laura was deeply moved. To ease the tension of the moment she laughed instead and asked, "So are you to be stationed at Lashkar Gah?"

"No, we are to be stationed at Farah which is some distance to the west of Lashkar Gah. The Brits are covering the Lashkar Gah area. Both places are all in the south of Afghanistan though. Tell you what, why don't you come and spend some time with us at Farah before going to settle in Lashkar Gah? That way you begin with a holiday and get to know more of the country before you get down to work."

Laura agreed to think about it. It was not as if she was going to meet up with anybody at Lashkar Gah. Lil and Greta had indicated they would be delayed on the way coming in. She would rather they started exploring together than loaf around for about a week on her own. Deep in her heart, she also wanted more of the company of Alex and Tim. Who knows what changes could occur in a week?

By the time they got back to the hotel it was late. Dinner was over so they got room service sent to their separate rooms. Deliciously tired, Laura fell into bed and dreamt of Afghanistan. It was a land full of controversies. In her dream she wandered about the hilltops looking for something which continued to be just beyond her grasp. She was not sure what she was looking for, but she did not feel frustrated because she was enjoying the hunt. She was confident she would eventually find whatever it was she was looking for.

The next day, she left with the marines to Qandahar. After a three-hour stopover, she flew on with them to Farah.

CHAPTER 4

∞

The United States Marine had a base in Farah which was officially known to all and sundry, friends and foes alike. However, outside the town on the northern edge of the city limits was another satellite base, housed in what had been a rich man's manor. It was built in the medieval times, complete with round towers decorated with ramparts. It housed some of the basics of the army staff especially the faction responsible for gathering and disseminating intelligence. It could also be self-sufficient. They had chosen this manor because it was outside of town, and easy to defend. It did not have a medieval moat but the mountain to its back was a sheer drop. The road coming up from town made a sharp bend coming up to its front gate with a long run which was almost two miles long. From the tops of the ramparts above a strategically located gate house which the army had converted into a very modern and efficient security post, one could see the whole stretch of that road. Although it was public property, anybody coming up to it could safely be regarded as headed only to that destination, since the only building at the end of it was the base.

Apart from the gatehouse, the army had also resourcefully converted the whole manor into an efficient barracks. Some of its numerous bedrooms had been converted into living quarters, offices, storage units, interrogation rooms, and so on. The dungeons had been transformed into an efficient medical unit and the chapel. It was rumored that there was a secret tunnel from the manor to the mountains, but it was never discovered. The army engineers suspected someone must have sealed it in the past. The grounds once had sturdy stables and beautiful gardens. They converted most of the grounds to games, recreational and practice courts, and shooting ranges. The outside buildings became garages, helicopter hangars, generator houses, and supply rooms. Some sentimental marines even created three gardens with park benches. As far as army bases went, this one was very small but quite charming.

Laura and the marines arrived at the base late at night. Major Grafton was the unit commanding officer. He had approved Laura's visit, and assigned her a bedroom suite near the top of the building. She did not quite appreciate this favor until the following morning when she woke up and looked out of the window onto a breathtaking view. She could not have had a more beautiful introduction to Afghanistan. From Dorothy Simmons' presentations, she had imagined Afghanistan as vast, craggy, bare mountain ranges either covered in snow or multicolored rocks. What she saw instead were rolling fields of green, with the silver sparkle of the Farah River in the distance. If she was a poet, she would have composed an ode there and then. If she was an artist, she would have brought out her canvas and begun to paint. Since she was neither of these, she did the next best thing. She brought out her camera and took as many pictures as she could. Feeling the pictures were too overpowering to keep to herself alone, she sat down and wrote an email to Katie to let her know she was now on Afghan soil. She attached some of the pictures she had taken so Katie could see how beautiful the place was. They had been warned about the sort of mail and pictures of Afghanistan which must not be sent home. This was not one of those.

She finally showered, dressed, and went down to breakfast. Apparently, her fellow travellers of the past few days all had an early start. She was alone in the mess for a late breakfast. She met a few friendly marines, but they all seemed to be hurrying about their own businesses. She encountered Major Grafton in what served as the library and asked if there was anything she could do to help in any place at all. "Oh, just show up for dinner" he said. "The boys behave better when there is a lady at dinner. I should rather be asking you: Is there any way we can entertain you before you go to face your duties at Lashkar Gah?"

Laura could not think of any way. Major Grafton was very likeable. Despite his tall and ramrod stature, he still appeared doddery with his greying hair and benign grandfatherly smile. However, he ran a very tight ship and his men loved and respected him. At his back they called him "Iron master." He warned Laura again never to leave the base unescorted. He told her she could make use of the library and other facilities within the base. "We try to run an open house. You can enter any room you please" he said with a twinkle. "Anywhere that you find locked is probably out of bounds."

She found no reason to leave the base at all anyway. Sitting at her window gazing out for hours would have been enough entertainment. From her window she often saw the marines leaving and coming back from their duties. She did not see any Afghans but sometimes in the distance, she imagined that she saw shepherds herding their sheep. In the evenings, she joined the men at dinner. Even though they were loud and boisterous, they were generally very polite and courteous in her presence.

For the five nights that she spent there, Alex and Tim remained her constant companions at dinner. Alex was in the intelligence unit. He told her he had been quite busy but would not describe what his duties entailed. There was a bomb explosion in a nearby village involving some British army personnel and the Afghans they were training. The marines went to help. Some of the wounded had been brought back to the base and some were flown out to Qandahar. Some were even flown back home. The ones brought to the base had just minor physical injuries, but they had sustained more severe emotional injuries. Tim was spending time with them individually and collectively. "I work with the medical staff "he told Laura. "They number only three at the moment, so they are glad for my input."

Laura was about to ask if she could volunteer but Tim forestalled her. "We will certainly call you if we need you. For now, Major Grafton gave us orders to treat you as an honored guest."

On her fourth night, two journalists writing for a British newspaper, Sarah Wright and Sam Ferguson came to the base for dinner. They had lots of stories to tell especially about how the Taliban were blowing up the road that the Indian Government was trying to construct from Zaranj to Delaram as a friendly gesture. "One thing you don't understand about these people is whether they love or hate themselves. Talk about biting the fingers that feed you," said Sam.

"Or shooting yourself in the foot" added Sarah.

"But you know the Taliban is not the true voice of the people. Most Afghans are against the Taliban" Major Grafton suggested.

"Well, if they feel oppressed enough then they should revolt" Sam insisted.

"It is not easy to organize an uprising against God. When people commit atrocities in the name of God, how do you fight the Creator?" Sarah put in. "History abounds with many similar situations."

"Yes," Grafton agreed, "the Afghan problem is greater than meets the eye. It is often difficult to see for sure who the enemy is and what the common man really wants. Even when you think you have nailed it, you might find yourself shooting at your ally."

They were actually there to probe Major Grafton about the recent bombing, and the allegation that the Americans were supporting local warlords and the opium trade. Major Grafton was too tested a diplomat to be caught out in any compromising quotes. He too had stories to tell and some of them he was careful to say he had heard from sources of questionable reliability. The rest of the evening passed in a political bandying of words until the journalists gave up and left.

The very next day, Laura caught a glimpse of the American-Afghanistan dilemma. Looking out from the window of her bedroom, she saw a horseman riding furiously towards the gate of the base. The sentries on duty shouted to the man to stop. They must have repeated the order in four or more different languages, but the horseman just kept coming undeterred. One of the sentries started calling out with a bullhorn but this had no more effect than their earlier attempts. As he came nearer, it became clear that the man was also shouting, and waving something as he came. He was not far from the gate when the automatic lockdown system activated. He had just a few inches more to get inside the compound, but the gate slammed shut in his face.

And then, just from behind the last turn he made, two other horsemen came into view. They were firing at the lone horseman. One of them was using an ineffectual pistol but the other one had a very deadly rifle. The sentries began to return fire and the pair fell back. They turned and rode away in a manner which showed that some of the sentries' bullets might have hit home. It was more hair-raising than any Old Western movie Laura had ever seen.

But the sentries were not the only ones who had succeeded. Almost in slow motion, Laura watched as the lone horseman fell at the gate and his horse fell on top of him. The horse twitched once, twice and then was still. Laura flew down the stairs. She was not sure why she did so or what she was going to do when she reached the gate. Before she got there, the sentries had reopened the gate, and were disentangling man from horse. She met Tim as she dashed out of the door, coming from the opposite direction. At her inquiries about the horseman, Tim invited her to come and have coffee with him and he would try to brief her.

"He is still alive," he informed her, "But he is very badly wounded. He caught a bullet on the shoulder which is bleeding briskly but is not a very serious wound. The horse falling on him broke some bones. He is being moved to the clinic for a fuller assessment now."

"Will he live?" She asked.

"Oh, he will be kept alive long enough to talk. After that, well, who can say?"

"But why didn't they let him through the gate? He almost made it. Why did they close the gate in his face like that?"

"They did not close the gate in his face. The gate automatically activates under such circumstances for security reasons," Tim explained patiently. "He could have been a suicide bomber. The sentries kept giving him warnings to stop but he wouldn't. The other option would have been to shoot him point blank. He might then have ended up worse than he is now. Even under provocation, we are trying as much as possible not to kill the natives. That is not our mission."

"Why? Why? Why?" Laura kept asking. There were so many questions which begged answers. It turned out Alex was among those questioning the man. Life at the base seemed to be generally affected by their strange visitor. The medics worked hard on him to keep him alive. The Army Intelligence worked just as hard to get at what he had to say. Laura tried to keep out of the way as much as possible. Tim had to see to the other men who were also being treated. For the first time they did not meet up at dinner. She was left to her lonely self to speculate listlessly. She went to bed early but did not really sleep well. This was the unpleasant part of Afghan life that she had been warned about.

The next morning however, Tim joined her for breakfast. He cheered her considerably by the news that the horseman was much better. He said the man had some information which he needed to deliver to the Americans but did not know how else to do it. All their contact drop-offs were being closely watched by the Taliban. They had followed him from the last place he went. Tim said that even as they spoke, Alex and a detachment of soldiers were on their way to take care of the situation the man had mentioned. It was that urgent.

Laura sighed with relief that the horseman would recover. At the same time, she trembled with fear for Alex and the others who had gone more or less into the lion's den despite Tim's assurance that this was what the men were trained for. After such a violent introduction, Laura was not very reassured. She did not have much time to dwell on it, however. That same day she had to leave Farah for Lashkar Gah. A British contingent was going by helicopter for some provisions and would be glad to drop her at the United Nations Offices at Lashkar Gah. From there she would take a cab to where she was to be quartered with the other ladies.

Alex was not there to say goodbye to her. Even Tim was not there. They had said their goodbyes after lunch. They agreed to keep in touch regularly, at least by Skype every Sunday. He held her hand and begged her to remember that they were just a shout away. "Don't ever imagine that you have no one in Afghanistan. We are all here for you," and then almost too softly that Laura was not sure she did not imagine it he added, "I will always be here for you, Laura."

Major Grafton was there to wave her off though. He told the sergeant flying the helicopter to take very good care of her. "Why, she has softened the whole place by a presence of just a few days. Be sure to come back whenever you can, Laura. Your influence is good on these boys."

Laura thanked him very much, and then she was on her way to Lashkar Gah.

CHAPTER 5

∞

Lashkar Gah is a major city in southern Afghanistan, the capital of the Helmand province. Like most cities of Afghanistan, Lashkar Gah had a very long history predating even the conquest of the land by Alexander the Great. Strategically located at a slightly lower altitude than the ancient cities of Qandahar, Farah, and Zaranj, commanders had always used it to quarter their armies. Lashkar Gah literally means "Army Barracks". It has its own fort at Bato and so the city of Lashkar Gah itself is also sometimes called Bato. In the middle of the twentieth century, as a friendly gesture, the United States Army Corps of Engineers built a thriving irrigation for the agricultural development of the city, province, and country patterned after the Tennessee Valley Authority. By the time the project was handed over to the Afghans, a directorship for it had been constituted which was semi-independent of the government and in some ways even more powerful. Afghans from other districts of the province, and other distant places flocked to it seeking arable land and employment.

Accompanying the irrigation project had been a development of parts of the city with American-style houses and wide boulevards lined with verdant trees. With just a little stretch of imagination, one could feel oneself in the suburbs of one of the American cities. At the beginning of the Afghan-Russian war, the trees had been virtually all cut down. Security walls had gone up all around the houses giving them the unpleasant appearance of impenetrable fortresses. Ostensibly, these security walls served to protect the people behind them, and so it did most of the time. At other times, however, they served the purpose of hiding the atrocities perpetrated behind them from casually prying eyes. It was just the Afghan way of life.

It was in one of such walled compounds that UNESCO quartered Laura and her colleagues. The original two-storey house had been skilfully partitioned into three separate apartments and the basement. All these were connected by a common entrance hall but each still had its own private entrance.   Laura, Lil, and Greta were to share the highest level which had three bedrooms, a shared bathroom, living room, and kitchenette. The middle floor was a self-contained apartment with its own amenities occupied by an Afghan family. Shamir worked with UNESCO as a security officer. His wife, Ayesha, worked at home, and looked after their seven and four-year old boys. The family could speak English fluently. Ayesha was contracted to help out in language and culture instructions for the foreign women. She was also to serve as their unofficial mentor. They had more dealings with her than with Shamir who was also a fulltime UNESCO employee like them. Their offices occupied the ground floor and the basement.

By the time Laura showed up, Greta had already called dibs on the large Master bedroom which looked out onto the street. Lil, coming a day later had taken one of the smaller bedrooms which looked out to the backyard. Laura was left with the other back bedroom. The view from it was not bad at all. It was quite restful. Her room was simply furnished with a queen-sized bed, a desk, and a moderate-sized closet. Apart from the swivel chair at the desk, there was also a comfortable armchair. She knew she would be comfortable there; and had no complaints at all.

The shared parts of the apartment were also comfortably large. The living room looked out onto the street, and the kitchenette looked onto the backyard. From the back they could see there were two other buildings in the compound. One housed the two UNESCO four-wheel trucks which would serve their purposes from time to time. Close to it was a low bungalow which they were given to understand was the security house. It had its own separate entrance from the street. There was a door from it to the common backyard but they rarely saw it open. The rest of the backyard was large, enclosing a few trees, two park benches, and was encircled by a paved track on which Greta was soon doing her morning runs since they were not supposed to leave the compound alone. UNESCO had laid much emphasis on this. They must leave the compound only in pairs or trios, even to perform official duties. Once in a while they could call cabs in an emergency, but this was only to be on very rare and carefully calculated occasions.

    To get to their offices, they had to go down a flight of stairs, pass by Shamir's front door and then another flight of stairs. They did not have any other office personnel. They did all the work by themselves. They had large desks and cupboards. Their office space was almost always cramped. After they received supplies from the main office, they had to sort through and allocate them to stations where they were needed. What they handled included school materials ranging from textbooks, workbooks, exercise books, teachers' guides to whiteboards, pens, chalk, dusters, and so on. Apart from these, they also stored some basic medical supplies, seeds, cookies, and candies. These later materials were often needed as incentives before they could launch into major projects. At other times, the people needed medical help, and the women would be the closest to these needs ever being met. Sometimes they met someone with the medical knowledge but who lacked the equipment and supplies. Their visits would then be doubly welcome.

    Lil as the statistician did the primary survey, determining where their help was needed, and where they would make the most impact and when. Laura as the financial analyst worked out the logistics, how much material would be needed to start the project, and to keep it going. Greta as the education expert sourced for the manpower, whether to move it in from another area or to refresh and reequip whoever was already on ground. She worked out the kind of curriculum that would work best in any given place. Afterwards Greta and Laura wrote their reports, which Lil analysed, arrayed, and projected on how best to carry on from there. Each felt the others' work was more important. This created a healthy state of interdependence among them.

A typical day began with each waking up in her room and doing whatever morning routine she had. For Greta this usually involved running several laps within the compound. For Lil it involved doing some stretch exercises in her room. Nobody really knew what Laura did behind her closed doors but whenever she emerged at about nine, she was as refreshed and as invigorated as her colleagues.

Earlier than nine, Shamir would have left for the office, taking his two sons to drop them at school. At nine, the ladies descended the first flight of stairs and knocked at Ayesha's door. She would welcome them into her living room and begin their language and culture lessons for that day.

Almost everyone in Lashkar Gah seemed to be multilingual. They could speak Dari, which was their native language; and Pashtu, which was the official language of the nation, fluently. They could also communicate in Arabic which was the language of religion. Indeed, a lot of the common phrases in either Dari or Pashtu were Arabic. They also had some smattering of Russian because of the Russian war and occupation. English was also spoken because they had been colonized by the British in the remote past and were currently occupied by the Americans and the British.

Ayesha taught them Dari and Pashtu, and the common idioms among the people. She taught them local etiquette and what was expected of them. She said things like, "One thing you must maintain is your respect. This starts from your appearance; in other words, how you dress. Whenever you leave the compound, be sure you are decently attired. To be decently attired means that no part of your body or hair is showing apart from your face. You might not need to wear a Burqa but you must try not to attract unnecessary attention to yourselves."

They came to understand their "queer" living arrangements. Ayesha explained, "As long as you are under this roof, you are ostensibly married to my husband, and we are all under his protection. Nobody can allude to you or insult you as being a loose woman."

"Oh yeah?" Greta asked. "When did this marriage happen?"

"As soon as you agreed to live here, and a contract was signed on your behalf by your guardian which in this case happens to be UNESCO."

"So, we are now your 'Ben' (co-wives)?" Laura asked. "Is this like a Mut'ah marriage?"

"Yes, you are my ben" Ayesha agreed without even missing a beat "but this is far from a Mut'ah marriage. It's more like a Misyar marriage."

"In that case," said Lil, "it's my turn to keep our husband company in the bedroom tonight."

"Did I also mention that once the marriage becomes sexual you must wait the mandatory three months or two menstrual cycles of Iddat before you can be with another man?" Ayesha asked.

"Get out of here" Lil screamed in mock horror throwing a cushion at her.

"I didn't think you would like that. I see how that Bjorn looks at you even in a photo."

Their sessions were like that. Ayesha did not just teach them the languages and culture of Afghanistan but also imparted a lot of local wisdom to them. Like the trio, she was also in her mid-twenties, but she had seen enough of life and suffering. Combined with wifehood, motherhood, and a natural tendency to be bossy, she lorded it over them. However, since she was also very good-natured, the ladies never took offence.

In the 1970's, Ayesha's father had been one of the directors of the Helmand-Arghanba Valley Authority (HAVA) which had been developed by the Americans. He had been rich and powerful. With four daughters and one son, he had insisted that all his children received the best affordable education even during the Russian occupation. He had survived the war with Russia but had been killed by his own countrymen even before the emergence of the Taliban. Ayesha was the last of his children. She had been fortunate to have married her distant cousin and come under his protection before Lashkar Gah fell to the Taliban. Apart from her teaching the UNESCO women and her own children, UNESCO was aware that she had more than her fair share of regular, exclusively female, visitors. Something clandestine, but not illegal or counter-productive to the UNESCO project, was going on in Ayesha's home. Her tenants never asked her about it. These other women came about three times a week after their own lessons were over. Sometimes they chattered and joked loudly like housewives on a break all over the world did. Some other times they seemed to be too conspiratorially quiet that one doubted if they were really there; most times though, they just talked in quiet voices so that their voices reached their office as indistinct murmurs of people working in a group or in groups. They never met nor spoke to Greta, Lil, and Laura.

Ayesha also undertook to do grocery shopping for the ladies and to provide them with one hot meal a day, six days in a week. two women, who turned out to be Ayesha's relatives, came to clean the house and compound about twice a week. They blessed Ayesha for alleviating their poverty by providing them with employment. They used every opportunity they got to practice their broken English on the UNESCO ladies. The said ladies on their part also determinedly practiced their broken Dari on the women with the outcome that both parties would usually correct one another amidst gales of laughter.

Their lessons with Ayesha generally lasted about ninety minutes, three times a week from Monday to Wednesday or from Tuesday to Thursday. And then they had to face the work for the day in their office. Apart from planning and writing reports, many times they had to sort and package materials for various schools or communities. Sometimes though, they would need to make a field trip. The driver would arrive around noon. If there was anyone to be left in the office, such a person would carry on with the job of sorting and packaging.

Field trips were necessary because Afghans were notorious for exaggerating situations and inflating quotations. The ladies had to see by themselves where the needs were, and whether the work they were doing was progressing or not. The drivers served the multiple purposes of interpreters and bodyguards, besides driving them. Despite their help with interpretation, the ladies found that when they could put in a word or phrase in Dari or Pashtu it pleased the people a lot. These attempts often caused their listeners to nod solemnly with their heads cocked endearingly to one side.

Afghans have Fridays as days of worship, worked half of Saturdays and used Sundays as their first days of the week. For the sake of their own sanity, the ladies worked mostly indoors on Fridays, took half days on Saturdays, for as Greta insisted, she had to have "Some Normal" on Sundays. On Sundays they got invited to the British Army Base or to another foreign embassy not just in Lashkar Gah but even to Qandahar. Greta always went as if her life depended on it. Lil went quite willingly enough because of the good company. Laura went sometimes because seeing other people happy helped her get out of herself. Other times though, she begged off. She spent more time on those Sundays with Tim and Alex via Skype if they were available, or just tucking up her feet on the couch with a book while watching the world pass by the living room window. She had stopped remembering her losses with a great deal of pain even though her eyes still remained sad and introspective.

CHAPTER 6

∞

Field trips could last anywhere from half an hour to three days depending on where they were visiting, and what they had to do. Many times, they had to attend a shura as part of the advocacy for their project. At first, they were very apprehensive, but they soon learned to enjoy these sessions. This was when they learned that these people had a form of democracy which had probably been forgotten by the West. They discovered that Afghan women were not as totally muzzled as the outside world believed them to be, at least not at the grassroots.

Drinking tea constituted a basic part of Afghan hospitality. At first, newcomers assumed it was a way of warding off the cold. However, at some times in the year, especially in the southern regions, the daytime temperatures could be quite high up to the 90's, and occasionally over 100. Even then, Afghans still served and drank hot tea. Once Ayesha told her pupils, "Even enmity does not prevent the serving of tea. Sworn enemies could sit down together to drink tea then get up, strap on their weapons, and take their positions for battle. A better indicator of friendship is the conversation that goes with the tea."

Whenever they went on a field trip then, they had grown used to never beginning any serious talks before the inevitable tea had been served and drunk. Their being in a hurry never had any effect on this. The only exception, they soon learned, was during the month of Ramadan when Moslems fasted. At those times, nothing is expected to go into the mouth from sunup to sundown. Although they would politely offer their Kafir (Non-Moslem) visitors tea, social decorum demanded that they demur unless they were in serious distress, which they never were.

If their field trip involved checking out the suitability of an existing facility, degree of implementation of a project, the inspection of available amenities, or things like that, they usually dealt only with a few people and did not spend a lot of time. Sometimes though, their visit would involve persuading people to buy into the idea of breaking free of traditional or religious confinements to get their girls educated. In that case, they had to attend a prearranged village shura.

A shura traditionally was a meeting of the village elders in which decisions were made for the good of the community. Each defined community usually had a head or a Khan but he was more or less like the people's spokesman and representative with outsiders. Big decisions were usually made by having a shura to which anybody who wished to come was present. It is true that women and children stood separately during these shura but the UNESCO women soon learned they were also allowed their own say in such meetings, either directly or through representatives.

Every shura began with the inevitable tea before the Khan called it to order. He then presented the case as he saw it. This was followed by a debate or discussion exploring the pros and cons of the case. A period of questions and answers then followed. The Khan would then present the decision arrived at. If anyone felt the Khan was misrepresenting their views or opinions, further debates followed until everyone was in agreement, a compromise was reached, or an impasse arrived at. If there was an impasse, everyone would be asked to go home and think it over some more. The good thing was that once a decision was reached in this way, everyone pitched in to help, supervise, and oversee the project. Everyone became accountable for the success or the failure of the project.

Following the shura would come a period of feasting. Once, the ladies asked Ayesha, "There is usually so much to eat. This means the people must have sacrificed their meager resources because of us. How do we get around it?"

"If you do not eat, they would see it as an insult" Ayesha informed them. "They would feel you are covertly saying they are not worthy to cook for you or that their food is not good enough for you. You must taste a bit of whatever they offer you and tell them how you relish it. Having said that, also make sure you leave a lot behind. Feting you is also an excuse for them to have a feast themselves after you have gone. It is not often they get an excuse to celebrate these days so please do not deny them the pleasure."

This advice was not difficult to follow. Afghan cuisine was very excellent, beguiling, and in a class of its own. They enjoyed the meals with their varieties of fruits, nuts, and staples. There was always too much presented so that even if they stuffed themselves, they would still leave a lot on the table anyway. However, after this advice they became even more mindful of the other villagers that also attended the shura and would have a feast after they were gone.

Children too were ever present at these shura. They were more open in their curiosity about the foreigners. The women had taken to distributing cookies and candies in small packets to the children. Greta introduced the idea that they should line up to receive the goodies from their hands while they exchanged a word or two with them in their native language. She felt this was a more humane method than what their drivers had suggested. The drivers had suggested that the ladies should just spray the goodies among the children and let them scramble for it. Greta felt this was too unacceptable, undignified, and inhumane. Lil and Laura agreed with her even though distributing cookies and candies could take them the better part of two to four hours sometimes.

Their advocacy was always about how important it was to have their daughters educated, and what role the community had to play to have this ideal come to pass. If the community was forthcoming, they then advanced ways of how this could become a reality sooner rather than later. In one hamlet they had visited just outside Lashkar Gah for instance, the elders agreed that not only was this a good idea but also a feasible one. "The mosque lies empty from when the morning prayers are ended until we come back from the farms. Why don't we use the mosque? We could add extra classrooms if there is a need to" someone suggested.

"And we have some teachers here who are now working in the farms. We could share their farm burdens if they will agree to educate the children" another suggested.

The discussions went on along these lines. The UNESCO ladies were fairly sure they had another success in the bag when there was a commotion among the women. Fatma wanted to speak. Apparently when Fatma chose to speak, people stopped to listen.

"I have a question, and it is this. Why are we talking about sending only the girls to school? Are our boys not to be educated also? If we give all this education to the girls, and none to the boys, what will become of the boys? Are we not condemning them to the dragon smoke? Besides, everyone knows it is unimaginable for the woman's urine stream to go farther than her husband's."

Fatma said she had one question only but had managed to ask several, ending with a proverb. A proverb in Afghanistan lent weight to any speech. It showed that the speaker had thought deeply about what he or she had said. Truly, all her questions really embodied just the one concern: she wanted to know why educating the boys was not an issue too. Fatma herself had five boys and only one girl. She, too, wanted a fair share of the communal cake. Her reference to the dragon smoke was real. Afghanistan was a top cultivator of opium. A field of opium yielded up to sixty times in monetary value, what any other crop grown in the same acre would yield. Caught in a cycle of poverty, the people were virtually forced to go on producing opium as far as there was a market for it. But growing opium did not necessarily mean consuming it. The elders went to great lengths to see that their young ones did not become consumers of the stuff, seeing firsthand how its use could destroy a person's life. That was what Fatma was referring to. Should the girls be sent to school and the boys left to the dragon smoke? It is universal knowledge that the idle mind is the devil's workshop. Besides, as she said, if they had high achieving girls, which husbands will marry them if the boys did not also achieve highly?

It was a veritable food for thought. By the end of the day, it was decided that a school would start in that hamlet. The teachers who had been there would be retrained along with any other persons wishing to have a teacher education. The mosque would be expanded to accommodate more classrooms, and the school would be for both boys and girls. It had been a successful shura. Greta, Laura, and Lil went back to the drawing board to make it a reality.

Later on, Lil brought up the point again. "You know what Fatma said made a lot of sense. Why should we educate only the girls, and leave out the boys?"

"Because somewhere along the line they already recognize the importance of educating the boys, so they do not need any advocacy there" Greta stated realistically.

"Yes, but in these outlying villages, no big effort is being made to send the boys to school either. They end up being drafted by the bad guys if they have no other choices. I believe oppression of women is almost inevitable unless the men are also properly educated. If they are well-educated, they are likely to respect the women more than otherwise." Laura added.

"And look at statistics" Lil added. She was always telling them statistics do not lie. "The incidence of girls-only schools which catch fire is much higher than the incidence of mixed boys' and girls' schools that do."

This was so true. Girls-only schools had a habit of bursting into flames in the middle of the night and everyone denied any knowledge of what had started it. Not only that, students and teachers in girls-only schools had been known to be assaulted on their way to, or from school; or even during classes. There were incidences of gunfire in the playgrounds during recess, and of bombs exploding in schools. These happened almost exclusively in girls-only schools. The harassment was so much so that sometimes schools would resume in the morning and then the students be sent home about two hours later from such an incident or the threat of one occurring that day.

Mixed boys' and girls' schools were a bit different. For one, the girls had relatives – big brothers, cousins, or even uncles who went to the same schools and protected them. The girls were required to be properly veiled with a hijab (a shorter version of the Burqa). Sometimes there would be a screen dividing the boys and the girls in the same classroom. However, such schools had less harassment than girls-only schools. One village Khan explained, "If there was no dead body, the buzzards would not gather. We don't want to give the Taliban or the religious police an excuse for poking nose into our affairs. It is not as if the screens would prevent the children from mischief if they had a mind to do any."

It was true. The reasonable elders were concerned about the girls getting an education. Who was to blame them if they were concerned for the boys also? Laura saw it as a healthy state of affairs. Fatma's contribution changed their whole outlook towards their project. They put it in their next reports to UNESCO but went on with that vital change in their advocacy while awaiting orders.

Not every shura had satisfactory outcomes. On one occasion, they had arrived at a village in the Nimruz province close to the capital, Zaranj. They had been welcomed very excitedly. Initial greetings over; and the customary tea drunk, they sat down to the shura. Talk progressed pleasantly. The villagers had heard about what they were doing for other villages. They were very eager to have such a thing done for them too. They had about forty school-age children, some of whom had to trek some distance daily to get to schools in a nearby village. They did not have any schoolteachers but hoped arrangements could be made on their behalf. There was an abandoned compound close to the village center which they could all work together to rebuild and make into a school. They were so full of enthusiastic plans, and the UNESCO team did not need to do any persuasion. In fact, they really had little to contribute. They were going to help the village source for teachers and provide the materials which they lacked seeing how enthusiastic they were.

Suddenly, without warning, a woman emerged from the opposite side where the women and children were. It was not standard procedure, but it was known to happen. Mostly, the women spoke through an appointed representative or at least indicated they wanted to speak, and then waited for recognition. As this woman came towards the center of the shura, a ripple of murmurs went round the gathering including the name "Hadjo". The UNESCO team deduced the woman's name must be Hadjo. Without preamble she addressed the elders seated at the crude dais. "How can you forget? How could you have forgotten so soon? Was this not how we roused the anger of the Taliban? Was this not why they came killing our sons and our daughters? These people come pretending to be our friends. When the Taliban come, and we cry for help where will they be then? They sing sweet love songs to us and then when we get into trouble, they turn their backs on us. What will we have left? How much more can we bear to lose?" She spat at their feet and left the gathering wailing what must have been a dirge.

From this point the meeting took a downturn. All hopes came crashing down. The elders began to hem and to haw. Where there were enthusiasm and certainty before, there were now a lot of promises to look into things. They were no longer sure of anything anymore. At the end of the shura, nothing definite was agreed on, no lasting arrangements had been made. The feast following the shura was so subdued it could have been a funeral. No one seemed to have any appetite for any food. Even the children did not show much enthusiasm for the cookies and candies that came afterwards. Indeed, there seemed to be very few children in view after the shura. It was as if their scared parents had hidden them away.

On their way back to Lashkar Gah, their driver explained to them that the Taliban had coerced the villagers to allow them to lay an ambush for the foreign soldiers there not so long ago. Hadjo's son had broken out to go to warn the soldiers, but they had not arrived on time. When they came eventually, they were very few and ill-equipped. The Taliban had proceeded to massacre them too. Not only that, but they had also turned round and proceeded to kill those whom they believed had helped the foreigners. Hadjo's family had been virtually decimated. These happened not too long ago, and the memory of it was still fresh.

The UNESCO ladies understood. They could relate to the villagers as well as to the poor deluded foreign soldiers who had underestimated their enemies and endangered their friends. They went back to Lashkar Gah and wrote their reports. They recommended that a repeat visit be made after some time to see if the people were more amenable to having a school. Up until they completed their stint with UNESCO, no school had been built in that particular village. Those who were minded to sending their children to school still did so to the neighboring village under much peril, and considerable hardships.

CHAPTER 7

∞

"Baada, Baada, nanananananana, mmm, ba koda…" Greta hummed, imitating Malali as she cleaned the stairs.

Malali laughed. "That, Afghan love song. Song for wedding… You wedding?" she asked Greta in her broken English.

"Not yet, thank you" Greta replied. "And you?"

"Me, old woman. Already wed three times," she said holding up three fingers. "Now no wed again but we have wedding Saturday. You come, you, and your friends."

"I thought you said you were not wedding again, or did I misunderstand you?"

"No! Sister's son wedding. You come to wedding. Ayesha bring you and your friends, yes?"

"Now, that is quite an impromptu invitation. Me and my dhosts will talk about it. Khoob?"

Malali laughed again. She went on with her cleaning while Greta went down to the offices.

By now in the course of their duties they had been to so many Afghan homes but had never for once been invited to one in Lashkar Gah itself except perhaps for Ayesha's. Being in Ayesha's home was no big deal. They were her co-wives after all.

Their language and culture lessons held in her living room. When Greta put the proposal to the others therefore, it was indeed food for thought.

"Just like that? They can give out last minute invitations to a wedding just like that?" Laura asked thinking of all the protocol this would have entailed back home. The guests had to be carefully numbered and selected. RSVPs had to be counted. Any extra guest was considered an unwelcome burden at the least.

"Apparently this is the Afghan way of doing things, 'Come one, come all', and the more the merrier" Lil confirmed. "I won't be able to come with you, though. This is the weekend Bjorn is coming to Qandahar. I'll be going to meet him there and stay over for the weekend." She had been harping on this expectantly for weeks.

"I also have plans with Tom at the army base this weekend. I don't want to call and cancel on him at the last minute like this" Greta added.

"And I am certainly not going alone." Laura said, somehow relieved.

They resolved to tell Malali "Thanks, but no". They had reckoned without Ayesha, however. She was the one who brought up the topic. "I heard I am to bring you along for the wedding on Saturday. Sorry it had to be Malali inviting you. I had meant to do so myself. The bride is my cousin's niece, and the groom is Shamir's second cousin."

"But we cannot come anyway" Lil told her. "Maybe you will help us tell Malali."

"And what kind of excuses do you have? You were not invited on time? You have nothing to wear? You have other engagements? What?" Ayesha asked almost belligerently.

"Those are certainly very acceptable reasons where we come from" Greta answered for herself and for the others. "You don't just land extra guests on a couple at the last minute. Besides, we have not made adequate preparations."

"That is certainly a Western way of thinking" she told them firmly. "An Afghan wedding is an excuse to entertain guests. The very fact that there are foreigners, no less than from the United Nations is certainly going to lend a weight of honor and add flavor to the wedding. The story will be told for years with nice embellishments. Those excuses are not good enough."

And so, they came up with the real excuses they had talked about among themselves. Greta and Lil had already made other arrangements; and Laura could not, and did not want to, go by herself.

"You know, sometimes three of you amaze me with your stupidity for such highly educated women. For instance, Greta, don't you think your Tom would welcome an excuse for attending an Afghan wedding? If for nothing, it will showcase the harmless ways in which the troops are fraternizing with the natives. Goodness knows the allied forces could do with such useful publicity. In fact, if his commanding officer knew he had such an opportunity, he would command him to go." Greta thought briefly about this and nodded. Ayesha's insight was totally correct.

"As for you Lil, what do you think Bjorn would prefer: to talk about how he visited Afghanistan and how the hotel and its grounds looked like every other Hilton all over the world, or to actually talk about how he not only saw the real Afghanistan but also took part in an Afghan wedding? Which one do you think would make a more interesting story?"

Knowing Bjorn as she did, Lil knew he would rather have the second option. He was always going on about the difference between a tourist and a traveller. A tourist, he said, only saw the dressed-up parts of a country which the natives wanted you to see. A traveller on the other hand, saw a place as the natives were used to seeing it. They saw it from the inside. Bjorn would definitely value attending an Afghan wedding on the outskirts of a lesser-known town, far above just an indoor stay in the big city, and promenades in their made-up parks and gardens.

"And as for you Laura, when are you ever going to wear those Afghan clothes you bought? A wedding would be a good excuse to wear them to convince your friend Katie that you are indeed having a good time here and not just pretending to."

Laura had told them all about Katie and how she was convinced she was going to be killed in Afghanistan. Ayesha knew the button to press for each of them. It was not as if they needed so much persuasion anyway. They had heard a lot about Afghan weddings and really wanted to see what it was like to be a guest at one. It was all agreed then and there. They looked forward to Saturday with a great deal of excitement. Greta sent an invitation to Tom whose commanding officer was more than enthusiastic at the prospect. Bjorn was excited at the change of plans too. He was glad to change his hotel reservations from Qandahar to Lashkar Gah.

Later on, they talked about it in their own living room. "What about gifts? It is surely too late to go looking for wedding presents now" Lil said.

"Oh, presents are not necessarily given on the day of the wedding" Greta reassured the others, having looked up that aspect of Afghan culture online. "It is something you give afterwards after the wedding frenzy is over and then the new couple could use them more reasonably. We can send our gifts through Malali about a week or two after the wedding according to protocols."

"What kind of gifts should we give them?" Laura asked. "Back home we would have got her household stuff for a bridal shower or given her Departmental stores gift certificates."

"How about we give a purse? We could put some money in an envelope and address it 'From your UN friends'. I bet she will keep the envelope for years to show off to her friends and to her grandchildren. It will be proof that the United Nations attended her wedding," said resourceful Greta.

"That makes a lot of sense. If we pooled resources together, we would make a bigger boom" said Lil quoting a local Afghan proverb.

And so they did just that. They gave the couple a gift of twelve thousand Afghanis in an envelope written "From Your United Nations Friends". In United States Dollars this was just about two hundred and fifty dollars but to the new couple, it was a small fortune. Like Greta predicted, the writing on the envelope was worth even much more to them than what was inside it.

About a month before, the three had gone to the local bazaar and bought for themselves some ceremonial Afghan clothes. This was now a time to air them.

No matter what she wore on the inside, outside or overall, a woman in Afghanistan is not considered decently dressed if she was not wearing pants. Like women all over the world tended to do, even the most constraining or conservative of clothing could be embellished with some frippery if the wearer had a mind to make it so.

By about noon on the Saturday, they gathered in their living room, similarly, and yet very distinctly attired. All of them wore the loose pants, narrowed and embroidered at the ankle. Over these were the beautifully made calf length gowns, closely fitting at the top and then flared into long swirling skirts from the waists. The tops had loose full sleeves gathered at the wrist like the pants were gathered at the ankles. The gowns clung daringly to the shoulders, exposing the neck, upper chests, and the upper backs. The most attractive thing about the gowns perhaps, was the intricate beading and embroidery. These were richly done at the bodice, chest, waist, wrists and ankles. In contrast, the long sleeves and the full skirts were absolutely bare of any beading and embroidery. This plainness enhanced, rather than detracted from the beauty of the attires.

Greta's outfit had a background of cream with decorations in green, Lil's had a background of yellow with decorations in red but Laura's own was perhaps the most eye-catching, with a background of coral, and decorations of mixed gold, red, green, and blue. They swirled and admired one another like little girls playing dress-up.

At about one o'clock, Ayesha came to hurry them up. Shamir had left about three hours earlier, taking the boys with him. He would drop them with his in-laws, come to pick up the men from the bride's residence to go to do whatever men had to do together before they came for the bride.

Ayesha also looked very prettily turned out. She wore a background grey, decorated with a rainbow of colors. She took a look at the girls, went downstairs again and came back with her jewelry box. Out came long, dangling earrings, intricate necklaces, bracelets, arm bands, finger rings, and nose rings. There were even pieces for their foreheads and their hairs. By the time they finished, they looked festive indeed. "We shall finish up when we get to the bride's residence." Ayesha said.

"You mean there is still more?" Laura asked. "I am already feeling overdressed."

"Nonsense," Ayesha said. "It is not every day one gets a chance to dress up. Let's just enjoy ourselves."

"Speak for yourself, Laura" Greta added, "I am feeling like a Persian princess of the fables. Where is that your ever-present camera? I'd like to have pictures and videos of myself before I ruin all this with sweat."

They spent some time taking pictures and videos of one another, alone and in groups of different compositions. Ayesha joined happily. They were so busily occupied by this that by the time the doorbell rang at four on the dot, they were startled.

Bjorn had rented a minivan for the duration of his stay and had come to pick them up as appointed. He let out a wolf whistle when he saw the women. "Wow! Let's get married right here, right now" he said to Lil.

"O but you already have as it is. You have four wives, right here, right now! Ayesha, please explain it to him" Lil teased.

"No, he doesn't" Ayesha retorted. "We have not made any agreements nor signed any contracts with him. So please cover yourselves up."

She showed them how to drape their scarves daintily over their heads. This veiled them but somehow made them appear even more seductive. Amidst giggles and titters they piled into the van. The ladies all sat decorously at the back so that Tom would sit in the front when they picked him up from the base.

At the army base, Tom also let out a whistle too "Tell me I have gone to a Moslem paradise, and I am to be taken care of by these beautiful women" he said.

"Tom, you big oaf!" Greta chided affectionately as she made the introductions. "How do you know we are not kidnapping you to go and do atrocious things to you?"

"Looking as you are, I permit you to kidnap me and to do whatever you want with me" He sassed back.

Ayesha now gave them directions to the bride's parents' house where the prenuptial events for the women were happening. As they went, she explained, "By now, the men and the bride's representatives will be signing the marriage contract at the groom's place. Shamir is waiting to take you there. The men and the women have separate festivities, and then we shall all meet up at the hall for the final events. Shamir will explain it all to you, Tom and Bjorn, as you go along. We shall meet up later."

As they pulled up to the gate, Shamir was already waiting. The ladies got down. Shamir got in and the men drove off. Inside, their senses were assailed by colors and smells. Even the very air itself had a silky feel and tasted of honey. They were immediately served with tea and a pastry snack full of fruits and nuts. "Don't eat too much" Ayesha cautioned them. "There will be lots of food later on."

The whole house was full of noisy women. They were drawn towards a back bedroom full of the evening light. The bride looked as if she was in her late teens or early twenties. She smiled shyly at them and greeted them in English. She was bedecked in silks and jewels from head to foot. An artist worked on her hands, painting intricate patterns on them with henna. There were other artists about, doing the same for the gathered women. Ayesha seated her guests close to the bride and ordered everyone to speak English or speak slowly in Dari so her guests could follow the conversations. Apparently, they were in the midst of giving marital advice to the bride. The advice included things like, "Do not run back to your mother every time you have an argument with your husband"; "whenever your husband looks at you after lunch cross your ankles left over the right"; "be sure you have emergency spending money and shop where things are cheap"; and "remember to say your evening prayers in front of a glass full of water if you really want a baby boy."

Of course, most of the advice was supposed to be silly and humorous. The more serious ones had been done in private earlier on. Some women appointed themselves to make sure that every advice had some silly comeback. For instance, after telling her not to run to her mother with every problem, someone quipped, "You may run back to your mother whenever you have counted up to ten problems." To crossing her ankles when her husband looks at her, "Please remember to sit down if you were standing!" and to making sure she always had emergency money, "And treat yourself to a silk once in a while…" while to the recipe for baby boys someone added, "Exchange the water with fruit juice for a baby girl" and so on.

At a stage they asked the foreign women if they had any advice.

"Be sure to send your daughters to school" Lil said.

"And if you have only boys, dress them up as girls and send them anyway" someone quipped.

"If you become bored, watch Bollywood" Greta added.

"But don't learn how to sing like them. Afghan songs are better" someone added.

When it was Laura's turn, she could not think of anything to say. Suddenly in a half wail which lent weight to the benediction she blurted out, "Be happy! Just be happy!"

Tears came to the eyes of those gathered. The atmosphere following this was not one which permitted a wisecrack. In a rather subdued voice, another woman repeated, "Be happy! Be very happy."

The mood soon became light again. They traded stories of other wedding ceremonies, real, imagined, and fabricated. They told of near disasters which might have happened. There were stories in which gowns were embarrassingly ripped, henna dye spilt on clothes; hands which became too reddened; grooms who rejected their brides and vice versa. For the benefit of the foreigners, they recapped the fables of Queen Soraya's wedding, and the wedding gift of Aminbullah which resulted in couples being made the kings and queens on their wedding days, and their every wish being granted. They all began to talk of what they had wished or would wish for on their wedding days, and the feasibilities of having these accomplished.

"I wished to have my father's bank account, but he just laughed."

"I asked for a car, but nobody had the resources to give me one."

"I asked to go to America, but nobody could get me a visa."

"I wished I had another husband, but my mother told me to just shut up."

And so on. Some had unexpectedly pleasant surprises.

"I wished my brother would come from the war front for the wedding. Later at the feast there he was with his friends. I forgot I was supposed to be the dignified bride."

"It was at the wedding my father gave me my scholarship to go to college."

"At my wedding I got a whole case of jewelry. I had asked for just one."

There were pleasant memories and some that were not so pleasant.

They worked on doing and redoing one another's make-ups. Things which the Western women had never even seen nor imagined were brought out and applied. Eyelashes became impossibly longer and were sprinkled with shiners that stayed. Lips became so many different colors. The eyelids were painted, and eyes lined and elongated. The Western ladies did not know half of these cosmetics nor how to use them. There were different brushes, pins, pointers, and jars. It all seemed so overwhelming. Different types of perfumes were tried, dabbed, sprayed, sprinkled, and so on. It was good the windows were wide open and the day breezy or they would have been suffocated. If they had felt overdressed when they came, they could not recognize themselves now. Hand mirrors, wall mirrors, rotating mirrors were all there for them to view themselves and to primp. Laura had brought along her digital camera and the gathered women spent some more time excitedly taking and viewing pictures of one another.

At last, emissaries arrived to say that the men had finished, and they were to escort the women to the hall. The hall was not far away. They tripped over in their high heeled slippers. The men were already there lining the left side of the path from the street, down the aisle of the hall to the raised dais where two decorated thrones awaited the bride and groom. In contrast to the women, the men looked almost drab. Some of them wore Western-style tuxedos, some dressed in simple shirt sleeves, but the majority wore the traditional Afghan dhoti with beaded mini jackets and lungee (head gears). Although most favored black, brown, or grey jackets, there were still subdued varieties of colors ranging from sober dark blues, green or maroon to very bright colors here and there. A few men even dared to wear mixed colors. They did not look bad at all. The women just looked more spectacular. Tom and Bjorn looked rather distinguished in their ensemble of Western suits combined with dark blue lungee that someone must have loaned them, or they had bought at the last minute because they were not wearing them earlier. They looked quite handsome and imposing.

The women arrived and started lining opposite the men, to the right of the path and the aisle. Lil made a move to go to Bjorn. Ayesha hissed at her. "What are you doing? That side is for the men. The women stay on this side."

Lil stayed back. She and Bjorn contented themselves with making eyes at, and smiling at each other. There was a twelve-man band playing soft music in the hall. Greta recognized the songs Malali had been singing. At last, when the guests were beginning to get impatient, the groom arrived. He was escorted by his relatives to one of the thrones. Shortly after, the bride arrived. She was heavily veiled, and in the company of her mother and her attendants. She too was enthroned. There were some speeches in a mixture of Dari and Arabic which the foreigners could not follow but Ayesha explained that the mullah was stating why they were gathered. And then the attendants took the veil which was covering the bride. Extending it, they covered both the bride and the groom. A jewelled mirror was passed under the veil for the couple to see each other for the first time in their married state. They murmured to each other, and Ayesha explained that they were making promises to each other based on verses which each had chosen from the Quran. When they stopped talking, the veil was lifted. As they gazed at each other, the hall erupted in cheers and jubilation. This was followed by a loud outpouring of music. In Afghanistan this was more than enough brazen show of affection.

"Aren't they going to kiss each other?" Greta asked.

"Such blatant demonstrations in public are quite disgusting, and do not mean anything at all" Ayesha informed her, "but we must also be careful. There might be mosque police about."

Lil looked around her, "All the women are unveiled. Won't the mosque police mind?"

"This is a wedding ceremony! Besides, we are all still decently covered" Ayesha answered.

They watched as the bride and groom fed each other with cake and grape juice. After that, they separated again into men and women to serve themselves from the heavily laden buffet tables. There was rice cooked in different ways, different types of meat on stick (kebob), paan (bread), nut and fruits, both fresh and processed in various ways and quite unrecognizable. There were different types of soups, gravy, and so on. For the amount of food on display, one would never have guessed Afghanistan had any shortages. Again, Ayesha pre-empting them, explained that the families must have saved for ages to have this occasion. They would also make further sacrifices in months to come to cover up this lavishness. Family and friends would also have pitched in to help. "But a wedding does not happen every day. We make the utmost of it whenever it does, especially if it is the first time for both. It is much different if either of them had been married before" she concluded.

As they were finishing their food, Ayesha explained that there would be dancing. "First there is a general dancing in a circle. That is Attan. Afterwards, there will be the dancing of married people. After that, all manner of groups will be called to dance. The wedding ceremony is now officially over so if you wish to leave at any time, just go and say goodbye to the new couple and go."

They stayed a bit after the Attan where all the guests formed a rough circle and danced to band music, sometimes even holding hands. Afterwards, they watched a few dances and then decided to call it a night. Ayesha said she would be coming back with her family so five of them left in Bjorn's rented van. They dropped Greta and Tom at the army base, Laura at the empty house, and then Lil went back with Bjorn to his hotel.

It was almost midnight when Laura got to her room. It had been quite a day. She was tired but too excited to sleep. She spent time clicking through the pictures and videos they had taken that day. It would make quite a viewing. She was glad she had a very large memory card. She uploaded them to her laptop and sent some off to Katie. After sometime, she decided to also send to Tim and Alex. It would make some interesting viewing, and hopefully lighten their days. On that thought, she shut down her computer and got into bed. All in all, she was very glad she had come to Afghanistan.

CHAPTER 8

∞

The day after the wedding, Laura woke up late. She had not heard Ayesha and her family come back but was not assuming she had the whole house to herself. She opened her window which had a view of the mysterious gate house but also a very nicely kept lawn in between. It was a very pleasant day. The sun was not yet very hot, and the breeze was pleasant. Back home it would be early spring and with this kind of weather people would not be able to resist the parks. Some very active people would even be on the beaches already or up mountain trails, hiking.

She enjoyed a leisurely breakfast, brought out a novel to read but just could not concentrate on it. She was to get on Skype with Tim and Alex around one in the afternoon. She made some tea for herself, complimenting herself for becoming a true Afghan. She did not really feel hungry but made herself an egg sandwich anyway. There was something the bakers added to Afghan bread that gave it a special flavor. Greta and Lil agreed with her that whatever it was, it tasted very pleasant indeed.

She found herself drawn to the wedding photos and videos. She thoughtfully admired the intricate henna artwork on her hands. They said it would take weeks to fade. Its purpose was to keep reminding her of the wedding. How apt! These people really knew how to appreciate the life they had. Who ever said money was essential to happiness? Memories assailed her, some of them unexpectedly bringing tears to her eyes. When she was younger, she had never understood why people cried at weddings.

She had now become one of those who cried at weddings without knowing why. Life was so touching.

Laura was still in that mood when Tim and Alex called her up on Skype. They were both in Alex's room. As usual he was still trying to straighten it up even as they came online. Tim was his usual neat self.

"How did your week go?" asked Tim.

"It went very well. The usual things except that we went for a wedding yesterday."

"Cool!" Alex said, landing on his bed with a thump. "I attended some weddings by default last year and boy, were they colorful!"

"This one certainly had lots of color" Laura replied. I sent pictures to you guys. What do you mean by default?"

"Oh, we got intelligence that there was to be a bombing at a wedding so we had to mount guard at several weddings which might be targeted."

"Did it help?" Laura inquired curiously.

"Oh, there was no bombing at the ones I was assigned to but as soon as we relaxed our vigilance, Wham! One happened. It was so sad."

"Stop depressing Laura by your tales. Laura, tell us about this one you went to." Tim asked.

Unlike Alex, Tim had a way of zooming in to her moods. She had actually begun to feel weepy at his tale of so much happiness gone awry. What if there had been a bombing at the wedding yesterday? She trembled at so much happiness being suddenly ended, hope giving rise to fear in an instant, just like that. Her thoughts were beginning to go along this lane when she was roused from her reverie by Tim. They had now opened her mail and were looking at the pictures together.

"Oh, I see the pictures you sent. You gals really looked groovy. Who did you know? Was it the bride or the groom?"

"Neither, but both of them are related to our landlady and to our cleaning lady. It was actually the cleaning woman who invited us."

"You can depend on Afghan hospitality. I'm sure no formal invitation was even needed. Their events are usually come one, come all" Tim said.

"Exactly!" Laura agreed. "We had begun to object but Ayesha overruled all our objections. We didn't even know the cleaning woman and our landlady were related to each other."

"Almost everybody in a small town is related to everyone else one way or the other" Alex said "but that is not even the main issue. You might even discover that some of the guests are beggars off the streets."

"The people I saw there looked nothing like beggars at all. They all looked too richly dressed to be beggars."

"Don't be surprised. One of the pillars of Islam is to give alms to beggars. One of the best ways of giving alms is to invite them to communal feasts and occasions." Alex rejoined.

"Yes, but you usually invite them towards the end to come and partake of leftovers" Tim said. "Even then, true Christianity could borrow a leaf from that."

"Talking of which," Laura said, "How was service at the base today? What did you preach about?"

"The service went well. More of the men found time to come. We actually looked at the parable of the Great Feast…"

At this point, Tim became a bit carried away. Laura had never met anyone who believed so much in what he preached as Tim did. Back home, Laura was not much of a churchgoer. Here in Afghanistan, where there was no church to go to, she found herself looking forward to these conversations with Tim. She had never truly appreciated the faith she was raised in until she came to Afghanistan, where there was nobody to discuss it with. In fact, religious discussions were prohibited even in private if it was not Islam. UNESCO had taken time to ask about their religious convictions and the strengths of them before they were taken on. They were strictly forbidden to discuss their religious profiles with any Afghan. Even among the troops, religious discussions or public demonstrations of religious rites other than the Islamic were prohibited. Only people like Tim who looked after the spiritual welfare of the troops were allowed to talk religion. Even then it had to be in strict privacy, in the army chapel, or hospital. But Tim talked of his convictions as a second nature, maybe even a first nature. As Laura had discovered in Miami, it carried into his everyday conversation and was so real that people listened. Even boisterous Alex became quieter when Tim "talked religion". It was uncanny. One listened to sermons and analogies without knowing one was in the midst of a religious discussion.

On this day too, with questions and answers, and talking about their jobs in the foreign land they found themselves, time passed. Before long, Alex was saying, "That was the dinner gong. We better get to the mess before it's all gone."

They signed off. With a sigh Laura realized that she was hungry as well. She heard the sound of Ayesha calling her sons to dinner and went to ransack the fridge for something to eat. Just as she pulled out a quarter chicken there was a knock on their apartment door. She went to open it and found Ayesha there, holding a basket. "I brought you some leftovers from the wedding. I figured you would probably be alone and not feel like cooking" she said.

"Oh Ayesha" Laura gasped, "You are a lifesaver."

Immodestly Ayesha replied, "I try my best, I do", and she went back down the stairs to tend her family.

"Thank you," Laura called after her. "I will bring the dishes and the jewelleries later."

"Take your time" Ayesha threw over her shoulder from the stairs.

There was enough in the basket to last all three of them some days. Laura helped herself to some nuts and cold meat, and put the rest away. Who said life was not good?

The next day was an Afghan statutory holiday to celebrate the first day of the Farmers' New Year, Nowruz. The celebrations usually lasted about two weeks but the first day was the most important. Workers usually had this first day off, and mid-semester breaks are usually announced for schools. There was not much to do in the office anyway. They had put themselves out to do as much as possible to clear their backlog and go a bit in advance. They had a few new projects brewing but they would need to do some field work first. They could not really do this since their Afghan drivers had to have the day off. They also had to do some skeletal work for the next two weeks before it became very busy again. Laura expected Greta to come back Monday evening. Bjorn was leaving by a flight the following afternoon to Qandahar, and then onward to Denmark so Lil would not be back until Monday evening either. She lolled about until she was finally able to settle into her book, and let it absorb all her attention.

She slept off with the book in her lap and had a queer dream. She dreamt she was at a wedding but someone outside and across the road was calling to her for help. As she went towards the voice, it kept going further and further into the hills. At last, she found herself surrounded by cold frightening shadows. She woke up shivering and realized her windows were open, and the lights were on. She got up, closed her windows, turned out the lights and crawled into the comfort of the sheets.

When she woke up the next morning, it was broad daylight. She seemed to have the house all to herself, but she could hear the whole town celebrating. She left her back bedroom to the living room from where she could catch glimpses of people out celebrating. The Farmers' New Year was also the official end of winter, and the beginning of spring. As for the conservative Moslems, it should probably be condemned for its pagan connotations but who did not welcome spring especially after a harsh winter? This was a good enough reason to celebrate. It was a time of giving gifts to one another, visiting, and appreciating the facts of surviving through yet another year. Laura would have liked to go to see what was happening outside on the streets, but she was mindful of the fact that she must never leave the house alone. She turned on the television and watched as people celebrated, turned out in their colorful garbs as they danced, gave speeches, and had roadside barbecues. She loved these people. She put together the things to be returned to Ayesha, listened carefully to see if there was any movement in the apartment below. When she could not detect any, she decided to postpone her going down. She divided her attention between looking out the window, watching the television, and reading her book. She resolved to walk around in the grounds later in the afternoon for some exercise but for now she was content to just sit idly.

Around noon, there was a knock on her door. Surprised, she went to answer it. Ayesha stood there. "I thought I was quite alone in the house" Laura said. "I was coming to return things to you."

"Well, I'm here. The boys went to watch a football match with their father, so I have some moments of peace" Ayesha said.

"O Wow!" Laura said. "I may as well get those things now." She went to pick them from the dining table where she had left them.

"There is somebody here to see you" Ayesha said, taking the basket from Laura.

"To see me?" Laura was surprised but opened the door wider. Ayesha did not come inside.

"It's a woman. She's waiting near the gate." Ayesha said. "It took all I could to even persuade her to come into the compound. If you want, I can send her away."

"Are you sure it is me she really wants to see? Did she ask for me by name?"

"What she said was, 'the Sad One that looks like us'. I assumed she could not mean Greta or Lil."

"What a description!" Laura sighed. She put on her slip-ons and automatically reached for a veil. As she came down the stairs, Ayesha threw her a cautious "Be careful" before going into her own living room.

Laura came down the stairs and opened the front door. Her visitor was just inside the gate. She could not see much of her. She was heavily veiled even for a respectable Afghan. Laura noted they were about the same height, and the woman carried herself well, projecting a quiet dignity. Without speaking, the strange woman gestured that they should move away from the door, towards the gate. Laura looked towards the gate and saw that she had come with a male companion. Laura was certainly not going anywhere with this woman. She was going to remain within the distance that Ayesha would at least hear her if she screamed. She moved about two steps from the door and then stood with her feet apart, firmly planted to the ground, indicating that she was not willing to go any further than she had already come. Her visitor noticed her hesitation. Without preamble, she launched into the reason for her visit.

"I am sent by Il-Dhost to bring you" she said in a very low voice, "We need your help."

"Who is Il-Dhost? Who are you?" Laura enquired, "And what kind of help do you need?"

"It is difficult to explain. You must come and see."

The woman's voice was low but her English was refined. She spoke with the musical lilt common among educated Afghans. "Dhost" according to Laura's understanding from her language classes meant "Friend", spoken with a slightly different inflection whether in Dari or in Pashto.

"You must understand; I don't know you. I cannot just leave this place and follow you without security. Please forgive me. Tell your friend I cannot come."

"We know about you" the woman persisted. "We have been seeking an opportunity to talk to you. We could not talk with you at the wedding yesterday. There were so many people. We must have your help. If you can trust me and come and see Il-Dhost, everything will be explained."

"I'm sorry. I cannot come with you. Please let your friend understand how it is."

The woman looked at her speculatively for some time, nodded mutely and turned. She went out through the gate and vanished around the corner with her companion. Laura went back into the house. As she went up the stairs Ayesha asked if she was finished with her visitor already and she simply said yes. Somehow, she did not feel like discussing it with Ayesha, and the latter did not probe. Laura just kept it in her mind and mulled it over. Back home, the expression which would be used for how she felt after this meeting would be "Creeped out" or "Weirded out". She could not, for the life of her have been able to describe her visitor afterwards except for her height. Even that was debatable. For all Laura knew she might have been wearing very high heels. She had not had a good look even of her eyes. She could not say what color they were except that they seemed to glow behind the veil. Her voice had been low and musical. Her English had been refined. Other than that, she could not describe her visitor. It could have been any of a thousand or even million Afghan women.

What disturbed her most was the woman saying they could not talk to her at the wedding. So they were a group, it was not a one-person thing. They were in an organized group. What was more, they had been there at the wedding, and had been watching her even before then. She did not feel terribly alarmed however; or stalked. Apparently, whoever they were, if they had meant to harm her, they had ample opportunity and would have done so a long time ago, at the wedding, or even that very afternoon. They knew where she lived and worked. She admitted to herself that she was uneasy about the whole thing but not unduly alarmed. She considered how she now felt about going for the wedding. After searching her mind, she did not find it in her to feel sorry that she had gone.

"Il-Dhost"! That was another reason not to feel alarmed. The person who wanted to see her was a friend. Same words had different connotations in different languages, but the general meaning remained the same. Surely, a friend was the opposite of an enemy. True, the emissary had not mentioned whether the direction of the friendship was towards Laura or not but hopefully it meant positive intentions. They wanted her help, not her death or something like that. She turned all these over in her mind and was still glad she had not gone with her mysterious visitor. That would have been foolhardy, but she decided she did not feel threatened either.

That night, Greta and Lil came back still basking in the afterglow of the wedding. Bjorn and Lil had decided to get married as soon as her stint was over. They were now trying to decide whether to make it an Afghan-style or a Swedish-style wedding.

Greta too talked of going to the next level of commitment with Tom which was saying something for Greta because she had the habit of dangling different men at the same time. The wedding certainly had a measurably positive effect on all of them. In the midst of trading feelings and stories, talking of Ayesha's gift basket, and returning her jewelleries, Laura totally forgot about her strange visitor.

Chapter 9

∞

Work soon resumed in earnest. Their sixth month and one year's assessments had been done. They indicated they had no trouble working with one another, and that they were making progress. By now they had covered as much ground as they could in their assigned area. Their proposal that Boys' and Girls' schools be supported while encouraging the enrollment of girls had been approved. They had planted, upgraded, and inspected many schools. They had attended a lot of shura, and written so many reports that even they, could appreciate the fruit of their labors. As they drew towards the end of their second year, they sought to spread their influence farther afield. Their reasoning was to do as much as possible within this time period so that the last nine months of their stint would be spent consolidating what they had already done. It was a very good plan. The UNESCO special projects in Afghanistan were also time-limited. At some stage they would also need to start training the natives to take over while they looked on from a distance.

The team had heard about Aid personnel being killed or kidnapped but these incidences were mostly in the north and to the east of the country. Two UN workers had been kidnapped, and their driver shot dead the previous month. Soon after this happened, Alex and Tim had begged Laura to be very careful.

"I have stayed in this country for almost two years now. I am so careful that I have not met even one Taliban. I hear talk about them, but I am yet to meet even one" Laura replied. "How will I sound credible when I get home?"

"You mean no one has come up to you wearing a sign that says, 'I am the Taliban!'" Tim teased her.

"Don't think they are bogeymen invented to keep you awake at night." Alex said more seriously. "They don't look any different from the people you meet on the street every day. Even ordinary-looking people might be spies in their pay. Just please be careful and watchful."

"Okay, I hear you. But what should I be watching out for? What are the danger signals? Is it the kind Mullah at the Bazaar, the man at the teashop, or perhaps poor old Ismail who comes to take away our garbage? Most of the men here wear bushy beards. They live by the Quran, and they do not threaten anybody. Should I watch out and be suspicious of all of them?" Laura asked heatedly.

"What Alex is trying to say," Tim pacified, "is not to take anything for granted. Always travel with a minimum survival kit; and whatever happens, try to get word to us."

"But of course, what else could I do? Even if I don't get word to you, you will eventually hear it since Alex is listed as my next of kin." And then she softened. "I know you are worried about me. I appreciate that. However, if we all live in crippling fear, the work is never going to get done. We all knew that kind of thing could happen when we signed up, but we keep praying it would not happen to us or to anyone we know. Don't worry, whatever happens, I am still hoping to come to Farah for Christmas, that is, if the invitation is still open."

"It is still wide open" Tim confirmed, pacified. "Alex is going home around Thanksgiving but should be back by Christmas, isn't it so, Alex?"

Alex grunted a confirmation and the talk shifted to other things.

Christmas came and went. Laura spent ten days at Farah. She enjoyed herself immensely. Major Grafton had welcomed her like long-lost kin despite the fact that he was chaffing under an enforced prolonged stay. He grumbled to Laura "I thought I was going to be here for only one year. This is my thirty-first month running. One would think someone has forgotten that I exist or that there are other very capable men in the United States Army to come to take my place."

"Maybe they just have not found one good enough for this sensitive place" Laura pacified him. "Besides, all your men adore you. Some other person might undo the good you have achieved so far."

"Whatever!" he growled, but he enjoyed the compliment. When the base hosted a dinner for all the foreigners who were in town including some journalists on Christmas Eve, he was his usual taciturn self, bandying words with the journalists while avoiding giving them any direct quotes, to their utter frustration.

At that visit too, Laura found herself attracted more and more to the quiet Tim, and less and less to Alex. True, by accident or arrangement she found herself more in Tim's company than in Alex's although the two were still often together. She noticed however, that even in her thoughts she was beginning to think of them more as "Tim and Alex" rather than as "Alex and Tim" as she had been wont to. If she was a teenager, she would have chided herself for having all the classic signs. She looked forward to seeing him. She could listen to him or talk to him for hours on end. Whenever he was in a room or came near, her heartbeat quickened, and her stomach turned flip-flops. She found herself watching his mouth when he talked and wondering what it would be like to kiss him. She grew warm all over wondering what it would be like to be held in his arms. She had no idea if he felt the same. He had always treated her with the utmost courtesy and decorum. She found herself wishing the visit would end quickly, and then that it would not end at all.

When eventually the visit ended, she felt as if her heart would break. Alex was to leave with a scout that morning to a hush-hush destination. He hugged her tightly and warned her again to look after herself, and to let them know at the base "if there is anything, anything at all which you do not like, cannot understand, or that disturbs your peace of mind. Do you understand, Laura?"

Laura said that she understood. She averred again that so far, everything she had seen, heard, or experienced had buttressed the fact that most of the dangers people talked of about Afghanistan were exaggerated.

Her parting from Tim later that afternoon was more emotion-charged. Tim hugged her too and she felt warm all over, and safe. Tim's hug was like a cozy blanket on a very cold day. She felt like never letting go. He held her lingeringly. "I wish I could keep you and come back each day knowing you are here. However, you know that even if I watch over you all the time it wouldn't keep you safe."

"Uh-hum" she murmured in agreement.

"But I commit you into God's keeping. He will watch over you and keep you safe. "

Laura murmured again. She was trying to hold back her tears. "Oh Laura," he moaned, "You will always be in my heart, always" and then he let her go. It was amazing how she even found her way to the army truck in which she was to hitch a ride back to Lashkar Gah.

At the last bend in the road, she looked back and saw Tim still standing there, his hand raised like a benediction.

She did not know it, but the men teased their chaplain tirelessly about his "Lady love". In his heart Tim knew he had never felt about anyone how he was now feeling for Laura. He also did not know what he should do about it. He knew how she had felt about Alex because she had told him at Miami. He also knew that all Alex felt for her was the filial love one had for a little sister, and nothing more. He too had confided in Tim. Even if her feelings had changed, was it not like stealing one's best friend's girlfriend? He was unhappy but also somewhat relieved when the visit ended. It was becoming too difficult to keep his feelings bottled up. Besides, they were at the battle front, more or less. He resolved to maintain as much distance as possible between them, at least until they finished in Afghanistan.

Why then did he eagerly count the days until it was time again for their Sunday Skype sessions? Even over Skype his heart leapt as soon as he caught sight of Laura's face. Why did he dream about her and long for her with an almost physical ache? Why were talks of love and marriage always creeping into his sermons these days? Most of all, why was he always wishing Alex would talk about her, and yet afraid that his true feelings for her would be exposed?

Back in Lashkar Gah Laura threw herself into the project to help her stop thinking of love in Afghanistan! She had no one to really discuss her feelings with. She was not even sure of what those feelings really were. Greta and Lil lived in a world of their own. Their values were not exactly what Laura would have chosen for herself, anyway. She realized they were all different, and she respected their diversities.

Ayesha was from a totally different culture, with different views and values. She had told them once that having one's mate chosen for her was much less tedious than sifting through life to find "The One". She said that a dutiful daughter was supposed to be content with the choice of mates her family made for her, and then get on with life. Whether this represented her own view or a projection of her cultural view, they had never established. Ayesha had strong views of her own on so many issues but believed one should have a realistically whole outlook to life from all angles.

Laura would have liked to talk it over with Katie, if for nothing else, to have this foolishness laughed out of her. However, Katie was not an internet person. She never used Skype and she felt that putting her feeling into writing was just not the same thing. Laura worried if she was even good enough for Tim. Would loving him not distract him from his work? She acknowledged that she now believed as Tim did, but her faith was at best in very early infancy while his was advanced. Indeed, until she met Tim at Miami, she had never thought of what it meant to be a Christian. With the restrictions she had met at Afghanistan, she had begun to really look into what the

Christian faith involved. Why was it rousing so much antagonism? She had searched the internet, dug into history, talked over Skype with Tim and Alex. She had finally come to a commitment all on her own. Commitment is followed by growth. Inasmuch as she knew she was growing, she felt she was not up to the stature of what Tim should have for a wife.

There it was again, the "W" word. She was not even sure of Tim's feelings. Surely just as many young women must consider themselves in love with their counsellors, such must be the case with pastors or spiritual mentors such as Tim was to her. Even the female marines she had met at the Farah base during Christmas all seemed to be in love with him.

"Hey Laura, are you alright?" Lil asked.

"She's in love" Greta announced. "She has been mooning around since she came back from the Christmas holidays. Spill it out Girl and let us get on with the work."

"What are you talking about?" Laura asked.

"I'm talking about the fact that Lil has asked you the same question three times and got no answer at all. I, for one, know you are in love, so I am asking you to spill your guts."

"I was just not concentrating" protested Laura.

"Exactly! So, my question is: 'why are you not concentrating?' Still waters like you run very deep. Now, take me for instance..."

"We are not doing personal confessionals here" Lil butted in.

Greta's love life went like a soap opera. She was so vivacious that she had a soul mate for every army contingent which came to Lashkar Gah. She also promptly forgot him once he shipped out again. Tom had lasted until he went back to England. Dick was now her reigning Flame. Lil teased her that Harry was on the roll next.

"What I asked" repeated Lil "is whether you think it wiser to go to Zokwa first before Gereshk. With Gereshk we would be concluding the areas around

Qandahar but with Zokwa we still need to visit six or more places, and we will need to be on the road for about three days."

"Let's finish with Gereshk by this week so we can devote the whole of next week to the Nimruz province" Laura said.

Lil nodded. "I thought so too. Greta still has a few things to tidy up. If two of us should go to Gereshk tomorrow, by next week we shall all be able to go to the Nimruz province together."

"Okay. That is settled then" Laura said.

"Good luck!" Greta said. "With the mood she has been in, you will probably find yourself with no good company on the road. Just hope she still remembers who she is sometimes."

The visit to Gereshk was uneventful. They had a restful weekend afterwards. On Sunday, as usual, Laura had her Skype conference with Tim and Alex. Alex mentioned he had talked with his parents earlier that day. "Mum said to let you know there was something of Allison's she was keeping for you. You are to be sure to go to see them as soon as you returned."

"What was it?" Laura asked curiously.

"She didn't have time to say. She was to drive Dad to hospital and was in a bit of a hurry."

"Hospital? He's been ill?" Laura asked, alarmed.

"Oh, old age problems, I guess. His prostate has been bothering him, but they don't believe it's anything too serious."

"Wow! Now I feel like going to be with them."

"You're very caring and compassionate" Tim said, and Laura blushed.

She mentioned the planned trip to Zokwa. "It should take us about three days. We will be back by Thursday. We've agreed to work hard to cover as much ground as possible and use our last few months to consolidate. That way, the team coming after us will have a solid foundation to build upon."

"It sounds like a very good plan for living life in general" Tim acknowledged.

"Is there anything this girl does that is wrong in your sight?" Alex asked Tim.

"Probably; but I haven't noticed any today, have you? You must admit that it is also right to give honor to whom honor is due" Tim said. Alex laughed, and Laura blushed again.

That was to be their last conversation for a very long time, but they did not know it. The next week, the ladies went on that field trip. They did not return as scheduled.

PART 2

CHAPTER 1

―――――∞―――――

Aziz came back to consciousness slowly. The first thing he became aware of was that something uncomfortable was jamming into his right hip. He shifted his position a bit to become more comfortable. He next became aware of the fact that he could smell the ground. It was an earthy smell of grass and rain which was not altogether unpleasant. Next, he became aware of the warmth of the sun on his body, under his body and all around him. That was when he fully came awake. He realized he was lying in an open field with maturing opium poppies all around him. Without moving a muscle, he did a mental check for any unusual aches or pains. There was none. He listened very hard for any human noises and could not hear any. He listened for the rumble of any moving vehicles. He thought he heard some, but they were rather far away.

He remembered clearly that they had come up to a roadblock manned by some mean-looking men with half covered faces who had not returned his friendly greetings. If he was still alive, that was good too. If they had dumped him where he was now, who knows, by some miracle the ladies might also have been dumped somewhere nearby. He did not hold much hope for this though. The ladies were much more valuable than him in many ways to any bandit or to the Taliban: to rape, to hold for ransom, as bargaining chips, or just for the plain symbolism of it. Nevertheless, if they had left him unaccountably alive, perhaps by the same token, they might have shown the same mercy to at least one of the ladies. Cautiously he called out in English, "Ma'am… Ma'am… Are you there?"

He peered into the bushes to see if there was any sign of color or movement. He did not really expect them to answer, and they certainly did not. Happily too, no other person answered. He was shaken, quite thirsty, and very bewildered. Idly, he thrust his hands into his pocket as he was wont to do whenever he did not know what else to do with them. That was when he felt the keys. The keys! The truck keys! That must have been what was digging into his hip. Aziz took them out and looked at them for a moment, expecting them to disappear magically or something. Automatically his eyes went to his wrist. They had left him his watch too. What kind of bandits were these?

By his calculation, they had come up to the roadblock before four in the evening, so he must have been out for about three hours or so. Already the sun was sinking, leaving a rosy blush on the western horizon, and long natural shadows everywhere else. The almost full moon was already clearly visible in the sky. He told himself that he had to get a move on. That he still had the truck keys did not mean a single thing. It probably meant the bandits had enough knowledge and the wherewithal to move the truck without the keys despite its many security locks. In fact, if by some miracle he survived the ordeal, and had a chance to report this misadventure, it might be assumed that he had a hand in the whole affair. Against this logic though, he still decided not to throw the keys or his watch away. Something good might still come out of it all. One never knew.

The sun was behind him, and the Northern Star to his left. He felt he was facing Kadesh and Lashkar Gah, and hopefully the direction they had been travelling. He started walking. He must have gone on for about ten minutes when he suddenly emerged from the poppy field. He felt he was on a road which must have been tarred sometime in the distant past and was still sometimes in use now. He certainly felt some pavement under his feet though the rest of the road was mostly ruts filled with rubble. If he continued on the path he was pursuing, he would find himself in the poppy field on the opposite side of the road. He looked to his left and to his right. His head swivelled fast to the left again. From the corner of his eye, he had caught a glimpse of… their truck!

United Nations vehicles are usually stark white with the UN insignia printed on the bonnet, the sides and on the roof in bold blue letters. It served the purpose of quickly identifying them from the ground and from the sky. Even in the gloom of early night, Aziz could see clearly that this was definitely the truck he had been driving earlier that day unless some other poor river was also in deep trouble. He almost cried out loud, and then started jogging towards the truck. Suddenly, he was checked in midstride. There was movement around the truck, and voices. He stopped, stepped into the field again, and hidden by the poppy plants, carefully crept towards the truck.

There seemed to be about three people at least around, and in the truck. Apparently, they had come upon it recently. Crouched in the field, Aziz listened to their exchange.

"It was certainly not here when we were going."

"And there is no blood anywhere in it or on it?"

"There's no blood, and there seems to be no signs of a struggle."

"Are there any papers or documents?"

"There's nothing at all. Apparently, whoever abandoned it here must have taken everything that was valuable."

"And whoever came upon it next must have then stripped it."

"Are there any pickings left at all?"

"There is none that I can see. We are probably not the first to come up to it." By this time all the men came into Aziz's view and went round the vehicle, appraising it. Aziz saw that there were four, not three men. By their dressing, they could be the village vigilante or the Taliban out on patrol. Each had a gun slung on his back. They prodded the vehicle here and there.

"Even the chrome fittings and decorations are gone, so are the mirrors. We are late, unless we want to take the chassis and the glasses, or to dismantle the doors."

"We don't have the instruments. Besides, what use would those be to us?" And to this none of them had an answer. Aziz kept on watching and listening.

They circled the truck again. "Perhaps we will get some credit for reporting it" someone suggested hopefully.

"To whom?" Another asked. "If you report to one side, you will be asked why you did not finish the job. If you report to the other side, it will be assumed you were part of it and that you know more than you are telling. It is better to leave it the way we found it. Let's just admit to ourselves that someone was faster and luckier than us."

With that, they hefted their guns and walked away down the road. Aziz finally dared to breath freely again. He had been lucky indeed that he had not been left inside the truck. He dared not approach the truck again, not knowing which other group might come up to it next. Since he had the keys, maybe he could take a closer look in the morning and see if there was anything he could salvage. Even as he arrived at this conclusion, the moon broke through the clouds, and he had a clearer view of the truck. That was when he understood that when the men said the truck had been stripped, it had really been stripped! It was just the husk of the truck which lay there. All the tires were gone. He had the keys, but he was not going anywhere in that truck!

He was weak and very thirsty. If he stayed where he was, he risked discovery by the people who had tied him up in the first instance, or the next group of curiosity seekers. On the other hand, he stood a better chance of being discovered by the allied forces when they started looking for the missing truck and its occupants. Nobody knew how long it would take for them to start looking, probably a week or so but sooner if someone reported them missing. He realized the crucial role he had to play. For some reason he was still alive, and his task was to report the misadventure, no matter how improbable, so that a search could be commenced sooner rather than later for the missing women. His report was going to be the trigger; and the abandoned truck was a good landmark to begin from.

Having resolved this in his heart, he seemed to get some energy to keep going. First, he determined there was no one still close to the truck. He then crossed the road and went into the poppy field on the opposite side. With the moon now almost overhead, he pursued the course he had been following. There were no ferocious wild animals to think of, but this part of Afghanistan had its own share of snakes, scorpions and bugs. The thought of these did not bother him at the moment. What he feared more was encountering fellow human beings. It would be difficult enough to explain his presence in the fields at this time of the night. Apart from that, this was Afghanistan, and one never knew who was friend or foe. Again, the friends of one's enemies are automatically counted as enemies.

He kept walking, mechanically putting one foot in front of the other. Sometimes he feared that he fell asleep on his feet, but he had lucid periods when he reassured himself that he was not just going in circles by looking at the position of the Northern Star. Sometimes he found himself in poppy fields, sometimes in wheat field. Sometimes he passed virgin bushes, and sometimes he crossed semi-tarred roads. Many hours later he thought he heard a call to prayer. Pausing, he determined that it was real, and coming from some way ahead of him, and then it ceased. He concluded it must be nearly dawn. By now he was stumbling along. When he was just about to give up and just lie down in the fields to sleep or to die, he stumbled into a clearing.

A dog barked at him half-heartedly but he paid it no attention. Right ahead of him, he saw that there was a mosque and men were moving about like ghostly figures within it by the light of the early dawn. They were just finishing their morning prayers. Where there was a mosque, there was usually a well or some other source of water for ablutions. Aziz zeroed in on a bowl which had been left by the side of the building. He saw another person who had obviously come late and was now only doing his own ablutions even as the other men dispersed. That was good. With any luck, he would say his own prayers alone and finish at a time when there would be no one to express too much interest in his sudden appearance. With the bowl he went to the water which had already been drawn up and left in a bucket beside the well and drank very deeply. That done, he went about his ablutions and prayers as slowly as possible until the mosque was totally empty.

Prayers over, he went to a corner of the mosque, fairly hidden by the shadows, and using his shoes as a pillow, fell fast asleep. When he woke up the sun was high up in the sky. The whole place seemed deserted. He emerged from the mosque, stretched, and reluctantly put on his shoes. His was quite a sedentary occupation. A nighttime of rambling in the bush left his feet sore and blistered but he was driven by a purpose now. "You can endure the pain" he told himself.

He saw the bowl he had used earlier. Going to the bucket, he filled it up again, rinsed his mouth, and took another long drink. He then went to the other side of the mosque and discovered he was not alone after all. There was an old woman there shelling nuts.

"Salaam Alekheim, Mother," he greeted.

"Alekheim Salaam" she replied. "Did you just come out from the mosque? I had no idea we had visitors over the night. I recognize you. We did a shura with you two months ago about having a school. We were not expecting you."

This was a good sign. At least he was not in a completely hostile territory. "And I come under difficult circumstances, Mother. Our vehicle broke down up the road and I must get to Kadesh."

"Ooh, that is bad" she clucked sympathetically. "Are the ladies in a bad place then?"

"The ladies are not inside it now, but I must get to Kadesh and get some help." At this stage Aziz did not know how much information was safe to share with the old woman and was being very cautious. Nothing he had said so far was an outright lie, but not entirely the truth either.

"It is a good thing the ladies are not there. These times are bad. There are bad people all along the road."

"If only she knew" thought Aziz, "if only she knew." Aloud he said, "So I thought I would just drink some water and be on my way again."

"You must have some tea," she insisted. "Today is a market day so the others have gone to Kadesh already. If you had come a bit earlier, you would have gone with them. As it is, most of the transport is already at Kadesh till much later in the day. Trekking there will take about three hours. You must have some refreshment before you set off."

Aziz was really very hungry, so he allowed himself to be coddled. He took three mugs of very sweet tea and ate the rice cakes which came with it. He expressed his profound thanks to the old woman who brushed it off. "It is good to see someone who eats a meal as if he really appreciates it. Won't you take some of the cakes for the ladies? They really liked it the time they came here."

Aziz gratefully accepted the cakes, wrapped in a bit of cellophane. He felt a bit uncomfortable at his apparent deception. Later he was very glad he took them. He also accepted a plastic bottle which he could sling around his shoulder. It could hold about half a gallon of water. He filled it with water from the well, and with rough directions from the old woman, he set off to Kadesh.

The woman had said Kadesh was a mere three hours' walk from where they were. This was perhaps so for the villagers whose muscles had been toughened by their strenuous ways of life. For Aziz who had gone soft through his own more sedentary lifestyle, this was a different matter. Besides, he had already walked through the night and had sore feet. The trek was no child's play. He decided that sticking by the roadside in plain view of everyone in the daylight would show that he was not any form of combatant, friendly or otherwise. When he set off, the sun was already blazing high up in the sky because it was almost one o'clock in the afternoon. He put his watch into his pocket to avoid tempting anyone; and wrapped his blazer round his head like a turban. Making a rough parcel of the rice cake, he tied it to the water bottle with his handkerchief and slung that across his chest on his grey vest which soon became very grimy with grease and dust.

It did not take him long to work up a sweat. There were very few vehicles on the road. Those that passed him going in the same direction were all fully laden with people and goods. They tooted at him and covered him in plumes of dust. He did not even bother to thumb a lift from any of them. He had no money to pay for transportation and could not afford to impart confidences explaining why he had none, or why he was on the road in the first instance. Surprisingly, he did not encounter even a single roadblock, legitimate or otherwise. He regarded this with mixed feelings of relief and frustrated anger.

He walked on. His feet blistered. At a time, he took off his shoes but the sand was too uncomfortably hot to walk on. Ten minutes of this had him putting them back on. He decided that wearing them was a preferable torture. There were a few dwarf trees by the roadside, and he resolved to use them as the markers of his progress. He would set his sight on one in the distance and mindlessly walk to it before sitting down for a bit of rest. He rationed his water by the mouthful and nibbled at the rice cake meant for the ladies. Most times he ate and drank, not because he was overtly thirsty or hungry, but just to give himself a sense of purpose and to keep going.

He marvelled at how far places were when one was not driving. Just when he was on the brink of despair, he saw the hustle and bustle that showed he was on the outskirts of Kadesh. The sun had almost set. Aziz headed to the place they were to have lodged the previous night, arriving when it was totally dark. He knocked on the door. As soon as it was opened, he collapsed to the floor, pulled off his shirt, his blazer, and his shoes and then he started sobbing. Bewildered, his hosts stared at him aghast. They managed to get him to bed, bathed his sore feet, and put ointment on his scratches, bruises and sunburns. He could not even eat. His host gave him some pills for pain and sedation, and he slept till afternoon of the next day. It was the sound of people returning from the mosque that woke him.

As soon as he came fully awake, he became agitated again, and did he have a story to tell! He insisted on reaching UNESCO officials immediately, but the offices were closed for the weekend. He asked to be taken back to Lashkar Gah or to at least speak to someone in ISAF. This was difficult to arrange but at last two local ISAF officials agreed to take him to the British command at Lashkar Gah.

At first no one would grant him an audience because so many crank calls and false reports were made daily. He had no formal form of identification, but he finally proved to the duty officers that he was who he said he was, and that the lives of three young female expats were at stake. Someone finally listened. Greta, especially, was well-known at the base but the ladies had not yet been missed. Aziz made as detailed a report as possible. They questioned him all through the night and made very copious notes. His story remained consistent. They satisfied themselves that he was not double dealing; and was actually sincere in his anxiety.

Finally, assuring him that he did the right thing and that something would be done to help locate the ladies immediately he was driven to his house by Saturday morning. As soon as she opened the door his wife demanded, "Did you not promise to be back since Thursday? What kept you? Couldn't you at least let us know somehow that you would be delayed?"

Amused, the ISAF official who had given him a lift home answered wryly on his behalf, "Aren't you just thankful he's even home?"

And then his wife took another look at him and burst into tears herself.

CHAPTER 2

∞

At the time Aziz was calling for the women in the poppy fields, about 200 miles away, Greta, Laura, and Lil were waking up from their drug-induced stupor. Their journey had taken them to Zaranj where they had been unloaded, still unconscious, from the truck and transferred gently, almost lovingly to clean beds with nice soft sheets. Laura had woken first, disoriented as to where she was. Greta woke next, and then Lil. In turn each sat up in bed wondering what had happened. The room they found themselves in was small and stuffy but not really uncomfortable. The room was large enough for the three narrow wooden beds it contained. Other than the beds there was no other furniture. The walls were probably mud or brick, but it was smooth and whitewashed. Their beds were pushed against each wall, and the door was centered on the fourth wall. There was only a single small window high up above the bed Laura found herself on. Through this window they could see by the almost full moon that it was night already.

"I think we finally hit the bottom line" Greta summarized for them all. "We are about to pay for all our sins in helping Afghanistan find her feet."

"What do you think they will do with us?" Lil asked of nobody in particular.

"Did you never read any of those Taliban horror stories? Don't you remember any of the things Lady Simmons said to us?" Greta asked.

"They might be holding us for ransom or as bargaining chips" Laura suggested hopefully. "We might still have some days to live while they discuss what we are worth, and what they will do with us."

"Ever the optimist," Greta said, "You are ever the optimist! I would like to hear what you have to say by the time they start getting nasty."

"Thank Goodness they left us all together" Lil said. "That is one good thing so far. They could have put us in separate rooms or sent us to different corners of the country."

"That is certainly a blessing" Greta conceded. "At least if we hatch a plot and decide to jump our guards, one of us might be able to escape alive to tell our story to the rest of the world."

Laura had been prowling about, examining the room they were in. There was the single window, but it was quite small and too high up. Only one door opened into the room but close to the door she had come upon a heap of things. By the faint moonlight from the window, she saw and suddenly exclaimed, "Here are our overnight bags. They left us our overnight bags!"

The other two came crowding round to see. Not only were their overnight bags there, their purses and other personal effects were also there. Incredible! They each went through their personal stuff exclaiming over and over as they made new discoveries. Not that it changed anything much but as Greta put it, "Nothing beats knowing you have your own change of underwear and your own toothbrush in a time of crisis."

They were still on their discovery spree when the door opened and a slender woman entered with a basin, wash cloths, and a cake of soap. She left as soon as she set the things on the floor but came back almost immediately staggering with a laden table-tray. The tray held tea, rice cakes, nuts, and fruits. There were paan, cheese, and milk. This was Afghan diet such as they had been used to. The woman who brought them said, "Eat" and then left the room.

They looked at one another. If they were going to die, at least their captors wanted them well fed beforehand. They did not even debate whether to eat or not. When all chips were down, death by poisoning was much better than starving to death. Besides, starvation would be by their own choice not their captors'. In any case, they were very hungry. Expecting a big meal at Kadesh, they had not eaten much at lunch. They therefore washed their hands as best they could with the water and soap, and fell on the presented meal with gusto. And so, even as Aziz trekked and suffered, fretted, and starved through that first night, the women had a hearty meal and waited for what fate was to bring them next.

In uncharacteristically unladylike manners, they ate all the food and drank all the tea.

"That was good" Laura said. "Now what happens next?"

"Didn't you ever read the story of Hansel and Gretel?" Lil asked. "Now we wait to become the dinner ourselves."

"Oh well," Greta said nonchalantly. "I wonder if that door is locked. What might we find behind it?"

She was going to the door to check when the door swung open as if on cue. The slender woman entered to clear up. As she was finishing up, another woman entered. She too was slender but taller. She said something to the other woman which the other occupants of the room could not make out. Turning to them next, she addressed them directly, in accented, but otherwise perfect, English.

"My name is Nazo. I must apologize for the unpleasant way used to bring you here. I assure you that no harm was intended. If there was any other way, we would have used it. We have a favor to ask of you. however, we will leave that till morning after you have rested. I am sure you are full of questions. I may not have all the answers, but I will try my best to answer as many of them as possible for you."

Her tone, voice, accent, and even her careful way of speaking rang bells in Laura's mind. Even her very appearance evoked memories. "Wait a minute" she said. "You were the one who visited me once and said your friend needed my help."

"You have a very good memory" said Nazo. "I was the one. It is still the same course we are pursuing. In due time hopefully, you will get to meet Il Dhost."

Lil and Greta looked hard at their colleague. They had questions for her but those could wait. "So, if you need our help, how come you are holding us prisoners?" Greta asked.

"You are not really prisoners. This door is not locked but it would not be wise for you to try getting out on your own. I will show you now, how to get to the amenities, but I must warn you not to try to escape. We are on the outskirts of the city of Zaranj. You should know though, that the area is full of gun-carrying men on guard. Some of them are ours. Those ones are under orders to protect you. "However, they would not be expecting you to wander around in the dark. They might actually shoot you before they realize they should be protecting you. Others are people who I can assure you have no good intentions at all towards you. You are not prisoners. You are free to come and go as you please, but you are well advised to be careful. Hear us out first. If you decide you do not want to help us, we will see to it that you are safely returned to where ISAF or NATO can safely pick you up."

They looked at one another. It did not sound to them as if they were very free but following Nazo's advice seemed the best they could do for the time being. She had promised them a full session of questions and answers in the morning. The best they could do for the moment was to have their own pre-meeting conference. For the moment they followed her out of the door and discovered they were inside the kind of Afghan-style compound they had been talking about earlier on their journey.

Their room was one of several which opened into a courtyard. She showed them a corner squat toilet, a rudimentary bathroom where they could bath with water from a bucket, and a well from which they could fetch water. Other than camping trips in their respective distant pasts, these women had never had it so basic. However, they were told this was all there was. Before the end of their ordeal, they learned to be quite proficient in using these basic amenities. They never took their Western luxuries and comforts for granted ever again.

Having eased themselves and washed up the best they could, they gathered again in their room. They found that leaving their door open like the other occupants of the compound obviously did, enhanced air circulation and relieved the stuffiness of the room. They did not feel in the least bit sleepy after their drug-induced nap. From the murmurs which came from some of the other rooms, they were not the only ones still awake. They spoke in low voices, not just to avoid disturbing the night but because they did not know who might be eavesdropping.

"So, you are in cahoots with our captors?" Greta asked Laura.

"Far from it but apparently we have met before now. She seems to know us all fairly well." Laura then told them about the strange visit she had the day after the wedding. "She said then that her friend needed my, or our help. She wanted me to come to discuss with the friend since they could not approach us during the wedding. I had no inclination to go wandering alone after strangers in Afghanistan especially ones who had been watching us covertly for some time, and at the wedding."

"And you never mentioned it to anyone?" Lil asked.

"I remember two of you came back to the house so excited with your own news. There was the wedding to discuss. What with one thing or the other it went completely out of my mind. It was not a request I was going to consider anyway so I didn't even file it away in my mind for any future reference."

"But now it has caught up with us" Greta said. "Did you mention it to your friends at Farah?"

"I don't think I did. It just did not seem that significant. It never came up in conversation."

"And there goes our last hope that perhaps someone will be looking for us." Lil said. "Do you think they have Aziz in the men's quarters or something? If we could team up with him, he could be our means of escape, and our guide back to civilization."

"You do know what happens in these kidnap cases, don't you?" Greta asked. "They usually kill the Afghan drivers and take away the expatriates for desserts. Aziz is probably being digested by the buzzards right now."

"Well, we could make it a condition to our helping them with whatever it is they want us to do" Laura said. "We don't have many bargaining chips."

They turned their minds to mull over what their captors could possibly want from them. At the end they fell asleep without really arriving at any solutions. However, they resolved on two things: first, they would ask for their driver to be part of whatever they were going to do. Next, they would ask that they should always be together to look out for one another. "There is something to be said for sticking together" Lil concluded for them all. "There is strength in unity."

Despite everything, they slept well. The following morning, they discovered that the compound was really full of women and girls. Closing their door was the only way of assuring themselves some privacy. Early in the morning there was a lot of movement and chatter which soon settled as the compound emptied. The woman of the previous night brought them some food, but they preferred just juice and fruits, having gorged themselves the previous night. Communicating with a mixture of gestures and in their stilted Dari, they soon learned her name was Soraya just like the princess of the wedding ballads. About midmorning, Nazo showed up with another woman whom she introduced as Nadia. Apparently, both of them were the emissaries of Il Dhost. Nazo did most of the talking but Nadia, though having a less superior command of English seemed to be higher in rank than Nazo, and more possessed of the facts. Nazo kept asking for her contribution or clarification.

"First of all," Nazo began, "we are not the Taliban. We are in no way connected to them and many times our interests are in direct conflict with theirs. They have a stronger might than we do. Since we cannot fight them openly, we try to subvert them. We are also not on the side of the foreigners. As well-meaning as they are, they do not fully grasp the Afghan problem. However, to be seen to be openly fraternizing with them is to invite the wrath of the Taliban. Besides, the friends of my enemies are my enemies."

"So, what are you in fact?" asked Greta.

"We are a group that looks after the interest of some Afghans who need the care. We are illegitimate in that we are not recognized by the government and dare not apply for that recognition. Most of our work is done underground but we do the best we can to better the lot of those who need it."

"You must know that if you are not legitimate then we cannot help you. That is one of the rules we must observe as UNESCO workers." Lil said

"That is our position exactly!" Nazo said unapologetically. "This is why we are taking these desperate measures. There is no way we can appeal to you legitimately, and yet we need your help."

"Does your organization have a name?" Laura asked.

"No. We are actually several different organizations which operate separately but sometimes we have a meeting point. We do not have names. The leader of our particular outfit is simply referred to as Il Dhost. Because of this, people have come to generally refer to us as 'The Friends'. We help out anyone in need just as a good friend should."

"So, when you kept telling me Il Dhost needed my help, you meant this person?" Laura asked.

"I did, and that is why we had to get you out to talk to you. We might keep you a bit long, but not any longer than necessary so please hear us out."

"When do we get to meet your leader?" Greta wanted to know.

"Eventually, but first let us tell you how we need your help. Have you heard about the Mut'ah system?"

They had heard from no less than Dorothy Simmons herself, before they came to Afghanistan. Ayesha had explained it more perfectly.

"One of the prime works we do is to rescue these girls who had been displaced and abandoned after such marriages. We actively seek them out, pick them off the street, go to collect them if we knew where they were, or raid a Taliban camp if we hear of one who cannot escape. Other people who pity them but are endangered by harboring them for long also send them to us. We have also gathered runaway wives, children, and other such oppressed girls. In the course of our work, we have faced our own share of disasters and losses. We have also had our own fair share of rewards, which are usually emotional, of seeing families reunited, and girls smile as they begin to live again. There is also the wonderful sense of achievement it brings, and so we press on.

"What we have at the end of the day are like large secret orphanages scattered all over the country at different locations. We try to locate the families of those who remember their way home. Sometimes the girls do not know their way home or are too ashamed to go home. We have had a few where the family rejects the child or are afraid of taking her back because that would incur the wrath of the Taliban. For such people we must arrange permanent placements and supports of some sort for their upkeep until they recover their senses of worth. Recently, a few of them got married. We were very glad, but this does not happen often. When they get married, we arrange for people to stand in the places of their parents, provide dowries, and so on."

At this stage of Nazo's monologue, Lil was almost in tears. Greta and Laura were also equally moved. "Does the government not help out at all?" Lil asked.

"What kind of help do you think this venture would get from the government?" Nazo asked. "The present government is so weak, and frankly corrupt. We know neither its agenda nor its stance on so many issues. The Taliban sees us as an anti-Islamic movement which encourages the people to go against the Sharia. We depend totally on likeminded individuals of which Afghanistan has quite a lot, I am glad to say. We have some friends in high places. They try the best they can to help. However, Afghanistan is also a very religious country. One must not be seen as working openly against God, as some of our actions are interpreted. Taliban is still in authority in many places. Where they are not, they are still feared." She paused, either from emotion or just for effect.

"So where do we come into all these?" Laura seized the opportunity to ask.

"We need an education curriculum, and educational materials. We have a lot of potential pupils but no materials or manpower. We have people who are ready and willing to be trained as teachers, but this must be done in secret. We need these things, but we cannot afford to pay you. What we would want you to do is to start us off on the right path. We will see how we can improvise as we progress.

"Secondly, after seeing how you took pictures at the wedding, we felt we could use some training in taking these pictures in attempting to reunite our girls with their families. Some of these girls are from across the borders, from Pakistan and Iran mostly, but some are also from Tajikistan and Uzbekistan. We have developed methods of smuggling people across the borders but sometimes it is terrible to go through the process of getting someone across the Pakistani border only to realize she's really from Uzbekistan or Tajikistan, or vice versa. If someone with the pictures could verify with parents that this was their long-lost daughter, and that they wanted her home, it will help us a lot. It would also make the risk more worth taking.

Laura now began to understand. But the digital camera and her laptop needed to be recharged from time to time. Where they found themselves did not seem to have facilities for such necessities.

"Sometimes we pass close to big cities or places which have electrical generators so we can do the recharging at such times if it is okay" Nazo suggested.

They asked for time to think it over but before they broke up the meeting, they remembered their bargaining chips. "What happened to our driver?" Greta asked. "We'd like to work with him."

"We had to let him go" Nazo answered blandly. "Somebody had to report that you might still be alive. We immobilized his vehicle, so he would not get help before you were safely out of view."

"He was not killed then?" asked Laura.

"Our organization does not go killing people unnecessarily. We made sure he was not anywhere near the vehicle so looters would not kill him. As for the rest, it is left for him to find his way to civilization and report you missing. The best we could organize was for someone to stay at Kadesh and report to us when he got there. We are still awaiting that bit of news."

"Are you aware of the hue and cry which will be raised over our disappearance?" Lil asked.

"We are more aware of that than you are" Nazo said as a matter of fact. "This is why you must help us as fast as you can so that we shall make you appear again."

"The Allied forces will come after you and will destroy your organization" Greta threatened.

"We have no doubt about the cleverness and the resourcefulness of the Allied forces, but we are on our own grounds. This country has so many hiding places. We are well-practised in evading the Taliban who are also natives of the land. We believe you shall willingly help us, and not blow the whistle on us before we are finished. That is why you must help us as fast as possible so we can return you before they blast us out of our covering."

Who could argue with that?

"We would also want to work together, and not be separated" Laura insisted.

"We would not dream of separating you. We understand that three of you work best as a team. Your team has done impressive work. Your reputation is spread all around the countryside. We have our very good reasons for choosing you rather than any other UNESCO team. We did our homework very thoroughly."

When they were again on their own, they decided that the task was challenging and intriguing at the best. They understood how they could not help legitimately but had to appear to be doing so under duress. Nevertheless, they felt there should have been a more civilized way of going about this business but of course any other way they did it, they would have other people looking into the affair, including their making periodic reports to UNESCO. They also reasoned that once UNESCO became a part of it, the organization would no longer be secret. Their angst was not for being known by UNESCO but by the malevolent Taliban.

They concluded that they would go along with the proposal but to start with, they would need basic facts and figures to draw up a plan. They would need supplies, and they would ask to be allowed to write notes to the outside world to let them know they were safe. When they told Nazo their decision later that day, she pronounced herself "very delighted".

CHAPTER 3

―――――∞―――――

Eventually, Nazo told them more about herself. It turned out she had been a practising lawyer before the advent of the Taliban. She had been forced to quit when the Taliban took over power. Although permitted to resume her profession, she found her underground work more emotionally fulfilling and decided to devote her time to it. She was certainly streetwise and knew her law well even as the lines kept shifting and blurring. She informed Greta, Laura, and Lil that their letters would be censored before posting. "No hard feelings or mistrust, you know, but we have to be sure you don't inadvertently give our positions away." They understood.

Greta wrote to Dick at the British army base at Lashkar Gah. "I am all right. We find ourselves in a tight position. However, we seem not to be with the bad guys. We have agreed to collaborate on a project which is by no means difficult. Hopefully, we will soon finish and be back. Keep the hearth warm for me."

Lil wrote to Bjorn. "I don't know what they will tell you, but we are treated well and actually feel useful. Hopefully, we shall soon be back on our major project but this one is no less important and we are glad to be doing it. At the end of it all we shall have more interesting stories to tell our children."

Laura wanted to write to both Tim and Alex but Nazo told her she was allowed only one letter. She decided to write to Tim. "We are not exactly in a predicament. Maybe this was why God sent me to Afghanistan after all. We might be in a position to do the best we ever could in Afghanistan. We do not perceive ourselves in any immediate danger and I trust you to explain this to Alex. Hopefully, we shall rejoin you all very soon."

They gave the letters to Nazo and thought they were posted the same day. However, it would be weeks before Nazo actually got someone to drop them off mysteriously at the post office at Lashkar Gah. They talked to her about writing to Ayesha or Shamir but she discouraged this.

By Friday they learned that they had some of their leftover school supplies from the truck. They spent most of the day sorting through what they had to work with. There were leftover Teacher's Guides, Greta's custom-designed curricula, some textbooks, workbooks, and exercise books. They even had a few classroom supplies, some cookies, and some candies.

By Saturday morning they came down to business. They had drawn up a list of questions they wanted answers to before they could put forward their plan; like how many pupils are they planning the school for? What was the age range of the pupils? How much, and what kind of education have they received so far? How many people were available for teacher education? How much did these potential teachers know already? Most of all, how willing and ready were they to be put through an accelerated pace?

Nazo and Nadia came to have another conference with them that evening. Apparently, there were about two hundred children living in that compound aged eight to eighteen years. They were all girls. There were about thirty-five adults. Two of the women had been teachers before the advent of the Taliban. Two other women were in training, and four others were willing to become teachers but had received only an equivalent of middle school education. Some of the other adults wanted to be literate too but not to have to go through regular schooling.

Of the roughly two hundred children, ALL were willing to learn. Some of them could read and write in Arabic; the teachers had been teaching them the Dari and Pashtun scripts. They all had some smattering of words in English. It looked like a formidable task. Most villages they had gone to had just about fifty children at most. Even in the bigger towns, they managed to find settings of a teacher to about twenty pupils. This was not going to be as easy as they had thought. "But" said Greta, "I have found that where the children are eager, the teachers love their jobs, and both parties have a set target, progress is fast, no matter the drawbacks."

"I think I get it!" Nazo replied. "We need three basic factors: eager children, gifted teachers, and specific goals. You will find out we have all three. We have also been getting good results. Our greatest challenge has been how to carry along people of different ages in the same class session. For instance, a teacher has eight-year-olds and sixteen-year-olds in the same classroom trying to do grade two work. The younger ones catch on fast, while the older ones are determinedly plodding along and getting frustrated because they are unable to get where the little ones are. If the older ones got it first, they could help the younger ones. However, this is not usually the case."

Strangely, Greta understood the scenario. She could even quote papers and incidences to support the phenomenon. However, what was needed here was a practical solution. Putting them in different classrooms was not going to help since there were not enough teachers. "What we have been doing is asking the smaller ones to come to school in the morning and work the fields in the evenings. The bigger ones come to school in the evenings after working the fields in the mornings. The teachers teach throughout the day and the strain is telling on them. We are not sure the bigger ones are making any real progress studying under so much pressure. They are already tired after working the fields all day. We will not even talk about the reduced efficacy in the fields. What we need is a program that would accommodate everyone and still not neglect their means of livelihood, something much more efficient than what we have now."

"How about the Accelerated Self-Pacing Curriculum?" Laura asked Greta.

"What's that?" Nazo asked.

"The ASPC! It's a recent curriculum that Greta is still developing" Lil explained, equally excited. "It actually targets gifted or backward pupils or pupils who do not really fit into any particular grade. Greta, talk about it."

"It might actually work in this setting." Greta concurred speculatively. "The role of the teacher is to get the child to understand a concept. The child then works with it, works around it, projects upon it, and broadens his or her interest in that one area until the pupil feels proficient enough, or becomes bored with it. The pupil could then ask for ways to advance in that particular area, or for an introduction to another area. It actually works best when the pupil is introduced to many concepts at the beginning and then he or she chooses the area which pricks his or her interest most."

Expecting Nazo to ask Greta to clarify this jargon, Laura and Lil were surprised when the description had an electrifying effect on Nazo and Nadia instead. They held an animated discussion in their native tongue which the other three could not follow. At the end Nazo explained, "This might be just what we are looking for. The vision we have is for everyone to know a bit of everything, and yet to develop a specific skill or interest which will eventually become an occupation or at least a means of sustenance. We don't have the outlets to challenge them with, but we would like each person to develop an area of interest which will speak to their natural talents as farmers or teachers or lawyers or craftswomen, whatever. Could you really help us to develop and implement this?"

"Okay, give us time to see how much we can come up with" Greta promised with a gleam of interest in her eyes.

"How much time do you need?" Nazo asked.

"Can you give us about two or three days?"

"Okay."

Before she left, Nazo cheered them up by the news that Aziz had safely reached Lashkar Gah and reported them missing to every possible authority. "There is a search now on for you. However, it is being done very discreetly. Authorities do not want the news to be leaked to the press because they have high hopes of finding you soon. They do not want to encourage other kidnappers."

Cheered by this news they were ready, even eager, to commence work and to work very hard. And so, it was as if they were back in their office in Lashkar Gah drawing up plans and proposals, permutations, and projections. They worked individually, collaborated, criticized, encouraged, and boosted one another. They made a lot of progress and thoroughly enjoyed the challenge. When daylight faded, they asked for, and received light in the form of kerosene lanterns. Not used to working by such poor lighting, they were finally forced to call it a day and decided to just talk about each person's progress and ideas among themselves and finish up by the next day. Very early the next day, they were at it again as if they were afraid of losing their trends of thought. Finally, by early evening they pronounced themselves satisfied. They had even set out how to impart this knowledge to the teachers of the teachers.

Up till this moment, they had not really had the time and the opportunity to get acquainted with the other occupants of the compound. However, they had heard them chattering, the noise level swelling or ebbing depending on the time of the day. They had no trouble believing that Nazo and Nadia were not exaggerating the numbers. They had also caught glimpses of the girls and women coming and going in flashes of color. Once in a while, some had stopped and stared at them boldly. If they returned the stares, they were mostly rewarded with shy smiles and giggles. Now it was time for them to meet with the eight women who were to undergo teacher education. Nazo told them it was starting from the following morning. That evening they decided to reward their hard work by just lolling about.

"Imagine, I could be at the army base right now having myself a good time" Greta remarked.

"I could have been completing an email and looking at catalogs with Bjorn now," said Lil.

Laura was about to talk about missing her Skype sessions when she suddenly sat up. "Did you hear that?" she asked.

"Hear what?" Lil asked. They all kept quiet and listened.

"I swear it sounds like singing" Greta said.

"If I did not know better, I would say it sounds like people singing the popular Christian hymn Jesus loves me but in Dari" Lil confirmed.

They agreed with one another that they were not having a group hallucination. They got close to the door, but the singing seemed to fade. They went outside and they lost it altogether. The compound itself was very strangely quiet and they seemed to be absolutely alone, which was a bit unusual.

The singing seemed to be loudest in their room or maybe from outside the high window. However, it soon ceased altogether. They looked at one another askance. They had known from their briefings, and since being on ground themselves that there was only one official Christian church in Afghanistan. That was the Roman Catholic Church within the Italian embassy which had been granted as a concession in 1921 after Italy became the first country to recognize Afghanistan as a sovereign state. American President, Dwight Eisenhower, in 1959 had asked for, and obtained permission to build a protestant church in Kabul as another concession for allowing The Islamic center to be built in Washington D.C.

The land for the Protestant church had been duly purchased with a 99-year lease and paid for in gold. In 1970 the foundation had been laid. The building had been erected with contributions made by Protestants all over the world. In 1973, however, the main church building had been razed during the civil crisis which had made Afghanistan a republic. The building was never reconstructed but Protestants in the expatriate communities in Kabul continued to meet for worship in other buildings on the grounds. Native Afghans were strictly forbidden to attend or to be seen unduly hobnobbing with people who went to the premises. Christian activities were especially taboo in Afghanistan.

"What did we just hear?" Greta asked.

"I think we just had a mass delusion" Lil answered.

"Of Christian songs being sung in Afghanistan" Laura added.

There was no way they would have asked their hosts what they had just heard. Discussing any religion other than Islam with an Afghan native was a criminal offence punishable by execution or extradition. Not that they would have minded being extradited at this phase, but they were very mindful of the law and the organization they represented. They had also become really very interested in their present project and wanted to see how it panned out. Besides, when the song ended, they had no evidence to support their claims to what they had heard.

That evening when Soraya brought them their dinner, they asked for an audience with Nazo and Nadia. "Later" she told them. The woman was not very voluble but what she withheld in speech, she more than made up for with smiles. The UNESCO captives liked her a lot, and apparently the feelings were mutual.

Nazo and Nadia did not come that evening. When Soraya came to clear away their plates and saw them clicking through pictures on Laura's camera, she showed so much interest that they included her in the session telling her stories of where they had been and what they had been doing. They showed Soraya how to operate the camera. She was a very quick and inventive learner. In just a little while she could even turn tricks with the camera, creating borders around pictures, changing backgrounds, merging several frames, separating pictures, and so on. She took a picture of the three women together. They all looked like happy campers rather than miserable captives. When the daylight finally became too poor for taking pictures she reluctantly left. They forgot to ask if their message had reached Nazo and Nadia. However, they did not care to have any serious discussions that day anymore.

The meeting took place the following morning instead. They attempted to explain what they had drawn up on paper but at a stage Nazo confessed herself totally bewildered. Nadia asked, "Instead of spending a lot of time trying to make us understand what is on this paper, why don't you just go ahead and put it into practice? The teachers and the pupils are right here."

Later in the day, they were told that a two-week holiday from class work had been declared for the pupils. Greta, Laura, and Lil were introduced to their potential students and just like that, they became involved in Teacher Education.

They had been involved in Teacher Education before but not this directly. They used a large room in the compound. Each day started as soon as the daylight was strong enough and the compound had quietened. The classes went on until daylight began to wane. They had two meal breaks, and endless cups of tea in between. Nadia and Nazo sat in on every class to interpret what the lecturers said to the students, and vice versa. After the first week, however, their input became less frequent because the teachers and the students could understand one another much better.

The students were very eager and quick to learn. The language skills of the lecturers progressed even faster than it had with Ayesha. By the middle of the second week, they felt it was time for demonstration teaching. The pupils were promptly called back to class. They returned reluctantly enough as pupils are wont to do all over the world, after a holiday. However, within a week they were learning very eagerly. Schooling had become a lot of fun. The teachers said it was noisier than usual but confessed themselves satisfied at their pupils' progress and eager inputs. The major challenge became how to get materials to keep up with the students' interests. Nazo and Nadia said they would work at this. However, the teachers and students were also very resourceful and inventive. They could improvise with just about anything. Their lack added to the education process.

Greta, Laura, and Lil stopped trying to count the days. They only marked time by the elusive singing which they worked out must be on Sundays. On such days, work was usually slow, and then everyone in the compound would seem to disappear. They were still hesitant about asking their hosts about this, but they appreciated the time off. They used it to improve on their teaching plans and work on some sort of reports. Each of them began keeping journals independently. Their individual journals showed they were not totally content at this time. Greta especially, chaffed at the bit for lack of physical exercise. The compound was not large enough for running laps. Joining Lil for her stretches just was not enough for her. Lil pined for the outdoors too, and for Bjorn. Laura longed most for a good book to read once in a while. She made her journal into a series of letters to Tim. She shared her innermost thoughts, and declared her love, secure in the knowledge that he would never get to read them.

Soraya continued to learn as much as she could about cyber photography from Laura. She learned about transferring pictures to the laptop and other storage devices. Nazo surprised them by producing thumb drives of different capacities one day. True to her word, she had somehow managed to keep the batteries of their gadgets charged. One day, she came with a digital camera similar to Laura's and asked if Laura could teach Soraya how to take pictures of those in the compound, annotating them. Within a few clicks, Soraya got the hang of it. She spent the rest of the day having fun with her new toy.

They must have stayed in that place in Zaranj for four or five weeks when Nazo came one morning and said they had to move.

"We're going back to Lashkar Gah?" Lil asked eagerly.

"I'm afraid not. I know I promised you that as soon as you have developed our curriculum you could go. What you have done here has been so successful that we would want to implement it in our other centers."

"And how many centers do you have?" Laura asked.

"We have several, but they are not all of the same size. You don't have to go to them all." She was elusive and diplomatic, but she tried to assuage their fears. "What we plan to do is merge several of the centers and congregate the people willing to receive teacher education. After they have learned, we will send them back to where they came from."

"That means about four to five weeks at each center" Lil gasped.

"I don't believe you will take as much time at the other centers as you did here. Consider this the pilot project. It becomes easier as you become more proficient and perfect the plan. Don't you think so?"

"And if we say no, will you then execute us?" Greta asked.

"We are hoping you would not say no. Il Dhost would be very much obliged to you."

"We do not owe anything to this your dhost. We don't even believe any such person exists. You are the main person as far as we can see!" Greta was on the warpath.

"Oh, Il Dhost exists, and is looking forward to meeting you. Consider the next leg of your journey as a meeting with Il Dhost."

Greta got up and prowled restlessly around the room, an unhappy expression on her face. As if reading her mind Nazo added, "And in this next phase, there is going to be a lot of physical exercise involved, I promise you. Please rest now, we will leave very early tomorrow morning."

"There's something else" Laura requested before Nazo left. "We will like to write notes again to those that are looking for us."

"Certainly" Nazo agreed, "but wouldn't you rather write the notes after you are settled than before you are moved?"

"Why can't we do both?" Lil asked.

Marginally hardening her voice Nazo replied, "Please, one favor at a time so that granting them will be easier." She had just neatly put them in their place, reminding them that they were still captives, all said and done.

CHAPTER 4

∞

True to his word, when the British commander received the report Aziz gave, he had set up a surveillance party to go to verify the driver's claims that same afternoon. They flew over the area that Aziz had indicated. They took aerial photographs of the immobilized truck, noted all the surrounding hamlets and villages, and came back to the base to make their reports. The three women, especially Greta, were well-known and liked at the base. The men were willing to do whatever it took to bring them back.

It was not until two days later, on Monday that they could make more practical moves. Working with ISAF, men were sent out in groups to nose about the villages and hamlets they had marked off from the air. They went to see if there were any unusual activities or foreigners held in any of the compounds. They also slunk through fields of opium and wheat in case the women were wounded and stranded in the fields, or if their captors were keeping them there. Such things had been known to happen in the past.

Another group was dispatched to their apartment in Shamir's house to gather whatever intelligence they could. Ayesha said she had been expecting the ladies since Thursday. She had asked Shamir that very morning to please report them missing at the office. "No" she said, "it's not like them not to keep to a schedule. They would have come back to the house before going for any other activities they have planned… I have had no trouble at all living with them. They have been model housemates and friends. Teaching them has been a pleasure… I have no idea at all of anyone who would wish them harm. They are very careful. I don't think they would have knowingly provoked anyone…"

She said that if the men wished, she could open their apartment and offices for them to look through their personal stuff in case they would find any clue to the ladies' whereabouts.

It was not until the following Monday, over a week after they disappeared, that the news reached the American base at Farah, including the futile efforts made so far to locate the women. Major Grafton was stunned. He knew terrible things happened in this country, but he had a rather soft spot for Laura. He had quite unreasonably assumed that the aura of purity around her was enough to ward off any kind of evil. He sent for Alex and Tim to come to his office behind the library after dinner.

"Please sit down, Gentlemen" he began. "I received some signals from Lashkar Gah and I'm afraid it's not very good news."

"Lashkar Gah!" Alex exclaimed. "It's about Laura."

It was a statement, not a question. The commander heard Alex but it was Tim's face he was watching as he spoke. He saw the young man visibly cave inwards. Tim did not know it, but he wore his heart on his sleeve as the saying went. Too quietly he now asked, "What did the signal say, Sir?"

"Laura and her teammates were kidnapped somewhere in the Nimruz province about a week ago. All the efforts to discover their whereabouts have proven abortive so far."

"Christ!" Alex exclaimed hitting his left palm with his right fist as if he would have liked to be smashing in someone's face. "Tim said something must be going on when we went for two weeks without getting any communications from her by Skype or by email."

"There is a peculiarity in this case however…" the two young men sat up again with hope. "The driver of their truck trekked back to report them missing. The Brits are convinced there was no foul play on his part. However, I will like you to go and question him again to see if you can jog his memory a bit more."

"I am ready to go any time you say, Sir" Alex said jumping up.

"Finish up whatever you have at hand now. Be ready to leave for Lashkar Gah first thing tomorrow morning. You will take Chuck and Randy with you."

"Sir!" he saluted smartly and left.

Tim remained seated. "I would like to go along too" he said to his commander.

"You know it's outside your jurisdiction, and this is Afghanistan. They will not respect your chaplain's badge."

"It's a risk I am willing to take sir. I just have to be there."

"She means that much to you?"

"Nobody, and nothing has meant so much to me in my life sir. I am willing to die for her if that is what it takes."

Major Grafton looked at the young man and his eyes softened. He had also been young once. He knew well what it was to be in love, and the futility of trying to hold back such ardor. "You have accumulated a lot of vacations and off-duty days. I believe you can go along with the search party but remember, you have duties here too; and you go at your own risk."

"Sir! Thank you, sir!" He stood up and saluted, his heart much more lightened. He went off to find out the arrangements being made by the others for the trip to Lashkar Gah. First of all, though, he went to his quarters and knelt down by his bed. He had a few things to discuss with God.

They temporarily took over the interrogation room at the British army base and began by going over the driver's report and the evidence gathered so far. They could not find any fault at all with what the British had done. At last, they requested a meeting with the UNESCO driver. Aziz was brought to them. To avoid any apparent intimidation, Alex and Randy stayed in the room while Chuck and Tim observed through the one-way mirror. Aziz went over everything he could remember of the incidence in minute details. They did not interrupt him until he came to the end.

"You said you became unconscious after they shot something at your neck?"

"Yes."

"Did they do the same thing to the ladies?"

"I have no idea. They were all sitting behind me. I did not turn around to look."

"When you came to, you were lying in the poppy fields, and you tried to find out if the ladies were also close by?"

"Yes."

"How long, and how far did you search?"

"Not very long, and not very far. I mean I must have spent about fifteen minutes or so wandering in different directions until the light faded and made it impractical. I tried calling out but there were no answers."

"So, they could have been there but still unconscious."

"They could have been there but not too close to where I was, and definitely not in the direction I had been searching."

"When you got back to the truck you reported it had been stripped."

"Yes, sir."

"Could it have been by the same people or a different set?"

"I have no idea, but the people I heard felt they were not the first set to have a go at the truck."

"These people could have killed you, but they didn't."

"The people I saw near the truck? They didn't see me."

"I mean the first ones who must have drugged you and kidnapped the ladies."

"They didn't. They also left me with my watch and the truck keys."

"Why would they do that?"

"I don't know. I have no idea."

"Where you discovered the truck was not where the roadblock had been?"

"No."

"Could you pinpoint where the roadblock happened?"

"I did. I showed it to ISAF. It was down the major road."

"So apparently they had got into the truck and driven it to the minor road. They then brought you out of it and carried you into the field before the truck was effectively immobilized."

"I think so."

"How many men were there?"

"I counted about four at the roadblock and then two others came out of the fields. They were the ones with the wrist things. There might have been many more. I don't know."

They questioned him on and on including about the village where he had taken refuge and received directions to Kadesh. They questioned him about his trek to Kadesh, and eventual return to Lashkar Gah. There were no inconsistencies in his story. The man sounded obviously sincere. Aziz was glad now that he had not tried to play any trick to make his story sound more plausible. He even shared these thoughts with them. The Americans merely nodded. At last, they let him go.

The British and ISAF ground teams had been to the surrounding villages and hamlets, some of them, more than once. They had even spoken to the old woman whom the driver had talked about. Her only remembrance of the ladies was when they had come for the shura, and at no other time. She confirmed the story of the driver. "That day, he did not appear as neat as the day of the shura. He told me that their vehicle had broken down up the road. I was worried that if he was looking so bad, perhaps the ladies were not okay. However, he said they were not waiting back there and I was happy for them."

When asked if there had been other visitors or any suspicious activities out of the ordinary around the place recently, she said no. "I should know because I am always here even when all the others go to farm or to market. There is nothing out of ordinary. I am sure of that."

The Americans meticulously went over their reports but gained no new leads. By late afternoon they went to the apartment where the women lived. Pre-warned, Ayesha met them at the door. She stood just inside the door while they methodically went through closets and drawers futilely looking for any clues at all. When they left to go to continue the search in their offices, Tim did not go with them. He sank into the armchair in Laura's room and moaned, "Laura, Oh Laura, just hold onto your faith Love, don't you let go."

He did not know that he had spoken aloud until Ayesha, still lingering at the doorway, addressed him softly. "She must mean very much to you." She was pretty much echoing Major Grafton.

"She does" Tim confessed to her. I love her very much. "Now I wish I could see her to tell her so. It's amazing how one never appreciates what one has until he loses it."

"You think you will never see her again?"

"I know that I will see her again, and very soon too. I have so much faith that I will. What I lament are the many opportunities I had to tell her how much she meant to me and never did so. Maybe if she had known, she would hold onto it at a trying time like this for whatever it is worth."

"I think she knows, and she is holding on. Women have a way of knowing these things even when they are not openly declared."

"I hope so" said Tim standing up to leave, "I sincerely hope so." He realized he must have been holding Ayesha up.

"Hey, for all this is worth, I think I should mention that Laura had a strange visitor once."

"She did? When was this?"

"It might not have any bearing on the issue at hand at all; but the day after my cousin's wedding, a heavily-veiled woman came to see her. It had never happened before so naturally I was curious. The woman did not want to come into the compound. I told her the ladies do not leave the compound alone either. She reluctantly came in and stood just inside the gate. I left the door slightly open out of curiosity; and in case Laura wanted anything. Laura came down, talked very briefly with the woman, and went upstairs again. She never mentioned anything about the visit. I thought about it afterwards and felt maybe it was somebody returning something she had lost or forgotten at the wedding. I thought it strange because if that was really the case, the person should have been more eager to speak with me. I forgot all about it until they went missing. I didn't even think to mention it to the British soldiers when they came."

"This might be a potent lead" Tim concurred.

He called out to Alex but even though they questioned Ayesha very closely about this strange visitor they did not get anything else other than that she was probably as tall as Laura, slender, and spoke in Dari to Ayesha. She talked about the man who had accompanied her, but he did not come near enough for Ayesha to have had a good look. The only concrete description she could give was that he was taller than the woman and had worn a dark blue kaffiyeh.

Crestfallen, they went back to the British base. The husk of the UN truck had been loaded onto a carrier and brought back to town. They looked over the vehicle and could not come up with any clues. The vehicle had been thoroughly vandalized. Even the engine was not spared but there was no sign of violence or even a struggle within it. It was worked over by people who knew what they were doing. They looked again at the aerial pictures and talked to the ground crew that had visited the villages and hamlets.

The man and woman whom Ayesha had described could have been any number of Afghans and did not ring any bells with anyone at the base. They asked Ayesha's permission to interview her relatives within reach who had come for the wedding. Nobody had noticed that Laura had dropped or forgotten anything at the wedding. They did not feel anyone had paid her any special kind of attention there nor knew of anyone who had gone to visit her afterwards. No, they did not have a guest list for the wedding. It was a typical come-one, come-all event. A lot of distant relatives had come from out of town. Some of the guests, they did not even know at all.

Having come to a dead-end in Lashkar Gah, they decided to visit the villages again. They tried to conduct a hush-hush investigation, but the curiosity of the villagers had been aroused anyway. It was inevitable that people would soon start claiming sightings, and even responsibility for the deed. Nimruz province was notoriously unstable. The Taliban kept claiming that they still had a stronghold there and were just tolerating ISAF. The Taliban warlords were well-known. Alex and his team decided to go to see the currently most famous of them. They went to beard the lion in his own den.

Neem Omatullah received his American guests with due hospitality. His men stood around nursing their guns in a show of power. The customary tea was served and drunk, and then they came down to business. The Americans told Omatullah, "We are looking for three foreign ladies. They disappeared somewhere around here about three weeks ago. The United Nations will be glad for any news at all concerning these ladies."

Omatullah was genuinely surprised. This was the first time he was hearing about this. He wished his own people had thought of this move first in order to warn off the foreigners.

He now said to the Americans, "This is news to me. Give me a week. I will send out feelers and see if any rival group has the ladies."

The team had no objections to his also making parallel enquiries. However, they went on with their own investigations. Every lead seemed to come to a dead-end. Even when Omatullah reported to them a week later, there were no fresh leads. They tried to console one another with the fact that "No news is sometimes good news."

People often have the mistaken belief that the Taliban was a bunch of ignorant, laidback mountain men frozen in the Middle Ages, who go about shouting Moslem slogans. Nothing is farther from the truth than this. The leaders of this extremist religious group were mostly highly intelligent, and often very highly educated men and women with first class education obtained from the United States, Russia, Britain, Canada, Germany, China, and other major universities all over the world. In their ranks they had professionals including engineers, doctors, computer scientists, pilots, and so on; with all the modern knowhow which man has invented or discovered. In addition to these were the foot soldiers consisting of men and women on ground that still had traditional expertise in tracking, mountaineering, and other basic knowledge by which the early man had survived living with nature in this rugged terrain down through the ages and through several civilizations.

The uniting factor for all these people was a fanatical desire to live according to the Islamic Law (Sharia) or their own peculiar interpretation of it. They had the backing of oil-rich Arabs, drug barons, other people more advanced in crime than the mafia, and even technocrats in Western societies and all over the world. They did not just have the technological knowhow they also had the equipment to back whatever they set their minds on to do. The allied forces had learned these lessons in bitter circumstances but still continued to underestimate them.

What Alex and his team accomplished therefore was interesting the Taliban in the case. By involving them, they further endangered the lives of the women they were seeking to rescue. Omatullah sent out emissaries to gather as much information as they could about the case. His methods were not as civilized as what the Americans were using. They got a description of the women, the circumstances in which the UN vehicle had been seen by those who had passed by it before it was finally taken away. They found out who the driver was, where he lived with his family at Lashka Gah, and which mosque he favored for Friday prayers. However, they decided there was no more information to be gathered from him. He might be useful on a future date but did not merit any more of their attention for the time being. Finally, they got the useful additional information that two UN satellite phones were also missing with the women.

"Track those phones" Omatullah ordered. "Whoever has the phones has the women and has done a very clever job. I wish to have people with such cunning and planning in my own camp."

And then, about four weeks after they disappeared, when UNESCO was about to make the news worldwide and start contacting their relatives, their letters arrived. There were three letters, one from each of the ladies. Greta had written to Dick at the British base, Lil to Bjorn, and Laura to Tim. The letters had come through the Lashkar Gah post office and there were many fingerprints on the envelopes. The letters were from the ladies all right. The handwritings were theirs. The fingerprints on the note papers matched what UNESCO had for them on file. The dates on the letters had obviously been cut off. There was nothing to indicate where they were writing from. There was also an accompanying postcard-sized picture of the three of them laughing, and obviously content. The picture came in a separate envelope addressed to UNESCO. It had no fingerprints on it at all.

After the letters and envelopes had been thoroughly studied and analysed, they were finally released to the rightful addressees. These addressees were all relieved and comforted but not totally at ease. To Tim it was like an answer to prayer and a sign from God that Laura understood. The women were obviously not in distress but something devious was definitely going on. That they were not free to leave was implicit in the letters.

Within hours of these analyses, Neem Omatullah was well-apprised of the situation. He had spies everywhere. He rightly concluded that the allied forces were also not having it easy. Despite threats and offers of rewards, he also had not been able to find out the whereabouts of the missing women. The satellite phones had not ever been turned on. "Continue to monitor those phones" he told his minions, "I feel they are a very important link. If they are with the women, they will one day turn them on to contact their base. However, we want the glory of capturing and killing them. If the phones are with their captors, they will know where the women are. Like I said, I want such people in my camp."

As the weeks passed however, and this elusive factor had neither contacted nor surrendered to Omatullah, he changed his song." If they are not working with us, then they are working against us. The friends of my enemies…" He left the sentence incomplete. If there was a faction out there that was capable of doing this thing, and had not contacted the Taliban for support, then they must be hoping for the support of the allied forces. Perhaps they were even then making negotiations which might be for the downfall of the Taliban.

Among the Allied forces, the search went on but at a more relaxed pace since at least there was proof that the women were still alive. No demands had been made and whoever was holding them did not leave an open door of communication. The

Americans returned to their base. Other duties called. The British called off the majority of their search parties. ISAF attached only a token number of men to the case. Il Dhost had achieved all these with expert cunning. The situation still simmered but the heat was off. The women were safe where Il Dhost wanted them, and they were being very useful.

CHAPTER 5

―――――∞―――――

When Soraya cleared up their dinner that night, she brought them each a Burqa to wear for the journey. She encouraged them to collect and pack their things "There will be no time in the morning. We leave before the sun rises."

They felt sad and deflated. They were hoping to be leaving to go back to Lashkar Gah but they understood they had no choice. They discussed different methods of escape, and of leaving trails for the people they were sure would be looking for them. Laura was very sure that Tim and Alex had the entire American garrison watching out for any telltale signs of them. Greta was sure the British would be looking out for them too. "We should watch out for anyone wearing ISAF or NATO colors, yell and then make a dash for it" Greta suggested. "We might not recognize those looking for us, but surely our pictures must have circulated by now."

They talked about the Hansel and Gretel Maneuver. Dorothy Simmons had briefed them on ways of leaving trails if they ever got kidnapped. They had paid attention when they were receiving those lectures but since they had never felt themselves in danger, the things they had been taught had become fuzzy in their memories. "And yet they are common sense things which would let even the most inexperienced know that surely we had been here" Lil said.

They thought of writing on the walls or leaving notes in corners so someone could follow their trail. "You can be sure someone will be in to clean up after us once we leave" Laura said.

For all the good that would do, they found sharp stones to work with. While Laura and Lil carved their initials close to the floor and the ceiling in their rooms, Greta went to the primitive toilet to do the same. They packed away their things, laid out the Burqa, and not feeling sleepy, just huddled and discussed ways and means of escape.

"We should use any opportunity we get to attract attention to ourselves" Lil said. "It's true we might attract the attention of the wrong people, who might be more evil than our present captors but we are more or less like captive slaves now, anyway."

They reminisced over their achievements of the past few weeks. Despite their predicaments, they glowed with a sense of satisfaction and pride. It was not the fault of the teachers or the pupils that they were in their present predicament, well, in a way, but people must appreciate good things when they happen. "When this is all over" said Greta, "I am going to use this ASPC method as a doctoral thesis."

Laura said she was also going to write up on how so much could be achieved with so little. Lil just wanted to go home and marry Bjorn. As she wept over this, the others wept with her. It was on this unhappy note that they all soon fell asleep.

Just as she said, while it was still dark, Soraya came to wake them up. She had a kerosene lantern which cast a bright glow and lots of shadows. She urged them to put on their Burqas over their clothes. "That is the good thing about the Burqa, it does not really matter what you are wearing underneath. Nevertheless, wear what you are comfortable in, and then put on the Burqa. I will come to collect you very soon. Do you want me to carry your bags now or do you want to bring them along with you?"

They preferred not to be separated from their bags for whatever little comfort this afforded them. It was scarcely five minutes later when Soraya came back. They followed her. For the first time since they came, they found themselves outside the compound. They did not have time to look back to study where they had lived for the past five weeks. Spread out in front of them was what appeared to be a whole village on the move. There were shadowy forms of men, women, and animals. There were sheep, goats, dogs, and larger animals which appeared like donkeys, horses, and camels. They did not have time to gaze at these for Soraya kept urging them on, "This way, this way, this way." They stuck to her as much in bewilderment as in astonishment. They got to a kneeling camel. "Our bags will be carried on this camel so you will know more or less to always home in on her. You can travel in any part of the camp you wish, but whenever we rest, come to where she is because that is where our bags and tents will be." Soraya lectured them. "Nazo said you might want to walk but these donkeys are also for your use when you feel like it." And then they saw four donkeys tied to one another. There was a slender woman standing by the head of the lead donkey. "Salaam" she greeted them in a low musical voice.

Soraya nodded to her and indicated they were ready to go. They noticed that the whole caravan had been in motion for some time. The young woman whom they soon learned was called Hafi asked if they wanted to ride on the donkeys or to walk. They preferred to walk for the moment. None of the three had ever ridden a donkey before.

They seemed to be in the middle of the caravan and were by no means the slowest. All around them were other women as well. Some were dressed in Burqas and some in the less confining hijab. Almost all of them had mysterious bundles tied to their backs, their fronts or to their sides. From the squirming of the bundles, it was obvious there were living things in some of them. Laura assumed they were all babies until Greta surreptitiously pointed to one woman and whispered, "I could swear that baby bleats!"

As the daylight became stronger, they saw that some of the bundles were indeed human babies but most of them were kids and lambs! "Ugh" said Greta in disgust; "Ooh" said Lil in admiration. Laura was too stunned to express anything.

Apparently, the kids and lambs which could not easily make the trek or that might slow down the caravan were helped along in this way by the women. The animals left a peculiar odor on clothes, but they somehow also provided mutual warmth. Before they came to the end of their ordeal, Greta, Laura, and Lil found themselves sometimes also providing these kinds of services especially as the days grew shorter and colder, and as they got to higher altitudes.

At first, they actually enjoyed the trek, having been cooped indoors for the past few weeks but then the strain began to tell on their unused muscles. They were about to give up and ask if they could ride on the donkeys when a halt was called. Apparently, they had come to a grazing land. It was a natural hollow, surrounded on almost all the sides by gently-rising slopes. The shallow parts of a river ran through it. The animals were let lose to graze while the people expertly erected some goatskin tents to provide sheds from the scorching sun. Soraya coaxed them to a tent on the edge of the camp. She set out refreshments before them. Before they ate, she took them to the tent that served as a washroom and showed them how to use sand as sanitizers after a little bit of digging.

The morning exercise must have been invigorating because they found themselves finishing the large meal set before them, and then they dozed off. When Soraya wakened them, the sun had shifted in the sky and become less merciless. "Nazo would want you to come to meet with Il Dhost" she told them. She led them to an outcrop of rocks some distance away from the camp and then disappeared again in the direction they had come. They saw Nazo seated on a rock by the grassy hillside. She embraced them like long lost friends but they held themselves quite stiffly remembering how they had parted. "I am so sorry for treating you badly" she began.

"Il Dhost has already chided me for my behavior. Now it is time for you to meet Il Dhost by yourselves."

That was when they became aware that Nazo was not there alone. The neighing of a horse drew their attention to a solitary tree farther up the hillside to which a magnificent chestnut horse was tethered. They did not know much about horses but this one appeared powerful and spirited even to the untrained eye. It snorted, tossing its mane impatiently as if raring to go. Close to the horse sat what must have been its rider in a lotus position, facing them. He did not look that impressive a man. They could not gauge his height or weight. Most of his head and face were wrapped in a winding turban which left only the eyes visible. From where they were, the sunshine was in their eyes. They could not even guess the color of, or the expression in the said eyes. He lifted a hand in greeting. They responded in like manner.

They now noticed there were other people in nooks and hollows all around them, obviously guards that were keeping watch. Before they could take all these in, Nazo gestured for them to sit beside her. They sat in such a way that Nazo sat some distance between them and the mysterious figure on the hillside. This was the way in polite Afghan society. Men and women ought not to have direct dealings with one another if they were not married or otherwise related. The man now said something softly to Nazo. Nazo carried the communication on to the women. Apparently, this was how it was going to be. Obviously, Il Dhost heard and understood what they said but would only talk to them through Nazo. Fine, this was Afghanistan. Greta, Laura, and Lil were not unduly offended.

Nazo said to the women, "Il Dhost wants me to thank you for your help, and all you have done for us. You will please accept apologies for myself, Nazo, treating you as if you have no intelligence. The right way should have been to let you know the kind of program we have in mind, and to ask if you would please help us out. Il Dhost insists that if you do not feel like helping us, we are to return you to Qandahar this very evening.

Nazo paused and looked at the women expectantly. They did not have the time or the language to confer among themselves privately. They had to speak their minds right then and there before Nazo. "We want to be returned now, immediately." Greta said.

Nazo conferred with Il Dhost again.

"We will be glad to do so but will you please listen to the rest of what we had planned? This present group you find yourselves among is a band of Kuchis. They are nomads. By the time you get to know this group well, you will discover that it has rather too many girls. This is one method we have of hiding the girls we rescue. It is also a very viable means of transporting them across the country or across the borders to where they belong. "Many of them are eager to learn. We are hoping you can set the teachers on a course like you did at Zaranj. We have twelve posts like the one at Zaranj, and a few other wandering groups but we are not intending to keep you to teach the methods to all these groups. Two women from your last class, and a few others whom we have invited from other centers have agreed to come along. They will understudy you and see if they can impart to other groups these methods that you used. If you can give us a chance, we believe that within a short time, we will be able to learn as much as you can teach us." Nazo and Il Dhost conferred again and Nazo transmitted to the women. "Il Dhost wants me to tell you that Christmas is just over four short months away. If you will help us, we promise that long before then you will be reunited with your loved ones, with our eternal gratitude and blessings."

The humility, the appeal, and the definite timetable threw the women off balance. Did they not appreciate the predicament the group had been in at first? Had they not voluntarily donated their time in the first place? In truth, they had enjoyed doing it the first time. Here also was a worthy experiment. Could the native women take over their work after they go? Finally, they each knew that their individual resolutions were in conflict with some of the concessions which they knew must be going on in the minds of the other members of their team. So far, the intentions of their captors had seemed noble. There was nothing that guaranteed it would not turn hostile at the drop of a pin. They did not have any bargaining chips at all. They had heard that the problem most captives faced was how to fill up the time. Here they were, being offered an opportunity to be creative, and actually add their own widows' mites to the rebuilding of Afghanistan.

After a prolonged silence, Il Dhost murmured again and Nazo spoke to them. "Il Dhost recognizes that perhaps you would want some time to talk it over among yourselves in private but the offer for a prompt return remains open but please, please, if you do not help us, these children might never, ever get such help again." If she had stopped there, the debate might have been long and hard but in an uncharacteristically broken voice, Nazo ended her oratory with a wail of "Please, please help us. Please!"

"Before Christmas, you said?" asked Greta.

"Long before then if you want to go; or if you judge enough progress had been made."

"We will think about it, discuss it among ourselves, and get back to you." Greta answered for them all.

"Thank you, thank you very much for not saying an outright 'No' and throwing it in our faces" was the humble reply.

And so, tacitly they had agreed to stay.

They soon learned that there were ninety-eight school age children in the camp aged eight to sixteen. Twelve of these were boys. There were actually normal families in the group but most were girls who had been rescued from unfortunate marriages and alliances. Some had been pregnant and had given birth while in the camp. Some others were just too young when they had left their homes. They either did not remember, and therefore could not go back to where they came from; or did not want to go back at all. Some others were hopeful of going back one day once they knew where home was, and how to get there. Notwithstanding this diversity, they were all roughly organized into families. Everyone knew which hearth to look to for a meal, and which tent to go to sleep at night. They all belonged to one another in the larger community but also had smaller units to be accountable to.

The three women never got an accurate headcount of the adults but discovered they were to be teaching fifteen women in all. After they gave Nazo an answer the day following their meeting with Il Dhost, they never saw her again on that trek until they were about to leave the Kuchis. It was Soraya who now saw to it that their gadgets were charged when they needed them to be. Nadia sat in on all of their classes but did not really do or say much. They were now more proficient in Dari and did not need interpreters for their lessons. The two women from Zaranj also helped out.

They followed much the same pattern they had at Zaranj but with their language refined, and their methods improved. They found they could actually do all the teacher education in less than two weeks. The classes too, being smaller, were easier to manage during the demonstration teachings. There was a healthy competition and challenge if there happened to also be boys in any class. Where they had thought the teachers and pupils at Zaranj very inventive and resourceful, these ones were even more so. From sticks and stones, they could fashion and create almost anything. The parents too, who were not directly involved in the schoolwork seemed to participate very maximally, providing very imaginative craft materials for numerous improvisations. Sometimes they would camp in a place where they could hook up to wireless internet. The pupils and teachers-in-training would gape in wonder at first as Greta, Laura and Lil demonstrated the wonders of the internet. They would then proceed to copy, and even outstrip what they were encountering even for the first time. They thought of surreptitiously sending emails but never succeeded for any known reason.

Soraya told them they trekked about fifteen miles each day. However, they had no way of verifying this. They set off while it was still dark each day. They went on till the sun became too hot or till they came to a good pasture. As the animals went to graze and people

went about their daily chores of fetching water, hunting for firewood, cooking, milking, or going to trade with neighboring towns and villages, the school tent would go up and learning would start in earnest. Just as at Zaranj, they took meal breaks and drank endless cups of tea, but they stayed right on course. When daylight faded, they stopped and relaxed in their tents, packed up their materials and personal effects, ready to set off again before dawn.

At first, they gamely trekked with the group. However, they soon accepted donkey rides and saw there was nothing to it at all. They each even confessed to having fallen asleep occasionally while riding the donkeys. Hafi laughed. She enjoyed taking care of the women. She saw to it that they were not in any real danger. Greta went for runs in the evenings. Soraya had got her men's clothes to wear during her runs. She showed Greta how to wrap her blond hair in a turban so that she could run unrecognized. Maybe people from outside the camp did not recognize her, but from within the camp she soon became daubed as "the He-woman who pursues the wind!"

One day, Laura felt that she saw the Farah Fort in the distance. She told Greta and Lil, "That could be the US Marine base at Farah. That window could actually belong to the room they assigned to me. From there I always thought I saw shepherds grazing their animals beside the Farah River."

Soraya saw to their particular needs. She never participated in the school sessions but would often entertain them after school with pictures and videos she had taken during the daytime. Taking pictures and talking about them seemed to have loosened her tongue, or perhaps it was the increasing familiarity with the women. She had become fast friends with them. She no longer spoke to them in monosyllables and smiles. She now seemed to sometimes have many more words than her pictures and could go on nonstop.

In some of Soraya's pictures people had posed for her. In some others she had captured people at unexpected moments. There was a shepherd snoozing in the fields with his charges grazing all around; a woman with Hijab flying behind her and a wooden ladle raised above her head in hot pursuit of a curious dog which had been nosing round the kitchen tent depicted in the background; camp elders thoughtfully stroking their beards during a shura, and so on. She even had a picture of Greta with a studious frown addressing her students; Lil all twisted up doing her stretch exercises, some of the women in the camp trying to imitate her with very amusing results; Laura surrounded by a group of children raising their flowerlike faces to her in rapt attention to whatever she was telling them. Soraya was really good. Under different circumstances she could have been an award-winning photographer. Laura told her she had far outstripped herself as her teacher. Soraya beamed.

After about a week on the road, a day dawned in which they did not dismantle to move early in the morning. The whole camp seemed to be in a mellow state. The animals still grazed but minimal work seemed to go on in the camp. Even in the school tent, the students seemed more languid than usual. They asked to be dismissed early. When Soraya brought them their midday meal she told them, "There will be worship this evening. Do you want to join us?"

"What kind of worship?" Laura asked.

"A Christian worship" Soraya informed them. "We thought you must have guessed by now. Our outfit is secretly Christian. If caught we shall be legally executed, I mean, beheaded or shot. However, this is what we have been called to do so we continue to risk it."

The women looked at one another as much to say, "I suspected as much" as to say, "What have we got ourselves into?"

"We shall love to join you and see for ourselves" Lil said.

"Okay, I will come for you when it is about to begin" Soraya said as she left.

She came for them before sunset. The entire camp, it seemed, had gathered close to the center. There was a campfire going but Soraya told them there were sentries on duty keeping a look out for any trouble. "Kuchis" she told them, "are known for their free style music and celebrations."

That night the people really celebrated. They sang and danced with abandon. Their language was just a dialect of Pashto so the women could follow the lyrics of the songs even though they did not sing any familiar tune that night. They sang about the goodness of God and of His son. They sang about the presence and work of the Holy Spirit in their lives. They sang about the blessings God showered on them day by day. Some people came forward to testify of these blessings amidst clapping and waving from the others. There were prayers and sermonettes; more prayers, more music and dancing, and then two hours later people began to drift back to their tents. Others remained to sing and chat around the campfire. "It's just like a good old Pentecostal revival meeting back home", Laura thought.

They went back to their own tent in very reflective moods. They did not even feel like discussing what they had just witnessed. The next day they were on the move again.

CHAPTER 6

---∞---

There was only one other worship meeting while they were on the road. They went along like before and left when the main events seemed to be over. Again, they returned to their tent in speculative moods which brooked no discussions. A few days afterwards Nazo came to see them at the camp. She wanted to know how the school had progressed, and what they thought of some of the women who had participated. Did they think some of the women could be trained to train others? Greta, Laura, and Lil reported as best as they could. They mentioned the names of the women they felt could become trainers themselves.

"Do you think you have concluded with this group? Are you comfortable enough to leave them and move on?" Nazo asked.

"I think so," said Greta.

"I don't think we can improve on what they have for now," agreed Laura.

"Yes," added Lil. "I feel so too."

Nazo then said, "The camp elders want to hold a feast in your honor when you have finished. Can I go ahead and give them a date?"

"Sure" said Greta.

"Why not?" said Laura.

"Okay" said Lil.

And so, it was all fixed.

The feast was no small matter. They discovered that whole goats had been killed and roasted slowly over wood fire throughout the day for the evening. There were different types of rice dishes, bread baked in different ways, cheese, fruits, and nuts. They were given gifts of decorated combs and embroidered clothes. The most touching aspect was when their students and pupils sang them songs that had been composed specially for them and came to tearfully hug them goodbye.

They felt it very keenly that on their side they had nothing to give, not even cookies and candies. An elder told them they had given something which would outlast any material gift. They had given their love, friendship, and an enduring education. He confessed he did not know that the camp women and children had been preparing gifts for them but hoped that wherever they went, they would carry with them the love and the appreciation of the whole camp. He then asked their permission to pray for them there and then.

The three women could never remember such a thing being done for them before, but they respectfully bowed their heads. The elder prayed in Dari. He prayed that God would bless them, always be with them, cause them to always see the light of His face, and follow the direction of His voice, no matter the cost. He asked God to bless them immensely for the work they were doing among His people in Afghanistan. He concluded his prayer by asking, "And when it is done, in a very short while, please cause that they will be reunited with their kin and those they love in the precious Name of Jesus."

The feasting, music, and dancing went on late into the night. They returned to their tent with their minds too full to even sleep. When they got there, Soraya had been packing for them. Apparently when Nazo decided they were to move, she saw no point in wasting time. There was no time for leaving Hansel and Gretel trails. They could not imagine a means of doing it anyway. In the original story, the children had also found themselves stymied the second time around. They had used pieces of bread which the birds found and ate.

They followed Soraya to a track just outside the camp where a truck and its driver were waiting. They piled inside with their bags, resolving to keep awake and mark the way they were going but in mere minutes they were all blissfully asleep, worn out by the events of the day and the feasting. When Soraya shook them awake sometime later, they could do no more than sleepily gather their things and follow her. They only vaguely noted that they passed through a courtyard and were shown into a room very much like the one they had at Zaranj. They had enough energy to just kick off their shoes and fall asleep again in minutes. After the clean open air, sleeping in a room again was like being caged. However, the soft mattresses made up for the bumpy pillows they had slept on while on the road.

The next day, Soraya gave them a quick orientation of their new living quarters. It really was very much like Zaranj. Here again, they discovered there was a little over two hundred children but there were now about thirty teachers willing to be trained. Nazo asked them if they could let the trainers in progress from Zaranj and the camp do the training while Greta, Laura, and Lil observed them. They were glad for this. For one they were beginning to feel depressed again. They had also all developed a bothersome cough which constantly tickled the back of their throats.

The trainers were good but a bit unsure of themselves at the beginning. With a little push and encouragement, they became better each succeeding day. Greta asked if she could resume her running but was told that it was not safe to do so. They promised to look into a way for her to exercise within the compound. Soraya made herbal tea remedies to help their cough. The tea tasted of mint, honey, and something else. They found out they rather enjoyed it. Whereas Greta and Laura got better, the less robust Lil grew pale and wan. Her cough deepened. She began coughing up yellowish phlegm which soon turned brownish and sometimes had streaks of blood. Her appetite greatly diminished, she craved lots of fluid instead. When she developed diarrhea and became feverish, Greta and Laura really started worrying. In their over two years in Afghanistan none of them had ever had an ailment more serious than a headache.

They asked for clean water, salt, and sugar. They made up oral rehydration solutions for her while the Afghan women looked on. She did not become worse, but she did not become better either. Greta asked Soraya to send for Nazo, Il Dhost, or whoever was in charge to get her help immediately. By now, their teaching had progressed to the point of classroom demonstrations. The native trainers needed the input of the foreign women. However, Greta and Laura balked at continuing until help was got for Lil.

Perhaps due to this, or because they were already going to do so, Nazo sent a message that she had made arrangements for Lil to be moved to the city. That night, Lil appeared even weaker than usual. Laura bathed her continually with lukewarm water which Soraya had provided. Greta almost wore through the packed mud floor in front of their room with her pacing. Laura tried to talk to Lil. "Very soon you will be reunited with Bjorn. Think of all the stories you will have to tell him, to your children, and to your grandchildren; stories of Afghanistan and how we got kidnapped. What is the first thing you would like to do once you set foot in Sweden?"

Lil smiled from time to time but did not answer back. Even speaking seemed to exhaust her. Laura felt that her breathing had become more labored as well. It occurred to her that when Lil was finally moved, she and Greta might not be allowed to go as well. Secretly, she wrote notes and stuffed them into the hems of Lil's shirt. She wrote things like "We are in Shindand now." "We seem to be heading north." "We saw Farah Fort a few days ago." "Il Dhost heads the outfit."

It was a laborious task doing this in the gloom of the solitary kerosene lantern they had been given. Although she whispered to Lil that there were notes in her clothes, she doubted if Lil heard her.

After midnight, they heard the rumble of a truck. Nazo and Soraya came to take Lil away.

"We are all going, right?" Greta asked belligerently.

"I'm afraid not" Nazo answered. "With Lil having to lie down in the truck there will not be much room. I promise to come back as soon as she is settled to tell you how it all went."

"I'm afraid you will have to take us along" Greta answered with an equally syrupy politeness. "You don't expect us to go on teaching with such a burden on our minds." Something else suddenly occurred to her. "You are taking her to a hospital, right?"

Reading her correctly Nazo replied with equal vehemence. "Of course, we are taking her to a hospital. Trust our integrity, she is going to get very good care. If we do not bring her back here it would not be because we killed her, it would be because we turned her free. Please trust me a little, Greta."

Greta was not ready to trust her at all but Laura coming up touched her arm. "A prolonged argument is not going to do Lil any good now. The sooner she gets help, the better." Greta saw the sense in this and quickly allowed them take Lil away. She followed Laura mutely to the open corridor in front of their room but would not go inside. They dragged a mattress out to the corridor. In whispers Laura told her of the little notes she had secreted away among Lil's garments. "Let us hope they find even one of them" she said.

The next day, school went on as usual. The Afghan women they had as students had seen enough tragedy and learned to live with it. They sympathized with Laura and Greta over their grief but knew life had to go on. Laura and Greta went on with their supervision but only half-heartedly. They admitted that the Afghan women were not just very good learners, but also very good teachers.

Meanwhile, mindful of the many responsibilities upon her shoulders, Nazo decided to take Lil to the city hospital at Farah. From where they were to Farah was about a three-hour drive. Taking her to Farah would ensure excellent care, anonymity, and protection from their base at Anar Darreh. Farah had an excellent hospital which served the whole province of Farah, as well as the neighboring provinces of Nimruz and Ghor. The next best choice would have been Herat but Nazo had her reasons for not going there.

This was her plan but as they hit the junction between Highway 1 and Highway 515 which would then take them down to Farah everything changed. Suddenly Lil stretched to her full length and started talking in her native language. She called out to her mother and said in English "We still have work to do at Afghanistan. We still have to finish."

Nazo panicked. If Lil had been stable, the Farah plan would have worked well. Delirious, she was not sure how much help she would get especially if she did not have a relative on hand to hound the besieged hospital staff. That was how things worked in the big hospital. The doctors and the nurses did their jobs well but because of the high volume of patient turnouts which passed through the hospital, the help of the relatives became quite necessary especially for hospitalized patients. Nazo could not afford this kind of exposure. She could not at the drop of a hat arrange for someone to impersonate Lil's relative. Again, with Lil now delirious, who knew what secrets she would expose?

Nazo was nothing if not a clever schemer. She made a cell phone call to Il Dhost to sketch out the broad outlines of her plans. The latter made suggestions to refine the plan, and instructions on what Nazo was to do exactly. Nazo in her turn gave instructions to the truck driver. About fifty minutes later, they were turning off a side street in downtown Farah.

Nazo had the driver go to an inn of questionable repute across the street from where they were parked. The lily-white name of the inn happened to mean "The Lotus". It was not yet quite day. The driver went into the shop. While drinking the proffered cup of tea, he told Abdul, the proprietor of the inn "My younger wife is having one of those women problems. We came all the way from the village to see the doctors at the hospital here. I have to go to the hospital to get a number for her. Please do you have somewhere she can rest a bit before the hospital starts accepting patients for the day?"

"Certainly," Abdul said. "For a prize it could be arranged for the poor woman to rest in the back room until the hospital opens to outpatients for the day. Yes, if you want to get a turn today, you better be at the gate before they open it, or the rush will be too much."

Some money exchanged hands. The driver obtained the key which would let them in through the back. Walking Lil between them, Nazo and the driver brought her to the appointed bed, made her comfortable and went out the same way again. The driver locked the door and returned the key to the proprietor. He said he was going to the hospital to take a number and would be back for his wife very soon.

"I've made a comfortable five hundred Afghanis" Abdul thought, "and so early in the morning too!" The day looked promising.

Their next stop was somewhere that Nazo made use of a computer and printer. They then went on to a teashop where drops were usually made for the American soldiers. She left an obscure envelope that read on the top "Lieutenant Alex Pearson *VERY URGENT*".

Nazo went down the street and virtually disappeared. She made the driver go on to Anar Darreh while she went to another teashop almost opposite The Lotus to wait in the shadows as a demure housewife might. She drank many cups of tea while awaiting developments. She waited till about two o'clock in the afternoon before she was finally sure that she was not going to put her Plan C into action.

At about ten o'clock that morning, the attention of a United States marine passing through town had been drawn to the envelope at the drop site. He would have waited until evening when he went off duty to deliver the envelope. However, it had been labelled as very urgent. It even had the name of a specific officer on it. Someone had failed to deliver such a message in the past and a major disaster had resulted. Besides, everyone at the base knew that Lieutenant Pearson was twisting himself into knots over the disappearance of the three UNESCO women and this might be related to the incident. He took the envelope straight back to the base, to Major Grafton. Major Grafton paged Alex immediately. Alex came promptly, with Tim in tow.

First, they verified there were no booby traps. It was not a letter bomb. Next, they dusted the envelope for fingerprints. Finally, they opened it. Inside was a copy of the picture which had come with the ladies' letters about two months before, showing them laughing. It also contained a single sheet of printed white paper. It read, "One of these ladies is very sick and is at the backroom of The Lotus Inn here in downtown Farah. The proprietor of the place knows nothing about the kidnapping."

Was this a trick, a trap, or a genuine lead? Which of the women was it? Why The Lotus in Farah? There was only one way of finding out. They had to go to The Lotus. That was how come that at about two o'clock in the afternoon Nazo saw two army jeeps stop at opposite ends of the street blocking it off. Eight United States marines fully armed and dressed to the hilt in battle gear jumped out and spread out, virtually cordoning off the whole street. She watched as two of them went into The Lotus. She listened as Abdul began to wail and protest in a high-pitched voice. There was a commotion as the patrons inside tried to disperse but were prevented from doing so. She watched as the back door of the inn was opened and two of the men carrying Lil on a mattress loaded her onto one of the jeeps which drove off even as another one arrived to take its place. At this point Nazo decided she had seen enough. She got up and left through a back door. No one could have described her. No one had taken any particular notice of her. Even Abdul had not known about her existence. She knew that everyone within that vicinity was in for a very long day. They would have a lot of questions to answer before the day was done. She, on her own part, had some other business to take care of.

Tim stayed with the group which had taken Lil away. At the army base clinic, the medics examined her and pronounced her to be suffering from severe pneumonia.

They did not have all the wonderful gadgets which modern hospitals then used but they had enough to set up intravenous lines, rehydrate her, bring down the fever and pump her full of antibiotics. Tim would have liked to stay on with her but as the saying went, "when it rains, it pours". A signal came from the British base at Lashkar Gah to say that a package drop had been made that morning at a motor repair garage just outside the town which the UN often used. There were really about ten packages wrapped in industrial cellophane bags. There had been an attached note stating that these were truck parts taken from the UNESCO vehicle on the way to Kadesh about ten weeks before. A check of the packages after confirming that it was not a bomb had indeed confirmed they contained all the missing parts: tyres, rugs, fittings, and even the engine parts. Everything seemed to be there. Nothing seemed to be missing except for the ladies themselves, their personal effects, and other UNESCO equipment which did not usually constitute a part of the vehicle.

The drop seemed to have been made in the early hours of that morning. Possible witnesses were still being rounded up for questioning but so far nothing had come of it. Major Grafton let the British know about the woman they had picked up just that afternoon. She had also seemed to have been dropped off that morning. Two leads in one day, in two different provinces, about three hundred miles apart, after such a long time with dead ends! Coincidences did not just happen. Someone was definitely trying to lead them in different directions at the same time.

CHAPTER 7

They came for Abdul in the dead of the night. There were three men, their faces wrapped in kaffiyeh so no one could distinguish their features. They entered his bedroom silently. When he saw two of them holding the mouths of his eight and ten-year old daughters Abdul quietly got up and followed without a protest. He did not bother to look at the devastation of the rest of his house. He cursed the five hundred Afghanis he had made that morning which had started all of this.

The American soldiers had questioned him for hours. He had finally managed to convince them, or so he believed that he knew nothing of the person who brought the lady, what he wore; the kind of vehicle he drove; nor even his name. He kept protesting over and over, "He just paid me some money and I did him a service. I swear."

The Americans had finally let him go close to midnight. He staggered home, trying to get some comfort in the refuge of his own home, feel secure in his own bed, but it was not to be.

They went in a single file down a long track that led outside the city. Abdul stumbled after the man who seemed to be the leader. He heard other footsteps following them. The footsteps of the men who had his daughters and heaven knew who else. They went towards the mountains they called Lor Koh, the safe motherly arms for her children, and the nemesis of their enemies. What it would be to Abdul that night? He did not dare think. He knew what could be in store for his young daughters. No matter what else he was, he had been a caring father who wanted what was best for his daughters. He had heard about what the Taliban did to the daughters of perceived enemies. Up till the present moment, he had believed this kind of thing only happened to the unrighteous or to outright enemies but what had he done in his life to deserve this? He had been an upright Moslem whose major interests had been making money to look after his family.

He bowed his head to pray but no prayers would come. These were the righteous fighters for all he had believed in up to that moment. They would force his consent, have his daughters wedded temporarily to the men that would ravish them to death that night, all in the name of God. He felt helpless because he could not do anything about it. When they eventually came to their refuge in the mountains, they did not even need to tie him up. Abdul was benumbed with defeat. He just stood there with his head hanging.

"Tell us, Shopkeeper, the things you forgot to tell the Americans" they began.

"I told them everything I knew, as it happened" he said dully.

"Repeat to us what you told them. We shall see how we can help your memory along."

He narrated again, probably for the fiftieth time, "The man who came into my shop was average-sized. He was neither too tall nor too short. He was neither too fat nor too skinny. He was just average in size and build. His dressing did not appear too rich or too poor. He was just ordinarily dressed. He ordered tea and said he had travelled through the night from the village so his ailing wife could see a doctor that morning at the Farah hospital. He said his wife was very tired. He asked if she could stay in the backroom to rest a bit while he went to the hospital to see to getting a number.

"Zakat! It was Zakat. One has to give to people in need. That is the command of Allah and the prophet, may peace be upon him!" Abdul said plaintively appealing to their religious sense of duty.

Ignoring his piety, his interrogator went on. "Did he say where they had been travelling from?"

"He did not mention the name of his village."

"How were they travelling? Was it by car, lorry, camel or donkey?"

"I don't know. I didn't ask, honestly. It never came up in our talk. There were other people in the shop, and we did not talk for long or very intimately."

"Did he say for how long they had been travelling?"

"Not exactly, he just said all night."

"Did the other men get a good look at the man?"

"I don't know. I cannot even remember who was there. They were also all travellers passing through town. It was still too early at that time for my regular patrons. I told the Americans this."

"What kind of illness was his wife suffering from?"

"I did not ask. He had said it was a woman problem."

"Was there any other person with the couple?"

"I don't know, but after he returned the key and left, I was hearing muttering from the back room. I assumed the ill woman was with a co-wife or another relative."

"Did you never go to check?"

"What right did I have to walk in on another man's wife? It is forbidden by the prophet; may peace be upon him."

This made religious sense.

"But when the Americans came to take her away, there was only one person?"

"So they said, I never got a good look myself. Somebody was already questioning me when they took her away. I did not get to see what happened in that back room when the Americans came."

"Are you sure there was only the one woman? We are looking for three of them."

"I swear by God. I have told you all that I know."

"Let's see if we can help your memory a bit. Bring the younger one."

From the shadows someone brought out Abdul's eight-year-old daughter, Amina. "Will you consent for Najib here to be the husband of your daughter, or would you rather have her dead? Islam forbids the killing of virgins. However, she is of age to marry."

The wild and frightened eyes of his daughter regarded him. Here was someone who had always implicitly trusted him for protection. She was betrothed to a distant cousin since she was a baby. That had been her protection in a way. One did not take advantage of a betrothed girl. Here he was, being asked to give her up to a forced marriage, to be followed by more shocking but religiously legal sex at that age. The alternative, although also heinous, seemed better by comparison. He could denounce her as no longer a virgin and watch her being beheaded. The dumb fright on her face was already a fate worse than death to her father. Defeated, Abdul raised his head and howled like an entrapped animal.

His interrogator slapped him hard across the mouth. His daughter whimpered, tears pouring down her face. Suddenly there were soft "whumphing" noises from the rocks. "Whumph! Whumph! Whumph!"

Abdul fell first, clutching his neck. His interrogator turned to see what was happening. He too fell. There were heavy thuds as other men fell in the dark. Abdul's older daughter screamed as the man holding her dragged her to the ground as he fell. The younger daughter stopped whimpering. She looked about her with eyes which had grown even larger, if it were possible. She seemed to be the only person standing there on the dark mountain. Her sister struggled up and two of them looked around them wildly. What had just happened? What were they to do?

Suddenly the night was alive with more men. Two men came and picked Abdul up between them. They commanded the girls to follow them. Other men brought up the rear. They went down a trail different from the one they had ascended. Some donkeys were waiting. They tied Abdul's limp body unceremoniously to one of the donkeys. They made the girls sit together on another one, and then they rode off. To the frightened girls, they were still in the same predicament. They were the captives of some vicious unknown men who were manhandling their father. They were headed away from their familiar city to an unknown destination. The only thing which had changed was that they were now together, and nobody was clamping their mouths shut. They were not free, not even to scream because their fates would then be sealed sooner rather than later. Their father too, was in no state to protect them. They kept weeping silently.

As day broke, their father began to stir. They found themselves in a camp of some Kuchis. They travelled along with them until they came to where they pastured their flock for the day. The girls and their father were led to a tent. As their eyes adjusted to the dim light, they also settled on their mother and their two baby brothers, Hassan and Hussein. "Madaar" they cried running to her and hugging her fiercely. "Madaar!" and they wept afresh. There were no words to describe the horror they had endured through the night, nor the relief they felt at that very moment. Their mother hugged them back, and they all wept together. That whole family would never be the same again. They had experienced firsthand the dark horrors of all they had been hearing about and thought would never happen to them. They had lost practically all they held dear up until that very day, materially, morally, and emotionally. In that one night, they had all aged at least twenty years. It would take some time, but they eventually would realize they had not lost everything. Some other more important things had been spared them. With time, they gained other things that were even more important yet. Every one of them would all come to cherish that night - eventually but not immediately.

If Lil had been taken to the City Hospital, one stiffly starched nursing officer might have ordered her clothes taken away immediately, and probably incinerated. At the army base however, every piece of evidence was very valuable. Even as she was being undressed and put in a hospital gown, some orderlies were taking away her clothes for analysis. They wanted to know everything including what type of sand grains were caught in the fabrics of her clothes; what kind of hair had been shed unto it and by whom; what kind of soap and water they had been washed with in the recent past, and so on? They would get a bewildering array of results on all counts, but the most immediate things they found were the notes Laura had secreted into the seams.

These were taken to Major Grafton who was at that very moment sitting with Alex, going over the frustration of their intelligence gathering at The Lotus, around it, at the hospital and other places they had been to in Farah. Nobody had seen nor heard anything that gave them a concrete lead. Those who had claimed that they saw something were so inconsistent in what they reported that it was absolutely of no use to the soldiers. Naturally, Alex was heading the intelligence on this particular case. When they saw the tiny notes, they both recognized Laura's handwriting. The notes read, "We are in Shindand now." "We seem to be heading north." "We saw Farah Fort a few days ago." "Il Dhost heads this outfit."

This Il Dhost was very clever but seemed to have been outwitted by Laura on this one. Their quarry was obviously at Shindand, heading north but wanted them to scramble about Farah or Lashkar Gah, hence the two confusing leads in one day. It was tempting to take a contingent of marines and go beating about the bush at Shindand hoping to flush out their quarry. However, that would not do. They were beginning to get a picture of whom they were dealing with. This was good as first steps went. The major task, they agreed, was to get Lil recovered enough to give them more to work with.

Lil continued to rave in her delirium. Tim was there keeping a benevolent watch over her and recording everything she said. There was an audio recorder, but he was also writing down his own impression of everything she said. Sometimes she spoke in her native Swede tongue or in broken Dari. Most times, however, she spoke in English. On very few occasions she would mutter in French or German, but this was not often. Whatever she said, the audio recorder registered, and Tim added his own impression as he heard it. At times she would call out to Laura or to Greta and give long spiels ranging from academic project reports to comic ditties. She laughed, she cried, but she never seemed frightened. Perhaps this Il Dhost was not that bad after all. However, nobody took anything for granted at all.

They debated the merits of transferring her to Qandahar. A video conference with the base hospital at Qandahar showed that the medical team at Farah were managing her well enough. A move might actually be detrimental. In any case, there was no helicopter immediately available for the next few days. She stayed at Farah then, since there was no urgent need. Two days later, her fever broke. Her breathing became less labored. She slept calmly through the night. Early in the morning on the third day, she opened her eyes and asked for tea! This was Afghanistan after all.

The medics laughed for joy. Tim continued to hover over her like a mother hen. He took care of her feeding and almost everything. Alex and his team wanted to interrogate her thoroughly, but Tim would only allow them subject her to short periods at a time so as not to tire her. Nevertheless, they learned a lot from her. Apparently, this group was basically like every other guerrilla war band in Afghanistan with the significant exceptions that they were Christian, and had some charitable plans especially for girls and women. In essence therefore, they were directly opposed to the Taliban. For the fact that they knew how and where to make drops for the Allied soldiers showed they had been around for some time., They were very well-organized. They also seemed to be very computer savvy and had access to computer hardware. They sounded good on the surface but that did not give them any right to go kidnapping unwary people. More significantly, Laura and Greta were still captives. Both of them needed to be rescued.

One day, sitting on the balcony of what had come to be called Laura's room at the base, she said to Tim, "You love her very much, don't you?"

There was no need to ask who she was talking about. She had just finished recounting yet another anecdote that had to do with Laura. "I do" he said, "I do. I just never got a chance to tell her."

"Oh, women tend to sense such things. She loves you too. Greta was always teasing her about it. She loves you but she feels unworthy of you."

"I'm sure you're wrong" Tim said sadly. "She has been in love with Alex since she was a child. She told me so herself. One does not go poaching on a friend's property."

"What she had for Alex was puppy love. What she has for you is the real, mature thing. Did you ever ask Alex what he felt about her?"

"It has never directly come up in conversation between us recently. I know he used to feel like her big brother but that was long before now. A lot has changed, you see."

Lil did not see so she pressed the matter. "You think Alex does not know how you both feel? Give your friends some credit, Padre. Your friends love you very much. Everybody can see that you and Laura fit together. In fact, tell me the truth, are you not caring for me now, even as a service to her?" Tim flushed, and therein Lil had her answer. However, she was too kind to continue to embarrass the poor young man as Greta would have. She merely continued, "I don't mind that at all, but you should look beyond what others might be feeling or thinking. Okay, maybe I will ask Alex on your behalf." Tim flushed even more, spluttered, and was at a complete loss for words. Lil laughed. She stopped teasing him, closed her eyes, and was asleep in moments. Tim left her to go and do some thinking.

The next time Alex and his team interrogated her, she asked if Alex could stay for a minute after the others left. Tim was hovering protectively close-by as usual. "Tell me Alex, how do you feel about my friend, Laura?"

"What do you mean how do I feel about her?" he asked.

"I mean, are you in love with her? Do you see yourself marrying her in the future, and spending the rest of your life with her?"

Alex roared with laughter. "What then will happen to Preach here who is so much in love with her it aches? I wouldn't dream of doing him that disservice. Laura is just like my little sister but Preach here will make her happy as long as they both shall live!"

Lil leaned forward to better see the face of the furiously blushing Tim who had been standing behind Alex ready to throw him out. "Did you hear that Padre? Your friend says his thinking of Laura in that way is to do you a disservice."

"Everybody knows Tim is in love with Laura except Tim himself" Alex said.

"What?" roared Tim in his own turn.

"Do you want us to sample opinions when we go down to the mess for dinner today? I bet you the first ten people we ask will confirm what I just said. I wonder that you have not made it official a long time ago or are you afraid of asking for my blessing as her next of kin? I might look into your financial records and decide you were not a fit husband for my charge, Preach!"

"I think that is enough teasing, Alex" Lil chided, "but you have just proven my point perfectly. You hear that Padre? Your way is clear. Make sure you don't miss the mark the next time you see my friend."

"Preach! O Preach!" Alex was still laughing as he left. Lil's eyelids had already drifted down in sleep.

But even as Lil was busy trying to pass her time matchmaking, not far from her window she had stirred up a big hornet's nest. Omatullah's men, humiliated from their encounter with the shadowy figures up the mountain, watched for any opportunity to recapture or kill her. They had reached a point of virtual frustration. Whoever they were dealing with, they no longer categorized as a potential friend. They were no longer even the friends of their enemies; they were now full-fledged enemies! Omatullah's men's only lead for the moment happened to be Lil. They wished they could have their own turn to question her and milk her for information as they were sure the Americans were doing then. They wished to interrogate her in a more secluded place than where they had Abdul. They knew there must be plans to move her soon. Once she left Farah, all advantage they had would be lost. But Lil never stepped out of the base even for one second. She did not have the energy to do so even if she could.

Unlike the Americans, Omatullah's men did not have the advantage of the notes Laura had written so they also had men keeping watch at Lashkar Gah, Qandahar, and around places in the Nimruz province where the women had first disappeared. They doubled their vigilance and waited patiently. At Farah they got ready to move in case the Americans followed any leads they might have got from the sick woman. They meant to recapture, and if possible, kill her and be able to take the credit for it.

Lil stayed a total of seven days at the Farah base. The day she was flown by helicopter to Qandahar, Bjorn had also arrived at the city by a commercial flight that morning bearing her mother's tearful messages. Their reunion was very moving. He held her and would not let her go. Ever slender, she was now like a pile of bones bound by skin since after her illness. However, she was growing stronger each passing day. She had a lot to tell him, but she kept falling asleep. If awake, she was content to just sit and gaze and gaze at him as if to make up for all the lost days. They spent days just talking.

Bjorn wanted her to come home immediately, but she did not want to go. "Unfinished Business" she said, and Bjorn understood. Her friends had not yet been released, and the time she had promised UNESCO was not yet ended. He understood this was something she just had to do. He did not begrudge her that satisfaction but they both agreed, and UNESCO concurred, that she did not have to go back to Lashkar Gah. She had a lot to do filing the report of the past three months and she was not strong enough to work for long hours at a time. Reassured, Bjorn went back to his business which had been more or less neglected while her whereabouts was unknown. His heart was much lightened. He had also noted a definite change in Lil. She was a different person, but in a better and more profound way. She was still sorting herself out and could not put it into words herself. Whatever she had become, Bjorn loved her even more for it.

Il Dhost was not a fool. It was necessary to move Greta and Laura at once. With the prevailing events and circumstances, and because their training had ended at Shindand, this became necessary. The very next day after Lil was taken to the hospital, they were informed they had to move. In her perception, Laura had mistakenly misled the American forces. She had mentioned they were heading north whereas, in fact, they were headed east. Following her clue, after Lil left for Qandahar, Alex led a contingent of soldiers to Shindand to nose about. Finding nothing, they extended their search to Herat which was north of Shindand but the trail was very cold.

Hot on their heels was the Taliban. They too ran into walls despite their more rigorous and less humane methods. From the shadows, Il Dhost observed the two parties and laughed quietly at all these wasted efforts. Il Dhost, however, was not in the habit of underestimating enemies nor of being careless.

CHAPTER 8

―――――∞―――――

Afghanistan is a land filled with mountains. It is also a land full of holes and tunnels. Some of these holes and tunnels are natural limestone caves. Some others had been created by centuries of mining ores from the rich mountains. Over the centuries, these natural and manmade holes and tunnels have become deliberately enlarged, strengthened, and in other ways refurbished by human hands, advanced tools and equipment, as places of refuge. At first, they were shelters from the elements sought by flock herders. Then they were used by poor families that needed to pay no rent to inhabit such foxholes. At other times, however, including very recent times, they had sheltered individuals, families, and sometimes whole villages from the ravages of war and other forms of persecution. It was said that some of these caves and tunnels had recently been modified and reinforced enough to hold hundreds of army tanks. These were being used by some top Taliban and Al Qaeda officials as bunkers and even headquarters.

No one individual knows all these holes very well. The Russians had tried following their quarries down those tunnels and ended up lost, trapped, or simply killed. They took to throwing Molotov cocktails down such tunnels to suffocate or even entrap the inhabitants with cave-ins. Sometimes they succeeded, wiping out entire villages of men, women, children, and animals. They made no distinction between the young and the old; the rich and the poor; the civilian and the soldier.

Most other times though, the people would have long escaped through other ways out of the tunnels. Sometimes, it is rumored, the escape route emerged in neighboring countries.

Somebody once advised the Russians not to beat out the information about the tunnels from informants as they were trying to do, but to make the informants go there with them. That was the only way of getting authentic information. They soon learned that the information about any tunnel was highly specific to an individual or an area. The informants did not deliberately misdirect them but really did not know. Even modern technology with sonar and heat detectors cannot always map out these tunnels. Many of them had also been technologically modified and enhanced, and really the terrain of Afghanistan is very rugged and uneven. And so even as the mountains of Afghanistan protected her children, so also did the holes and the tunnels of Afghanistan.

Greta and Laura became introduced to the tunnels. On the day they moved, they left after dark. They were driven for some distance and for a long period in a truck. They came down and rode on donkeys. Still in the dark, they came to a house. They went in through one door, came out through another, went into a very dark room, and were met by some people who gave them battery-powered flashlights and led the way. They walked until their ankles were aching. Just as they were on the verge of collapse, they climbed some stairs and were suddenly blinded by daylight. There was a truck apparently waiting for them close-by. They climbed in, closed their eyes and were dead to the world until Soraya shook them awake some indeterminable time later.

Greta and Laura got out from the truck wearily and then immediately came wide awake when they saw they were in front of one of those mini palaces that looked as if they belonged to the ancient Persian Empire. They were shown to a rather opulently furnished room.

It was nothing like where they had been living for the past three months. It looked like a leaf torn from Arabian Nights - Illustrated. Their bedroom was as big as a football field with an inordinate number of throw rugs and silky cushions on the floor. There were decorated pillars, nooks, and arches here and there. The large windows looked onto a very beautiful garden filled with colorful flowers and imaginative fountains. The twin bed they were to share was large enough to accommodate up to six people and still have room to spare. It was tastefully piled with quilts and the famous Afghan rugs.

Three steps down took them to their bathroom which had all the modern facilities. There was an indoor toilet that actually flushed, a small shower stall, and beyond it, a massive bathtub. It was as big as a small swimming pool, resting delicately on decorated claws. They found out eventually that it even had a Jacuzzi. Large continuous mirrors took up almost every other side of the bathroom.

They returned to the bedroom. On the ornate coffee table, tea things were set. There was even a turbaned and bejewelled maid ready to pour it for them. "Are you Morgana?" Greta asked her in English, not expecting any answer.

"I could be, but around here people call me Asmaa" she answered in perfect English with a slight British accent. "You are guests in my parents' home. Would you want to take some tea now or have a bath first? You could also do both at once, if you like. There is a bell here which would always bring someone to serve you. The house has an intercom system, but it takes some getting used to. If you would like to join us for worship, please ring the bell and I will come to take you after you have freshened up. I wanted to order some food for you. However, Soraya thinks that is her exclusive department. She will be here soon, I guess. Is there anything you need before I go?"

They were still too dumbfounded and could not think of anything they would need. After she left, they kept looking around and discovering more and more delights in their surroundings. At last, they settled for tea, and then showers. They would take their time to explore the bath later to see if it really worked. If only Lil were here! Laura took pictures to remind them later that they had not dreamt it all. As it turned out they did not need to use the bell nor the intercom. Soraya came with their meal. "When you are comfortable enough you can also eat in the dining rooms. One of them is a very organized and formal affair. The other is an informal and riotous affair. You will probably experience both before you leave here" she predicted. "I cannot stay with you for long. I want to attend the worship service. Today we have some baptisms."

"We would like to come too" Laura said. Quickly she corrected herself. "I would like to come. Greta, would you like to come too?"

"I would love to come" Greta said.

"Okay" Soraya said, "I will come back to clear away your dinner plates and then we will go together."

For the first time, the discussion was out in the open. "You know" Greta said, "I never gave much thought to Christianity until we were about to come to Afghanistan, and they started all that brouhaha about not proselytizing, during our briefings. Even then, I didn't think much about it until we were kidnapped. Now we have seen Christianity in different settings ranging from sheer poverty to vulgar opulence or whatever you'd like to call where we are now."

"Me too" Laura confirmed. "If you had asked before I volunteered for this if I was a Christian I would have replied 'Of course' but it took one conversation with an army chaplain to get me really thinking more deeply about it. Since coming to Afghanistan, with Christianity being outlawed and everything, I took time to search the internet and read it up. One day I just fell to my knees and asked, 'God what would you do with a poor sinner like me?' My views and perspective on life has not been the same since."

"If you had told me this three months ago it would not have made much sense. I probably would have laughed you to scorn but yeah, what would God do with a poor sinner like me? I am a sinner that came from Martin Luther's own country to this land where Christianity is all but banished?"

They paused to contemplate, each in her own thoughts, in companionable silence but not for long. Soraya came back and briskly hurried them along. They followed her through unbelievably long and ornately decorated corridors. They came to the very large kitchen where Soraya unceremoniously dumped the plates in a sink. They hurried after her as she descended flight after flight of stairs and turned round corners. At last, they came to a very large hall in which there must have been roughly about three hundred people gathered. Opposite the door they had come throughways a large, glassed bay window which let in the daylight. It looked over a grassy knoll through which a slow-moving stream flowed. They saw Asmaa and went to sit beside her. "I see Soraya brought you" she commented unnecessarily but companionably.

The worship service had already begun. It was quite solemn compared to the ones they had attended on camp. They sang two hymns in Dari which sounded familiar. Laura and Greta tried to sing along in English. They also sang some simple repetitive songs to the accompaniment of instruments and the clapping of hands. Instead of a series of sermonettes, there was one sermon which lasted about thirty minutes. Some prayers were said, and then the people who were to be baptized were called to the front of the congregation. There were six men and three women. First, they talked about their journey to faith and their decision to be baptized.

Their stories were all touching. There was the man who had persecuted his brother. "I was going to report him to the mosque police but decided to first explore this forbidden religion and find out what it was all about. I became convinced myself that this was indeed the Way."

Another man talked of how he had a disturbing dream that the path he was following would lead him to destruction. "A voice told me in the dream that I should go and discuss with Harunabullah Musa about the right path to follow. I did, and now here I am."

One woman talked about how she was running away from an oppressive marriage, and someone took her in. "Every other person avoided me because of what my husband could do. Rahima's family took me in. As I stayed with them day after day, I observed that their method of worship was different. I became curious and asked. They told me what made the difference and so I too, have become a follower of Christ."

Another man talked about how he was in prison with a man who was being punished for being a Christian. "All the beating did not change his mind. I wanted to know what gave him so much confidence. He introduced me to Jesus Christ, our Savior. I believed."

They went on and on.

By the time it was over people were weeping openly, Greta and Laura among them. All nine of them said they wanted to be baptized as a confirmation of their faith. They had read in the Bible that this was what Jesus wanted His followers to do.

Escorting them to the bank of the stream just outside the meeting place, the pastor stepped into the water. He dunked them one after the other into the stream, and baptized them in the Name of the Father, and of the Son, and of the Holy Spirit. Thereafter, he reminded everyone that they were not just being baptized into the death and resurrection life of the Lord Jesus Christ but also into His suffering and His church militant here on earth. He said that each of them was to find out how to best serve Him as evidence of their belief.

Like almost everything Afghan, they were to end with a celebratory feast. Picnic baskets appeared and the grassy lawn assumed a very festive look in the dusk. When Greta and Laura turned to look at the meeting place, they saw that it really was a cave which was disguised to look like a house. It even had what looked like apartment buildings on either side of it.

"Do those buildings also open onto this knoll?" Laura asked. "I see only windows and no doors."

"Oh" explained Asmaa. "Their true entrances are actually on another level, one: two streets away, and the other about a mile away."

"True entrances?" asked Greta.

"There are also secret entrances which come up at other places. From our house, we can get into those buildings without coming out on any street. All the buildings around here actually belong to my family."

As darkness gathered, the group began to break up and disperse. Asmaa and Soraya came and handed them battery-powered flashlights. They went back into the meeting hall. Again, turning round corners, and climbing flights of stairs, they eventually returned to their dreamland bedroom. "What a day!" they told each other as they crawled between the quilts and fell asleep. When they came slowly awake the next morning, they were glad to discover they were still in the same bedroom. Soraya brought them tea and they asked if that giant bathtub worked.

"It does" Soraya said, "I know for sure they use it. The water that drains from such tubs is circulated for flushing the toilet and scrubbing the floor. There is also something you can inflate by the sides of the tub to make it smaller if you feel it is too big for you. Would you want to run a bath now?"

"We were just wondering," said Laura.

"Take your time to enjoy this place" Soraya said. "I have it from the grapevine that you are going to have close to seventy students. However, I mustn't run my mouth. Asmaa is coming to talk to you later. I have also been asked to inquire if you would want to go jogging again, Greta? We will need to make arrangements for suitable jogging clothes."

Greta did want to go jogging again so Soraya went to report this. Asmaa came about two hours later, still wearing her turban and lots of jewels. Apparently, this was her normal everyday dressing. She brought jogging gears for Greta which consisted of sweatpants, the matching sweatshirts, and two abbreviated hijabs. This was another kind of female veil. It stopped just at the shoulders. She also brought designer running shoes for the two of them. "In gratitude" she said and then immediately added, "We truly appreciate all you have done for us. Hopefully after here we will definitely return you. We have news that Lil is recovering well. She is now holidaying at Qandahar. Il Dhost will come by with some more news later in the week, and to also convey appreciation. I also need to tell you about what we plan in the next few weeks.

"We hope you will finish the training of the teacher trainers by watching them at work and telling them how to improve. There will be twelve such trainers now. We will be grateful if you can divide work for them so that each has a particular specialty in certain areas. Such a person will be able to improve herself and to train others in this chosen area."

Greta and Laura had not even thought that far but the proposal made a lot of sense.

"There will be sixty-four people to be trained. Some are coming from other locations far from, and near to this place. We have about three hundred and sixty pupils on ground for demonstrations. We appreciate that you might need to go over your plans to create a reasonable schedule. Would you want to take some days off before we start? Your students and their students are already here, except for two who are arriving tonight. They're also in a holiday mood but whatever you say is what we will have to work with."

The proposed schedule sounded reasonable to Greta and Laura. They felt two to three days would be enough to re-organize, especially as Lil was not there to do her part.

"How are we going to get materials?" Greta asked.

"Just write a list of the materials you think you will need. We'll see how we can source for them" Asmaa answered her. In her turn she asked them, "Would you want to eat with us this evening or would you prefer that your food always be brought up here by Soraya?"

"Oh, it will be good to eat with the others" Laura said. "We don't want to feel isolated."

"It will help us get to know our students better too" Greta concurred.

"Okay I will let you know when we're ready" Asmaa said as she left.

They brought out the plan they had used so far and began to work. Soraya came by later to show Greta where she may jog. Laura came along for the walk. They were shown a paved lane lined by trees on either side, with the mountains behind the trees on one side and a stone wall on the other side. "It is well-protected. The guards have been told to expect you from time to time" Soraya said. "It is important though that you always dress in what Asmaa gave you so nobody shoots you by mistake. Whatever you do, do not ever jog beyond the gate."

The last was a tall order. Greta came back to tell Laura. "I jogged for about two miles and never even caught a glimpse of any gate of any kind."

Dinner that evening was in the informal dining room. It was just as riotous as Soraya had promised it would be. The size of the room was immense in dimensions with really high, vaulted ceilings. It could have easily accommodated ten times the number of people present if the tables were arranged end to end and across. The tables, however, were arranged in a U form near the center of the room. Asmaa sat at the connection of the two limbs. She beckoned Greta and Laura to come and sit by her. There were up to a hundred people present, both male and female. Everyone seemed to be talking at the same time. How they were able to hear, understand, and respond to one another was a mystery. When the food was all set on the table, Asmaa rang a bell. All talk ceased at once. She asked someone to say the grace. Bowls were then passed around, and people served themselves.

Laura and Greta were curious about Asmaa. She very easily talked about herself. It turned out that she really was descended from the most recent Afghan royalty because there were so many. Her parents had gone to live at Dubai just before the troubles with Russia and they hardly ever visited home. She and her brothers had been born in that very house. From Dubai they had been sent to Britain for higher education. One brother now lived in India, and the other in Britain. Both were doctors. "I met my husband at Pakistan. We both decided to come back here to live. He is an accountant turned politician, so he resides in Kabul most of the time. We both believe that some people must come back to try to rebuild this country from within. Believe me, it's not an easy task at all. Sometimes those who wish you the greatest ill are those you are bending over backwards trying to help."

Asmaa had two daughters and one son. Her children were currently in their teens. Three of them were living with her in-laws at Pakistan while going to school. "The girls are to leave for Britain early next year for further studies. My brother will be their legal guardian there. My son will be going to join them next year or so."

Greta exclaimed, "I had assumed you were in your late twenties, or early thirties at the most."

"Thank you" Asmaa said. "I accept that as a compliment. I actually turned forty-two a few days ago" she said.

"Say that again" Laura requested in amazement.

Asmaa laughed and told them, "I am flattered."

She said she was glad to be involved with Il Dhost and to contribute her own bit. She did not want to let them know the extent of her involvement because of the sensitive position of her husband in the nascent government. "You will also be debriefed by your government after your return. The less you know, the better for all of us, including yourselves." Her only regret was that she was not sure if her children were being raised with true patriotism. She was confident she was raising enough people to go on with her work, should anything happen to her.

She told them that most of the people at the table at that moment were their students. A few of the faces, they already recognized from previous encounters. To their surprise, she told them that some of the men would be joining the classes but most of the men present were guards. As long as the students were on the property, they helped out with housework and preparing their own meals. Her house staff served for when she hosted formal or state dinners. Laura and Greta would stay hidden on such occasions, but they were welcome to have a run of the house otherwise. Someone would tell them where it was unsafe to go, and when.

She then asked how far they had gone with their preparations and was happy to hear they had made good progress and would likely finish by the next day. They told her how they were hoping to divide the supervision between the two of them and then come together for the final criticisms.

Even after the food was eaten and the dishes put away people lingered, enjoying one another's company. Finally, Asmaa rang the bell again, and asked someone to pray. The person prayed a prayer of thanksgiving. She asked for God's blessing on their endeavors, His protection for the persecuted, wisdom for themselves and their leaders. It was not a very long prayer, but it seemed to cover all the bases. Asmaa asked people to use that outline and continue to pray in their closets. She then bid them all a goodnight.

The pattern was set for the four weeks they stayed there. They chose to always have their meals with the group. In time they learned to even talk and make as much noise as all the others. To them it was a novel way of unwinding at the end of the day. The only time they felt uncomfortable was sometime in their second week when Asmaa asked Laura if she would offer the prayers before they started eating. Laura did so but Greta told her afterwards, "If she ever picks me, I will stop joining the informal dining sessions."

But towards the end of their four-week stay, Asmaa asked Greta to pray, and she did. Laura told her afterwards, "You really did a good job of it. I'm sure God had been waiting to hear your voice!"

To her surprise, the unflappable Greta burst into tears.

CHAPTER 9

―∞―

Towards the end of their first week, Asmaa told them that Il Dhost was around and would like to have dinner with them. For this occasion, dinner would be served in the formal dining room. They had never been in the formal dining room and were quite curious about it. They were duly impressed by its stateliness. The heavy polished oak tables arranged in an E fashion. The formidable-looking high back chairs had velvet seats. There were also silver chandeliers and gold-handled cutlery. They could understand state dignitaries being hosted to dinners here.

Il Dhost sat at the far end of the crossed bit of the table while Asmaa sat at the opposite end with just enough space for Greta and Laura to sit at that end of the table with her. Just as at their last meeting, even though they were sure Il Dhost understood them very well, everything he had to say to them was said in a low tone to Asmaa for onward transmission to the ladies. As before also, he was dressed in the traditional garb common to Afghan men consisting of a dark jacket over a greyish white caftan long shirt and pants. Again, only the flashing eyes were visible through the swaths of kaffiyeh round his head and face but now they could see that it was a greyish green in color. They did not even see his nose and beard and wondered how he could breathe through all the wraps.

"Il Dhost wishes to thank you very much for being friends of the organization and wants you to know that we are forever obliged to you. Il Dhost hopes you know that this organization will always serve you in whatever way it is within its power to do so."

Il Dhost murmured something. Asmaa said to them, "Il Dhost appreciates that there are some promises we cannot keep as humans. However, we pray the eternal hand of God to always guide and keep you."

More murmurs. "Now Il Dhost wants you to know that your friend is doing very well and has brought some pictures to reassure you to that effect. At this point Asmaa handed over some pictures she had obviously been looking at before they came in.

Laura and Greta took the pictures and looked at them together. In the first set of pictures, they saw a very gaunt Lil standing beside a UN helicopter. There were a few marines in the background. Laura felt sure she recognized Tim's profile in one of them. In the next set of pictures, they recognized Qandahar International airport and a much recovered, but still very thin Lil standing with Bjorn who was trundling a small travelling suitcase. They saw Lil hugging Bjorn, and then Lil waving to Bjorn. It was like a picture story series.

"Il Dhost apologises that close-up pictures were not taken but that the aim was to also get the background to prove the pictures were not fake. Il Dhost wants you to know your friend is well-recovered and is staying at Qandahar for now at least. She has given much information to the Allied forces. There is no doubt Lieutenant Pearson will soon be hot on your trails. However, you will be reunited with your friend long before he reaches you here."

"Lieutenant Pearson? Il Dhost knows Lieutenant Pearson?" Laura asked.

A light of amusement came into the eyes of Il Dhost. Asmaa transmitted. "Il Dhost knows a lot of people and has had the pleasure of close dealings with Lieutenant Pearson though he might not remember it. There will probably be further dealings in the future. Il Dhost wishes for you to carry personal greetings to Lieutenant Pearson when you return."

There was not really much to say. Il Dhost assured them again that they will be reunited with their friend long before Christmas. "In fact, sooner than that if we can help it but we hope you shall also always consider us your friends too wherever you may be, and whatever happens."

Il Dhost did not stay to eat with them. They were served in the formal dining room anyway which gave them some quiet to discuss what they had seen and heard with each other.

Assuming that classes would be held in the castle, they were surprised to be taken to some secret chambers which might not exactly have been in the castle. In fact, as Soraya later informed them, the classes held about a mile away from the façade people saw at the castle. On the first day of classes, Soraya came to collect them from their bedroom. Just like the day she took them to the worship, they went downstairs, corridors, and corners. Finally, they burst into what could have been another disguised cave, and there were the students already waiting. In case they needed to ever go back on their own, Soraya showed them how to recognize marks on the wall which would direct them to their bedroom. However, she told them to try as much as possible not to wander off on their own or they could get lost, and starve to death.

That first day of classes, Laura and Greta divided the sixty-eight students among ten student teachers. They chose to partner with the two teachers they had started with from Zaranj as supervisors. They briefed these two on what to observe and record. For the rest, they put them into two sets for the training, one on practical teaching, and the second on planning and administration. From their observed strengths and weaknesses, likes and dislikes, it would then be determined where each might put an emphasis, and possibly take on as a specialty.

It was a simple plan. The students were very enthusiastic. At the end of every day the supervisors compared notes and generally agreed on most things. By the end of the first week, Greta and Laura exchanged those who were understudying them to determine where their own specialties should be too. The third week was demonstration teaching with the three hundred and sixty pupils. By the fourth week they were putting finishing touches. They let the trainers pick and demonstrate their perceived specialties.

The whole process had been so rewarding, especially because of the eagerness of the student teachers and the pupils. Greta and Laura drew up their recommendations and it exactly matched what their understudies also did. Awesome!

They continued to attend the "Cave Meetings" as they came to call them. Unlike when they were with the Kuchis or at Zaranj when they could time the regularity of the week by the signs of worship, the meetings here were very irregular. Sometimes they happened two days after the last one, sometimes it would be five days. At one time, they had counted up to ten days before Soraya came to ask if they would like to come for a meeting. Soraya explained that other smaller worship meetings took place but that even those had to be staggered and irregular to maintain secrecy. Many of the Christians held reasonably high positions in the society here. They had to show a face to the world which must not be endangered unnecessarily. "Maybe one day I will take you to a prayer meeting which we attend in the kitchen of a police chief" Soraya promised them. They never got that opportunity before they left. However, they began to understand the dangers the Afghans had to go through in order to practice their chosen faith in a hostile land, and how precious this faith became to them because of this.

One day, they were told not to leave their room by the door they usually went by. Soraya came to conduct them through the French windows of their room. They went through the beautiful garden they enjoyed looking at, through another courtyard, into a garden shed, and down some stairs. They now came to familiar corners and corridors and went on until they came to the school and to their waiting students. For the next few days too, Greta was not allowed to go jogging. They did not eat dinner in the informal dining room but in another hall off the main school building with their usual dinner companions except for Asmaa. However, they still had a Cave Meeting on one of those days.

Soraya explained that Asmaa's husband, Khalid, had come from Kabul with some house guests for those few days. He was aware of what she was doing and her involvement with Il Dhost but did not want to be fully apprised of the details in case he ever had to be interrogated. Greta and Laura never got to meet him throughout the entire duration of their stay.

On their last day of classes, after they had taken feedback from their students and consulted with their co-supervisors, their students informed them they had planned a "Thank You Feast" for them. They were not unduly surprised at the spread of food, the magnificence and the usual abandon which greeted them. It was the normal Afghan way. There was dancing and merriment, singing and skits by the children. They presented Greta and Laura with three Afghan rugs. They said one was to be for Lil, even though she was not physically there. They prayed over them. Having enough command of the language and Afghan expressions now, Laura and Greta also prayed for their students and "hosts". Asmaa begged them not to take any pictures for security purposes. However, Soraya took lots of pictures instead. Soraya now had two people - a young man and a young lady, that she was training. They were doing a good job of understudying her too. As before, Greta and Laura fretted that they had nothing to give in return, but the people assured them that they had given plenty already by just cheerfully sharing themselves.

The party broke up late but the people did not mind. There was no serious work the next day. Most of them were to return to their stations the day after. The next morning, Asmaa came to them just as they were finishing breakfast in their rooms. "I understand you were asking if it is possible to use these bathtubs" she asked.

When Greta and Laura confirmed this was so she said, "You may want to do so today or tomorrow because you are to go back to Qandahar in three days' time."

Three days' time! Their ordeal, if such it had been, would end in mere three days! They had been expecting it but now that the chips were down, they did not know whether to be happy or to be sad. Some parts of their captivity had actually been wonderful compared to their entire stay in Afghanistan. These weeks in captivity had even been some of their high times in Afghanistan. "Maybe I should have left it till the last moment to tell you" Asmaa said "but if it were me, I would want to prepare ahead and do last minute things."

They could appreciate that, but by the time Asmaa left, Greta felt too restless. She dressed up and went jogging although the temperature was becoming unbearably cold even during the days. Laura usually liked to sit for hours gazing at the garden and writing in her journal. That day she decided to take Asmaa up on her offer. She rang the bell for the first time since they came. She asked the maid who appeared how to prepare a bath. The maid offered to run the bath for her. Opening a panel which they had not known existed, she proceeded to measure out mysterious salts, perfumes, oils, and other things Laura did not know. She was informed it would take about half an hour to run the bath. If she wanted to stay in it for long, she should begin by using the shower stall first. There was also an automatic massager afterwards if she so chose. The maid offered to stay to bath her. However, Laura was not used to such things. She firmly refused the offer, but she indulged herself in every other thing that day! By the time Greta returned, Laura was all mellow and too languid to even lift a finger. Greta swore that the next day would be her turn. She took everything they had to offer her. "I might never get such a generous offer again" she reasoned.

Soraya came to say goodbye the following night. There were tears, gratitude, and promises. "You will never know how much you have touched my life" she told them.

"But you touched our lives even more" Laura told her. This was really true and not just a reciprocation of sentiments. Greta gave her the ring she always wore on her little finger. "This is so you will always remember us."

Laura gave her a small New Testament Bible in Dari which Tim had given her a long time ago. She had always carried it in her purse, never knowing what to do with it but cherishing it anyway because it was a gift from Tim. Soraya was overcome with tears.

On her own part, Soraya gave them prints of some of those pictures which she had taken while they were on the trail, and during the Thank You Feast. She made sure they were the ones which did not show the faces of the others clearly. They were all very happy pictures.

The next day, they left the house before it was even dawn. Asmaa asked them to dress in their Burqas. She gave them flasks of tea for the road, and a picnic basket of food and fruits. In addition to their overnight bags which were now full to busting, there were two duffel bags that Asmaa told them contained things that had been taken from the UN truck in the first instance including, she told them, the satellite radios and Lil's stuff.

"Your trip has all been planned" she told them. "The hope is to get you to Qandahar by tonight. We will check you into the Sheraton. There is no knowing what may happen on the way. However, you should know that your satellite radios are all charged and ready to use. Please do not turn them on or use them unless you really have to. Inform your driver if you have to use them while you are in the truck. You might endanger our whole network if you don't follow these instructions precisely. We pray that you don't do that. Once you switch them on, you can be tracked by them as I am sure you are well- aware. The hope is that those tracking you would be friendly elements but remember that unfriendly elements could also be tracking you and might get to you first.

"We will not ask you never to talk about us. In fact, your talking about us may even help our cause but please remember that the information you have, in the wrong hands, may endanger many lives."

She hugged them very tightly and kissed them on both cheeks, French fashion. She handed them into the back of the trucks and thrust a picnic basket at them before she slammed the door. What she had failed to tell them was that the tea in the flasks was spiked with an opium compound. Because the weather was quite cold, even as day broke, they had both finished the content of their flasks and were fast asleep. They did not wake up even though the road was very rough and the ride quite bumpy. They could never describe their journey or the direction they took. They came across a few roadblocks but not as many as they would have if they had gone through the major route, Highway 1. At each roadblock, the driver always claimed they were his wives, and they were on their way to the next town. Seeing as how they were decently and modestly dressed in Burqas nobody had any cause to doubt him or to delay him for longer than necessary.

By the time Greta and Laura woke up, they were in Tarin Kowt. The driver informed them they would rest at an inn there because he planned to enter Qandahar after dark. They ate from the picnic baskets. The driver went to refill their flasks from a teashop. This time the flasks had tea which was not spiked. About an hour later, they took off again. They drove into Qandahar at about seven in the evening. Their driver told the bellboy about their reservation and asked for their luggage to be taken up to their room. The driver shook their hands and bade them goodbye out in the hotel parking lot. He had reason for not wanting to be caught by the security cameras in the hotel lobby.

"Remember to wait until morning before you turn on the satellite phones to call UNESCO" he told them as he left.

Their room in The Sheraton was much less opulent than where they had slept for the past few weeks, but much more comfortable than what they had been used to before then. They were surrounded by all the comfort that modern technology could offer them, yet they found sleep elusive. At first, they undressed, took showers, and wore back their normal clothes. They turned on the television set in their room, realizing that throughout their period of captivity they had not watched any television but had not really missed it. They flipped through channels but could not concentrate on anything. Local news did not interest them; neither did international news, nor a movie, a soap opera, sports, or anything else! They tried to talk, and found themselves wandering meaninglessly from one topic to another until finally Greta asked, "Why would they not want us to call UNESCO immediately? Why do we have to delay until morning?"

Laura had no answers. Greta really was not expecting any. For security reasons, they felt they were far better off in a UN facility than where they were at the present. If it was to protect Il Dhost's outfit, surely an hour or two would be enough for their driver to have made a getaway. Greta paced up and down trying in vain to make sense of the situation. Laura was sleepless too but was more serene, as usual. There are some people who go through life questioning very little. Not much adventure might come their way but at least they tended to live longer. Laura was such a person. She asked Greta now, "Why don't we just pray about it?"

Even though neither of them was quite experienced in this business of praying out loud they had managed it well enough when occasion demanded it of them.

"Lord God please grant us peace. Let us know the right thing to do" Laura prayed out loud.

"And while you are about it Lord, please give us some rest tonight as well" Greta added.

Greta's prayer was answered almost immediately. Neither of them knew when they slept off. The television was still murmuring in the background when they opened their eyes simultaneously and saw that it was bright daylight. In fact, it was eight o' clock in the morning according to the hotel table clock. This was confirmed by the television anchor person about to start the news hour.

"Okay, here goes," Laura said. "It's time to turn on the satellite phones, call UNESCO, and go back to work."

She proceeded to turn on the phone when Greta suddenly said "You know what? Turn off the phone. I'll call the front desk for a cab, and we're getting out of here. I've got ants in my pants. I just can't stay put."

Laura turned off the phone while Greta requested a cab from the front desk through the hotel intercom. They did not dress in their Burqas but wore simple veils over their acceptably modest clothes as Ayesha had taught them. They shouldered their overnight bags, toted one duffel bag each, and found out that they were not heavy at all. They got to the lobby just as their cab was arriving at the front doors of the Sheraton. Assuming that they had no outstanding debts, they did not even bother to check out at the front desk. They both got into the back of the sedan cab and asked the driver to just go.

"To where?" the driver asked in heavily accented English.

"The United States Army base" Laura answered mechanically. Greta looked at her searchingly but said nothing. She had no objections to that particular destination. It was as good as any for that time.

The driver eased into the busy morning traffic. At nine o'clock on the dot they arrived at the gate of the base and began to go through the routine security surveillance procedures. They still had their UNESCO IDs and security check was going smoothly. Laura went first. Just as Greta was being processed, there was the sound of a sudden blast which made them, and the guards at the security post to duck down in alarm.

"Looks like another bomb blast" said the young US marine checking Greta in.

"Yes" agreed his colleague, "and it seems to be coming from The Sheraton. Poor bastards!"

Greta and Laura could not get through that gate fast enough. They asked to see the commanding officer immediately. "We need to be debriefed" Laura said, "and it is very urgent!"

PART 3

CHAPTER 1

∞

Their mission completed, the American officers did a little shopping at Herat. Totally off-guard, they wandered leisurely on to the road to Shindand hoping to get back to their base at Farah later that night. That, in itself, was a grave mistake. While in Afghanistan, they had been warned to never be off their guards. So far, the men who were tailing them were happy. The Americans were acting quite as expected. In a while they would be outside the city limits. The topography between Herat and Shindand was so bare and flat with absolutely no hiding places. It was a good place to lay an ambush for a totally unprepared foe. Omatullah's men had been planning this for weeks and were unexpectedly rewarded in this outing. These particular Americans had some information they wanted. Lulled as they were by a false sense of security, they would definitely make very easy pickings. This was the kind of laxity they had hoped for.

They approached the city limits, the hunter, and the hunted. Suddenly, there was a loud explosion in an open field almost in front of the Americans. The leader of the enemy squad swore. Whoever had set off the explosive had destroyed all their plans with just a single stroke. Immediately the Americans became alert. They jumped out of their jeeps. In minutes they had scattered, become almost invisible, and were in combat mode. If this had happened in the open country where the ambush had been laid, they would have had only their jeep as a very flimsy covering in the circumstances. As it was now, not only did they have adequate covers, but they would also become more alert as they left the city. The enemy squad leader swore again. Calling his men off, they set about trying to find out what had exploded, why, by whom, and to what effect.

The Americans also did their own investigations and both parties arrived at the same conclusion. What had exploded were harmless fireworks near a marketplace. They saw the remnants of it, but bystanders claimed not to see who was responsible. The rest of their questions were therefore moot. The Americans reorganized. They chided themselves for their lapse in vigilance. They took the incident as a warning and decided to re-plan their route and general itinerary. They did not leave Herat until the next day. When they left, they went by Anar Darreh instead of by Shindand.

Alex, leading the American squad, absorbed most of the blame. They had successfully completed their official mission. Their heading to Shindand was to nose about a bit, still trying to get any leads in the mystery of the continued disappearance of Greta and Laura. It was more of a personal mission. He had no call to lead his men into danger. From Anar Darreh he sent the other men straight back to the base and decided to hike on to Shindand with only Randy for a look around. He was not aware of the people tailing him, mistakenly confident in the fact that his going to Herat was primarily because he was following a lead on the still-missing UN workers. The explosion and his subsequent change of plans threw them, through no effort on his part. They had to regroup and therefore did not follow him to Anar Darreh or to Shindand.

More alert now, Alex detected the sound of people coming on the trail before they were upon them. Whoever they were, they were not being stealthy about it so maybe it was just chance. However, due to their military training, Alex and Randy were very suspicious of coincidences. They hid on opposite sides of the trail and cocked their weapons. Having worked together for long, both of them had perfected a method of wordless, soundless communication with each other. They did not have long to wait. Soon enough, about four men came into sight leading their donkeys. Donkeys are a common means of transportation in this area with its rocky, uneven terrain. There was nothing abnormal about this. What was abnormal was that the men leading the donkeys, even though dressed in traditional Pashtun attires were speaking very good English. And then there was the content of their conversation.

"The men were headed this way" said one of the men with the donkeys. "They must be somewhere nearby."

"Il Dhost said to let them know there is important news" another rejoined.

"What if we don't see them? How do we then deliver the news about the missing UNESCO women?" asked yet another.

They were obviously keeping up conversation in a loud voices hoping to be overheard by the Americans.

"We can only do the best we can. If we don't see them, we will go back and report. What else can be done?"

"The instruction is that if we don't find them then maybe they will find us. Under no circumstances are we to sneak up on them. They are supposed to be well-oiled killing machines."

Yes, Alex did not believe in coincidences. These men wanted a meeting with them. They said all the red flag words like Il Dhost, missing UNESCO women, and so on. He allowed them to go a bit beyond their hiding place while motioning for Randy to stay hidden. Rising, he dropped to a path below where the men were sure to pass. With his gun in the crook of his arm he confronted the men. They stopped as soon as they saw him. "Okay, where is this Il Dhost, and what news do you have of Laura and Greta?" Alex demanded.

"Aha" said the man in the lead. "We were told you would probably find us. Lieutenant Pearson, I believe. I am Raziq."

"Let's cut to the chase! What news do you have of the women? Where is Il Dhost?"

"Il Dhost is just as eager to meet with you. If you would just come this way, please..."

They turned and went back the way they had been coming. Alex brought up the rear, keeping a careful look out for any sudden movements. He signalled for Randy to follow but to stay hidden. They rounded a few bends and came to some rocks which seemed to have been deliberately arranged to hide a hollow. Some other rocks were scattered about as convenient sitting spots. The lead man halted and simply said, "We're here."

Alex turned around and carefully surveyed "Here". Sitting about three meters opposite the entrance they had come by was a figure, dressed in the true Afghan fashion with a turban round the head exposing only twinkling greenish grey eyes. But the figure was not alone. He could see telltale signs of other figures hidden behind the rocks and the sparse bushes. Counting the ones he came with, there must have been at least twelve of them. The man who had called himself Raziq now said, "Il Dhost bids you welcome, and says won't you tell your friend to please show himself? We do not underestimate you but if we wished you harm you would both have died before now."

There was sense in that. In any case, Alex and Randy were hopelessly outnumbered in the present situation. It was infinitely better to throw themselves at these people's mercy and assume this was a friendly meeting. He signalled for Randy to come out. At the same time, he asked, "What does your friend want of me?"

The be-turbaned figure murmured something and Raziq transmitted. "Il Dhost wants you to know that we are very grateful for what these women have done for us. Il Dhost spoke with them about three weeks ago, and they were in good spirits. Even as we are talking now, they are on their way to Qandahar. Before you reach Farah, they will be at Qandahar."

"If you appreciate them so much, why kidnap them in such a tawdry manner and keep them prisoners for all these months?"

Il Dhost did not wait for interpretation but murmured something which Raziq then transmitted. "Sometimes, prevailing circumstances force us to do things in ways we otherwise would not have chosen. When you reunite with the ladies, they will answer most of your questions, and clear up most of what you would want to know. For now, though, Il Dhost wants you to know that you stirred up a hornet's nest as you would say in your own country. Enlisting the help of Omatullah put his men hot on your path. They hoped to find the missing women before you did. We managed to save the family of Abdul the teashop owner at Farah where the other sick woman was dropped. We saved you from an ambush yesterday by setting off an explosion to alert you. Hopefully, when the women surface, Omatullah's men will stop dogging your steps, hoping to discover where they are."

So this was how it was to be, thought Alex. They talked and Il Dhost understood them but only spoke to them through Raziq. It was all good by him provided he got some answers eventually. "Why are you telling me all this now? Why should I believe a word you say?" he asked.

"You know in your heart that I am telling you the truth" Il Dhost answered through Raziq. "This will be confirmed when you hear the good news of the women's return to Qandahar. You can, of course, check it out but we are telling you this now because what you started, only you can finish. Once you have information that the women are safe and sound, send to Omatullah to thank him for his help in safely getting the women home."

"But that would be a lie!"

"And yet it's not too far from the truth. If he had been more efficient and did not have us to contend with to undercut his schemes, they might even now be in his camp with no prospects of leaving there alive. No, we saw to their abduction and their safe return. However, we want you, Lieutenant Pearson, to be the one thanking Omatullah for their safe return. There is also the added incentive that you get a close look at his set up again. You can gauge his strength when you go to thank him in his den."

"You must believe I have nothing better to do. I do not want to give an impression to Omatullah that we are now friends."

"You are right in some aspects. Nevertheless, is it not better to know what moves the tree than to keep guessing that it must be the wind? However, we do have an ulterior motive. Letting him know personally that the ladies are back will take the heat off of us for protecting the ladies. We hope it will pacify him enough to stop hunting us."

Alex began to understand. This Il Dhost was a very clever schemer. It was very important for Omatullah to assume that it was the Americans who had the ladies all along, or that had rescued them. This way, he would not go seeking this rival group. Wryly he asked, "And should I also give him your compliments when we meet?"

"Again, as you say in your country, 'this meeting never happened!'"

"Okay" Alex agreed. He was amused despite himself. "This meeting never happened."

"Il Dhost is very happy we all understand ourselves. Now that we have all become friends, perhaps we could take some tea, and then we shall show you the quickest way of getting to Farah."

And so, Alex and Randy had tea with the men who chose to show themselves. There were probably others on sentry duty. After tea, true to their word, they showed them how to get to Farah in four hours or less depending on how fast they could hike. It involved scaling a few mountain apices, going through a tunnel, and fording a stream. They would never have discovered that route themselves. As they parted, Alex asked, "So will we ever meet again?"

"We have met before", Il Dhost informed him, "and we are always watching out for you. If you ever need to meet us and we're not there, just leave a message with Laura and Greta. Tell them to mention it to their landlady."

"So, their landlady was involved in all this!"

"Not directly, but women talk. We pick up what we need to."

Simple, very admirably simple! They parted. Il Dhost and his men dissolved into the mountainside like wraiths. Alex and Randy went back to their base, and to the news that the women were even then at the Qandahar army base. They also went back to the news of the explosion at The Sheraton barely minutes after the ladies left there.

CHAPTER 2

∞

Alex made a full report to his commander including his misjudgement at Herat, and his eventual meeting with Il Dhost. They both agreed there was something to be said for Alex going to "Thank" Omatullah. It was going to be strategic on so many counts. Major Grafton also agreed for Alex and Tim to go to Qandahar to be part of the team debriefing the three women. By now Lil had come to join them at the army base. Although nobody had yet found any direct link between them and the bombing at Sheraton, the three women were still much shaken from the event. They would not turn on their satellite phones even experimentally but rather turned them in to UNESCO for overhauling and reformatting. They cogitated upon the fact that for over two years they had been in Afghanistan, including the four months of their captivity, they had never felt this insecure.

Lil was glad to see the other two and catch them up on what she had been doing as well as catch up on their last post in captivity. They talked of what to do with their remaining few months in Afghanistan because UNESCO expected some sort of response from them. After their gruelling experience, they were told, they could be released from their contract if they so desired. Their plans had been to start training some natives to take over after they left, or to start making extensive notes for the next UNESCO team which would replace them. They were supposed to be discussing these issues. However, they could not keep their thoughts on track. They kept going over the last instructions their captors had given them, trying to read between the lines. They still made no sense of it at all.

Two days later, before their usual morning meeting with those debriefing them, the young sergeant looking after them announced, "You have some visitors from Farah." Laura jumped up almost involuntarily and stood there, trembling. Greta and Lil gazed at her teasingly. Barely a minute after the announcement Tim and Alex entered the room. Without planning it or even meaning to, Laura found herself in Tim's arms. He hugged her tightly and kept saying, "My darling, O my darling. I have missed you so much. I have missed you. I love you, Laura. Do you know how much I love you?"

They wept in each other's arms. Laura was no less voluble in returning those endearments. For some time, they were oblivious of their spectators who were weeping right along with them. Finally, Alex cut in. "Don't I get even a hug?" he asked.

Tim finally loosened his hold. Laura gave Alex a hug and a perfunctory kiss on the cheek. "Hi Alex" she said.

Alex turned to Lil, "Did you see that? Did you all see that? Should I not protest about this injustice?"

Lil laughed. "Cut it out Alex. You know how this works." She got up to hug Tim herself. "Hello Padre! I hope you remember me. Allow me to introduce Greta, the third member of this Terrific Trio!"

Greta and Tim shook hands. "You know" Greta told him, "She just would not admit what was so clearly written all over her. I am glad to finally meet you in person Mr. Chaplain?"

So much for private declarations of love as each had planned! They had a lot to say to each other. They did so for those few days they were together at Qandahar. For the moment however, they contented themselves with gazing into each other's eyes while Alex outlined his plans for debriefing them.

Alex spent a lot of time questioning the ladies together about what they had gone through. They were relieved to be talking about it as well. For the first time each of them began to appreciate the others' perspectives in the whole matter. This kind of debriefing had a lot of psychological benefits. They admitted that even though they did not feel totally free and in charge, they had felt neither oppressed nor intimidated in any way. They talked about the services they rendered, and the friends they had made. When Alex talked about his meeting with Il Dhost, and the requested meeting with Omatullah, some of the last instructions they received began to make sense. "And that bomb blast was really meant for us" Greta said, "but I think the spirit of God rescued us."

Coming from Greta, this was really a testimony of God's goodness. They went into that aspect of their captivity too. A lot of the information they had, they dared not make public. Alex would not even put them in army records which might someday be made public. "There are Christians in Afghanistan" Laura summarized for them all, "but the more impressive thing was that we came from our countries with Freedom of religion, to meet Christ in Afghanistan with all its restrictions on Christianity!"

That was a major factor. All three acknowledged the changes which had occurred in their lives as a result of this adventure they had. It was Tim's high point to "Debrief" them on this aspect or as Alex put it "To disciple or to catechize them". However, three of them deeply appreciated this input as well. It concretized what they had come to believe. He also answered many questions which they had. Greta wanted to be baptized in Afghanistan in the way they had witnessed. Tim said he would look into that plausibility but felt it might not be advisable. Lil wanted to be baptized too but wanted to do so with Bjorn. When they talked on Skype later that day, Bjorn was actually, and unaccountably, excited about the idea.

They all agreed that Il Dhost's suggestion of Alex going to "thank" Omatullah might really defuse the situation, provided all of them in the know kept quiet about what they really knew. They talked about Ayesha being a link. "I always felt there was something clandestine about those meetings she held in her house" Lil said.

Agreeing to this however, was taking their return to Lashkar Gah for granted. Whereas they had felt uncertain about it before, this prospect now gave them a good reason to return. "We could propose to UNESCO that selected women be sent to us for training at the house. That way, we still go on with the work without taking any more field trips" Laura suggested.

It made a lot of sense to the others. They agreed to work from this angle. UNESCO accepted their proposal but instead of Afghan women, they were sent other expatriates who were to understudy what they had achieved in their entire stay in Afghanistan, including the practicability of the methods they claimed to have used during their period of captivity.

Alex and his team left for Omatullah's lair after two days. Army chaplains had no call to be at such meetings, so Tim stayed with the ladies for two more days. He escorted them back to Lashkar Gah then went onwards to Farah. He left, a happily engaged man with a very promising future.

Ayesha was beside herself with joy. She would have called a big Afghan party there and then except for reasonable restrictions. Shamir was no less excited. However, he was a man after all and so his rejoicing was more subdued. He flushed and sputtered when Greta asked him how it felt to have four wives again. Their boys danced around the ladies with excitement. Fortunately, they had remembered to bring along lots of candies and cookies from Qandahar. They spoiled those boys shamelessly.

Three of them had decided not to tell Ayesha everything. As it happened, she was the one who brought up the topic about a week after they returned. "So, you have been with Il Dhost" she began. It was not so much a question as an opening statement. "It is a camp which we support from the sides because it helps displaced girls and women. The Taliban is not happy with them. We try not to talk about it at all so we don't implicate ourselves."

With that, she let them know she did not want to know the details of their abduction. She would be glad if the topic remained closed. It was probably her own way of saying that anything mentioned in relation to Il Dhost was to be considered a message to be passed on. This was indeed cloak and dagger stuff. Until they left that household, they could never say for sure if Ayesha was one of the secret Christians of Afghanistan or not.

When the Americans visited Neem Omatullah, he fully expected reprisals, or at least inquiries, about the Sheraton bombing. Omatullah's men again put up their show of power. However, the Americans were alert enough to notice that some of those blatantly toting guns seemed to pay special attention to what the Americans said, and even how they said it. The Americans noticed by the body language of their hosts, and the direction they kept glancing that they probably had more men, more weapons or some other significant equipment hidden nearby.

Omatullah's men were therefore totally thrown off balance when after the customary drinking of tea, the Americans began with, "We came to thank you. The women we enlisted your help with finding are safely back to their base. They were well-treated, and we are sure your hand was in their adventure all the way. This is the kind of cooperation we are asking for. We are very grateful for their safe return."

They had said a lot; and they had said nothing at all. The content of their speech was very open to free interpretation.

"We are glad they are safely back" Omatullah replied. "We assure you that we had nothing to do with their kidnapping. Islam is about peace. We are very glad when everyone is at peace."

They exchanged other meaningless pleasantries. The bombing at the Qandahar Sheraton was not mentioned at all. After about a total of more than two hours, the Americans got up and left. Later on, they discussed their impressions about the visit. There was someone or something bigger than Omatullah in that compound. Maybe it was there on their first visit but they had not taken notice because they were too preoccupied with getting the women back. Maybe it was a new development but there was definitely something there. They resolved that Omatullah's compound, habits, and movements deserved a closer surveillance.

On their own side, after the Americans left, Omatullah and his men discussed the absurdity of the visit. "They either came to spy on us, or the women reported missing was just a pretense to draw us out. When did we ever aid in the investigation? What did we really find? In all probability, the women never left the army base at Qandahar except for the one who was planted at the inn at Farah. That is why it was easy to rescue the Innkeeper and his family from our hands without leaving any traces. There is no rival group. They either wanted to pitch us against one another or to get some information out of us."

They asked one another how much information the Americans might have gathered from that visit. After due rumination, they reassured themselves the Americans had not learned much after all. They decided to be more vigilant however. They would capture the women for real if they ever made any other forays into their territory again.

CHAPTER 3

With the women now found, and safely within the confines of Lashkar Gah, life went back to normal or what passed as normal for Alex in Afghanistan. One Monday, Major Grafton sent for him. "There is a rumor of insurgents around Shahsak. ISAF is asking us to check it out with them. I want you to do a reconnaissance while Dreyfus takes a main body out with ISAF. You can pick three people to go with you."

In other words, it was business as usual.

Alex picked his men. Theirs was to be the unofficial part of the venture. They dropped off their vehicle at the ISAF headquarters at Shahsak and hiked off into the hills with their survival kits. They took little note of the signs of people passing through the area because of course it was inhabited. Their business was to note any abnormal activities.

By Thursday, they found a couple of goatherds and their hardy charges heading downhill. With broken English and broken Dari all round, they exchanged pleasantries, candies and cheese. The Americans apologized for not having cigarettes, and the goatherds moved on.

Almost immediately afterwards, they came to a plateau and there were about six men on horses. The horsemen were on alert and seemed to have been waiting for the Americans. Alex recognized Il Dhost in the middle of the group by those flashing green eyes which fascinated him so much. They checked their advance as the two groups regarded one another warily. At last, Raziq spoke.

"We have been waiting for you Lieutenant Pearson. We thought you would have been here since yesterday evening. Il Dhost says old age seems to be slowing you down."

"Tell Il Dhost that old age or not, I am finally here. What is this all about?"

"We know what you are looking for. We could get you there sooner if you would come with us. If we get there on time, we might prevent an ambush on the ISAF forces coming behind you."

"Certainly! How long will it take us to get there?"

"Maybe two, maybe three days."

"What? Can't we get there faster or is Il Dhost also being slowed by old age?"

At this Il Dhost laughed, or did what Alex assumed was laughter for his whole body shook and his eyes twinkled brighter. Raziq answered, "Il Dhost thinks that is a good joke. No, just as it was probably not age but caution which delayed your ascent. It is caution which must delay our progress. It is of no use to give your enemies warning that you are on the way except if that would win the battle."

"When do we leave then?"

"Right now. We are all set to go. So are your men, we believe."

And so, they set off as a group. Some of Il Dhost's men rode double on a horse until they came to a point where they all dismounted and rode on donkeys instead. Some other men emerged from the dark to take the horses away. The Americans carefully marked the course they were following.

They noted that they travelled in a northerly direction, and yet eastwards at the same time.

Sometimes they went through a rocky tunnel for a short distance; sometimes they passed mountaintops seemingly very close to the stars. At last, close to dawn Il

Dhost called a halt. "We will rest here for about eight hours" Raziq said, "and scout out the land. We don't want to run into any traps."

Their resting place was a natural cave overlooking a grassy plain. Il Dhost's men took their positions a little separate from Il Dhost which seemed funny to Alex. It was too much of a portrayal of traditional respect even on the battlefield. As they huddled in their group, Alex talked with his own men and made arrangements for keeping watch.

"Keep your eyes open" he told them. "We shall compare notes later. Rotations will be every two hours. I will take the second watch."

He did not need to expand on this order. They all understood him very well. Alex determinedly went to sleep. Something niggled his mind, but he could not put a finger on it. He awoke after two hours, refreshed. He noted that those who went to sleep before him in Il Dhost's camp were still asleep but those on watch were very vigilant.

As he watched, Il Dhost stirred. A corner of the covering slipped from his face. Alex saw that the face was totally and uncharacteristically beardless! It was even soft and girlish.

Something stirred in him. He felt a familiarity he could not account for. It was very brief, and then Il Dhost turned and faced away again. Alex was not quite sure of what he had seen, given the shadows and the number of men between him and Il Dhost. He felt embarrassed. It was as if he had been caught playing "Peeping Tom". He took over the watch. The person handing over shook his head "No". There had been no abnormal occurrence while he slept.

They spent one more day travelling. By the following night, Raziq signified that they had come very close to the enemy camp.

He asked that Alex and his men accompany them to where they could spy on the insurgents. They duly set up their equipment so they could monitor the men's activities. Because one of the Americans could speak Pashto and Dari well, they also set up listening and taping equipment. At this point, Alex thought Il Dhost and his men would leave. When he voiced this thought however, Raziq asked him, "How then will you safely get off the mountain?"

Of course, they had their satellite equipment which told them at what latitude and longitude of the earth they were located. The equipment also told them how to home in to base. Nevertheless, there was nothing like having a native as a guide. "Besides," added Raziq, communicating what Il Dhost had just said, "in case your backup does not arrive on time, is there no comfort in knowing that someone friendly has your back?"

The Afghans only briefly watched them setting up their equipment before melting into the surrounding rocks and sparse brushes. The Americans only knew they were there because they had said they would be. They set about the business at hand. They gathered information, location, plans, and strategies of the insurgents. Alex then proceeded to code the information and transmit it as a squawk to both Major Grafton and to Lieutenant Dreyfus. What they did with the rest of the information was up to them.

Alex decided that he and his men would stay a day more to see if they could get additional information. With the satisfactory glow of a task accomplished, he set up a round-the-clock watch for his men and decided to explore where he was at present. He wandered off the major path, following what he felt was the sound of running water. He had no reason for doing this other than plain curiosity.

He had not gone far when there was the shrill of a whistle. It was obviously a signal.

Alex automatically crouched low, hid behind a stone, and crawled forward, his weapon cocked in his hand. Peering round the trail he had been on, he caught sight of someone hastily winding a turban around his head. Another step closer and he recognized Il Dhost. Il Dhost turned with those flashing green eyes which intrigued Alex so much. Now were they flashing from surprise? Alex could have sworn it was from anger. Again, he felt he had seen those eyes before. Remembering his surprise glimpse of the previous day he asked, "Now I meet the great Il Dhost alone face to face. Tell me, is there something that you are hiding?"

Before he had the opportunity of getting an answer, Raziq stepped out from behind a nearby bush. His eyes were brimming too, but with something which resembled amusement. "Ah Lieutenant Pearson, you surprise Il Dhost doing private meditations. Was there something you wanted?"

"Nothing particularly" Alex answered. "However, I sure would appreciate a private audience with Il Dhost if I may."

"This is certainly private" Raziq reassured him. "What was it you wanted of Il Dhost?"

Deciding nothing would be gained by forcing the matter, Alex left his suspicions to himself. He changed the topic instead and said, "We really appreciate your help on this mission. I have sent the outcome of our intelligence gathering to the necessary people. We will be ready to leave whenever you choose."

Raziq looked at Il Dhost who continued to say nothing and still looked peeved. "We will discuss this among ourselves, Lieutenant Pearson. "We will get back to you as soon as possible" Raziq answered at last. "Was there something else you wanted?"

"Only to take a look around, and at the mountain stream I seem to be hearing."

"That would be over that way" Raziq pointed. Alex went in that direction, Raziq and Il Dhost went in the opposite direction.

That evening, they had what could only be described as a camp meeting. Il Dhost and his men let Alex and his men understand they were close to the town of Sayghan. They were really between the bigger town of Bamiyan, and Kabul where there were also army bases. They could go to either place to request transportation to

Shahsak where they had left their own vehicle, or undergo the gruelling journey they had just undertaken, in the reverse.

Two of his men were for going to Kabul and getting back to base that sooner. Alex and Randy undertook to go back to their vehicle at Shahsak. Il Dhost's group also divided up. Raziq explained that some other tasks awaited them. Some of the men going to those tasks would see the two Americans delivered at the army base at Kabul, and then go on from there. Il Dhost, Raziq, and the rest would escort Alex and Randy back to Shahsak.

The journey back to Shahsak was uneventful except for the fact that Alex wanted to ride at the rear and get a good look at Il Dhost. However, Il Dhost also seemed to have the same plan. Out of necessity and the demands of the trails, sometimes one succeeded, and sometimes it was the other. By the end of the second night, Il Dhost and the others melted into the mountainside as only Afghans could. Raziq and the only other man left to guide them informed them that they were virtually out of danger. As day broke, they were looking over the town of Shahsak. Without further directions, they could home in on the ISAF headquarters where their jeep was.

Alex chaffed at something. "Say goodbye and thanks to Il Dhost on our behalf" he told Raziq on parting.

"Something is eating at you" Randy told him as they walked to their jeep.

"Like what?" Alex asked.

"Il Dhost. The man got under your skin somehow, and you don't know what to do about it."

"I don't know what you're talking about."

"You sure do, only you can't explain it to yourself yet."

"Maybe, but that is not your business!"

"You're right. Let us discuss what our business really is."

They spent the rest of their journey discussing their impressions about the venture they had just undertaken, and a bit about the men they had undertaken it with. They soon got to Farah and reunited with the rest of their team.

CHAPTER 4

∞

Major Grafton invited Greta, Laura, and Lil to the Farah base for Christmas. They were very glad to accept. For Greta this was her first time at the army base. However, she was already very used to such settings. For Lil it was like a homecoming. All the men remembered her fondly. They exclaimed over how well she was looking. For Laura, this was home, more or less. She enjoyed playing hostess to the other two. Major Grafton embraced her like a longlost daughter. He said to her, "Now I can really have you as a daughter-in-law, I hear. Preach has made a wise move but we all saw it coming except the man himself. If he hadn't made the move, I would have commanded another of my men to marry you so we can keep you in the family."

Laura blushed and laughed but she was too happy to really be embarrassed. Tim beamed. He had never felt the need for a leave nor to take off-duty days. It would be nice to take the ladies round the countryside with what he had accumulated but Farah was not that safe. He organized hours of proselytizing for the "Lady Disciples" as Alex called them. They benefitted from his tutelage and found depth in the services he organized for the men at the base. They went along with him to minister to the sick who seemed to get better more quickly in the presence of the ladies, to the amusement of the medical team. The three ladies talked again about getting baptized but did not like the bathtub baptism which Tim proposed. "You know you cannot have open shows of religion even for yourselves in Afghanistan" Tim told them. "Besides, we cannot have you in freezing river water at this time of the year."

That made a lot of sense. The temperature was really very unfriendly, not to talk of the razor-sharp winds off the mountainside. However, Bjorn was still not there. They agreed that before they finally left Afghanistan by July, Bjorn would come. They would see then if they could not organize a riverside baptismal session, masked as a private picnic!

No matter how busy they had been during the day, Tim and Laura always found time to go off together in the evenings after dinner. They wandered the gardens alone in the dusk and cold. He took her in his arms, and she felt right at home. He kissed her, and she felt all the right sensations. "Chaplains can become tempted too, you know" he told Laura one day. It was one of those moments when they found it rather difficult to let each other go.

"Let us get married as soon as possible. What will it take?" Laura asked.

"Well, we are discouraged from getting married while on tour, but I believe ours is a special case."

"Why should people be forbidden to get married when they want to? It is a breach of human rights" Laura was indignant. Her American spirit was aroused.

"Actually, I think fraternizing with the natives is what is forbidden; and it is for sensible security reasons."

"Why? How?"

"For one, their religion forbids their girls marrying non-Moslem men; but their men can marry girls of certain non-Moslem religions including Christians. Anyone who breaches that rule could be killed, brutally. Can you imagine how terrible it would be to know you were the cause of the death of the one you love? In Iraq I knew a few of the men who secretly converted to Islam so they could marry since the ladies were forbidden to convert to Christianity; but that is on the one hand.

"On the other hand, many of the ladies go into that kind of marriage for convenience. They use their marriages to get passports to the States. Once they arrive there, they sue for divorce. You won't believe how much easier it is to get a divorce in Islam. However, they wait till they get to States where they have even more benefit for the divorce. Our men are so naïve and vulnerable. Being far from home, they actually fall prey to all manner of scams."

"But you said there are special conditions? Are there no genuine cases?"

"You are looking at one right now. If we, or any expats, want to be married now, we get a special license from the base commander. The base commander either performs the marriage himself, or he gets the army chaplain to do it."

"So, we can do it" Laura exclaimed. "Let's do it!"

"Sure, why not?"

And so, they found themselves planning for a wedding. Greta and Lil were excited, and Alex no less so. Even Major Grafton was excited. They wanted a date in the New Year just before they went back to Lashkar Gah but Alex wanted to be able to finish an assignment and be there to give Laura away. "Oh! I wish Bjorn could be here too" Lil said.

"And won't it be fun to get Ayesha here?" Greta added.

The plan started snowballing out of their control, bigger than what they had planned. At the end, the wedding had to be postponed because a lot of other things happened.

Alex was following a tipoff. There was a gathering of insurgents between Farah and Anar Darreh. He took three people to go to investigate this about four days after Christmas. They hiked up the Farah side of the mountain and started sweating from the exercise despite the cold. Alex lifted a finger signalling the men to be quiet. Something was disturbing the peace and quiet. They looked again. About a hundred feet in front of them, they saw it – it was the corpse of a man dangling from a tree. They cautiously circled it. After another fifty feet, they saw another corpse on the ground, this one with its throat slit. Alex almost let a moan escape because he recognized this corpse. It was one of the men who had escorted them to Sayghan. They were in enemy territory then. As they moved cautiously forward, they became aware of movement in the glade in front of them. It was Il Dhost holding court. There he sat, surrounded by about a dozen men. Alex would have hailed them but felt the need to be cautious. If their lookouts had been killed, then the enemy was not far away, and they had not been warned. Remembering the trick they had used to help him at Herat, he signalled to one of his men to come nearer, asked him to return to the corpse on the ground, and throw a grenade around there. He counted in his heart while keeping watch on the people in the glade. They still remained oblivious of any danger. They seemed to be arguing intently about something.

Just as the grenade exploded, the men in the glade all took cover. They disappeared among the trees and rocks. At the same instant, some other men jumped into the glade shouting and cursing. They began shooting and lashing about with mean-looking knives. They had almost been upon their quarry. Noise of battle erupted in the bushes. The Americans from their hiding places, had front row seats. It took a lot just to keep watch on one another at the same time. However, they warily looked on, taking note of where the action was happening.

The skirmish went on for about an hour, and then a deafening silence followed. It was either the men had all killed one another or were regrouping for a second onslaught. There had been no noisy gunshots but soft whumps of silenced guns or other weapons, and the grunts of men either engaged in strenuous physical activity or merely dying.

The Americans waited about an hour more before daring to emerge to investigate. Behind every rock, almost every bush there were signs of prostrate men, either unmoving or severely wounded. They came upon Raziq. "Il Dhost" he whispered hoarsely. "Have you seen Il Dhost?" Alex said he had not. "There was no signal." He said hoarsely.

"Your sentries were eliminated. We saw them and sent the signal."

"Well done. We need another signal now. We need to clear off this mountain. More of them are coming."

"I have four men here. How do we help?" Alex asked.

"Water… If I have some water, I will be able to call the signal."

Alex could manage that. He held out his drinking canteen to Raziq. After he had taken a mere sip, he let out a piercing whistle. Alex propped him up on a stone and went back into hiding with his men to see what would happen next. They did not have to wait for up to fifteen minutes. Some people came up the mountainside with donkeys. They went from man to man on the ground sorting out their own. The ones who were wounded were loaded onto the donkeys and taken away immediately. Next, they checked out the inert ones. Some of these, they also loaded onto donkeys. Raziq was among this latter group. From where he was, Alex could not tell if he was dead or alive. He signalled two of his men, "Follow them and mark where they are going but don't become involved. Report back at the base. We will come later when we find out what is going on here."

Although he had been watching carefully, Alex had not seen Il Dhost either among the wounded or the unmoving. He scanned the clearing but saw no sign of him. He signalled to Randy that he was circling round again. It was quite by chance that he saw the figure behind the stone. He had concluded there was just a pile of rocks there when there was a groan. He stopped, checked and saw it was human. As he watched, it groaned again and he saw that it was Il Dhost himself with his left arm lying at an awkward angle, obviously dislocated or broken. His face was covered with blood but he could not see where the bleeding was coming from.

Recalling all his training in First Aid he now approached the figure. Obviously, he was alive. That was why he was groaning. A quick check confirmed he was breathing well enough. The neck did not seem broken. Nevertheless, Alex gave the best simulation that he could under the circumstances of log-rolling him. The bleeding from the head seemed serious enough. There was only one way to find out how bad it was. He unwound the turban and gave a gasp as masses of hair the color of deeply toned honey came tumbling out. Il Dhost was a woman!

This was a real surprise. However, he did not waste time dwelling on this. He saw that there was a cut just above the hairline which was not as bad as the bleeding had suggested. He tore the turban in two unequal strips. With the thinner strip he splinted her wounded shoulder to her body. He wound the larger strip round her head again to cover both the wound and to hide her glorious hair. He wondered how to move her. He had subconsciously been aware of movement nearby as he worked. Now, he saw one of the men with the donkeys returning. Apparently, they had come to look for other survivors or for Il Dhost in particular. Before Alex could decide whether to call out or keep hiding, there was a sting at the side of his neck. Even as he lifted his hand to rub it, his vision blurred. He slumped beside Il Dhost. Everything became dark.

That evening, two of the men reported to Major Grafton at the base. They talked about how they had followed the donkeys until they disappeared round a bend. Some men then confronted them, demanding they went back peacefully the way they came unless they wanted trouble. The mysterious men had then escorted them some way, turning back only when the Farah market was in view. The Americans had been told to be non-combatant unless they were provoked or were defending themselves. They had not been provoked at all, so they had complied in order not to rouse unnecessary hostilities. Besides, they knew they were hopelessly outnumbered. They returned to the base just as Alex had told them, to report everything to Major Grafton.

When Alex and Randy did not return to the base that evening, Major Grafton was not unduly worried. When the next day ended and they still had neither returned nor called in, he became faintly alarmed. By the third day, he called for the two men who had gone with them. These both felt they could get back to the point where they last saw the donkeys. However, just as Major Grafton was deciding to organize a search party to go looking for them, Randy came stumbling in; and did he have such a story to tell!

He had seen Alex loaded on a donkey, seemingly still alive but unconscious. He had been torn between following the donkey and securing their field equipment. The decision had been made for him when he noticed that the people on the ground were beginning to stir. When he heard the sounds of footsteps returning, he did not know which side would come next for their fallen men. However, he was sure of one thing: the American field equipment was safer with him than with either side. He had made for a safer hiding place after securing his, and Alex's equipment. By the time he returned, he could see neither hoof nor hide of the donkey which had taken Alex away. He spent part of that first evening and the whole of the next day fruitlessly trying to tail them. At last, he had decided that the best course of action was to take their field equipment and head back to the base for reinforcement.

The only good news he could give was that he was quite sure it was Il Dhost's men who had Alex, not the other side. With that, the whole base had to be content for the time being. Major Grafton allowed Tim to tell the women as much as he thought they should know. One thing was for sure, all wedding plans were postponed for the moment. Even the New Year had to be welcomed on a very low key compared to the previous plans which had been afoot by the base to celebrate the return of the UNESCO women.

CHAPTER 5

―――――∞―――――

When Alex came to, his first sensation was of a terrible thirst, then a blazing anger. He then noticed that all over his body was afire. He lay still and took a mental stock while moving his body parts limb by limb. Yes, he had a terrific headache. However, nothing seemed to be broken. He was not bound in any way. He seemed to be lying on a soft but narrow mattress. The bed was not quite long enough for him. He stood up gingerly and reached for his boots. His head swam but he managed to put on his boots. He was in a small room with just that single bed, and a door opposite the bed. Steadier on his feet, he reached the door and pushed it slightly. The door opened and he found himself in a courtyard. There was a jar of water by the door with a plastic cup on top. From experience, he knew that Afghans stored their potable water in this way. His thirst was such that ignoring the cup, he lifted the jar whole and drank very deeply. Refreshed, he turned back to the room. With the door still open he did a quick surveillance of his quarters. His kit was not there. His weapons were not there. He reached down to his socks and saw that even his knife had been removed. He swore under his breath. At least he was still fully dressed in his own clothes. His whole body seemed to be bruised. He judged that a whole day at least must have passed but he was not quite sure.

He left the room and decided to explore the courtyard. The very first person he saw was Il Dhost but O what a totally transformed Il Dhost! She looked much better as a woman with her rich russet hair tumbling over her shoulders. It showed a broad forehead despite the bandage she wore. Beautifully arched brows were above those glittering green eyes with naturally long and dense eyelashes. With her pert nose and full ripe red lips, she could have held her own in any setting of beautiful women anywhere in the world. Alex was touched by her beauty but what was uppermost in his mind was anger at his mistreatment. "How dare you?" he hissed through clenched teeth, "How dare you have me drugged like some wild animal and brought to your infernal citadel?"

Green eyes now flashing with anger she flung back at him. "How dare you? How dare you invade the privacy of our home without invitation? And what are you doing in this part of the compound anyway?"

"Oho! So, you do have a voice which even speaks English! I certainly did not come here on my own nor ask to be brought here. What business did you have masquerading around the countryside dressed like a man, and having other people speak on your behalf when you could speak perfect English?"

"And what business do you have questioning me over how I choose to live my life in my own country? I speak to whom I please, how I please" She lifted her right hand to rub her temple as if speaking with Alex gave her intense headache. Her left arm was encased in a sling better than what Alex had previously fashioned.

Her companion drew her closer. For the first time Alex noticed the older woman. The two women looked so much alike that the other one could also have been Il Dhost; except that she was older, a bit shorter, had a few pounds on Il Dhost, and was obviously not carrying battle scars. As she ministered to the younger woman, Alex deduced they were probably mother and daughter. She murmured something to Il Dhost and then turned to Alex. In perfect English she said "Hello, Lieutenant Pearson, we have not been introduced properly. I am Serisha. This is my daughter Zohra." She stretched out her hand graciously. Alex would have been a lout not to have shaken it. "Both of you had a very grueling day yesterday" she continued.

"Instead of taking it out on each other, why don't you both just eat and then go to sleep. Things always appear better in the morning."

Her voice was quiet but authoritative as only a mother's could be. Zohra answered "Yes Madaar" while Alex turning, went back the way he had come. He really was tired. He needed fully functioning faculties for the ordeal he knew would soon be at hand. Serisha herself brought him supper of a rice meal, paan, vegetable stew, and the inevitable Afghan tea. He ate everything. Pulling the mattress to the floor, he lay down and fell asleep. After all, if he had been on the mountain that night, he probably would have had worse sleeping arrangements.

It did not occur to Alex to question if any part of the meal was drugged, considering the group's modus operandi. With the power of hindsight, he concluded it must have been, because he slept dreamlessly afterwards. When he awoke, he felt refreshed and totally free from all pains. The only problem was that he had completely lost all sense of time. He did not know what day it was or how many days he had been in the lair of Il Dhost.

Somebody named Raju came to show Alex where the conveniences were. In a mixture of broken English and Dari, he let Alex know he was to come to a gathering somewhere else in the compound. He took Alex on a route opposite to where he had encountered the women the previous day. About a dozen people were already there when they arrived. Instinctively his eyes searched for Zohra, but she was not there. Serisha and another woman whom he eventually got to know as Nazo were there. All the others were men. Raziq was there too, as were about two other familiar faces whose names he could not remember. They were already drinking tea. Alex was served some tea as well.

It was Serisha who opened the discussion. "First, Lieutenant Pearson, let us begin by apologising for the unusual way in which you were brought here. Believe it or not, the person who decided to do that on the spur of the moment had only the friendliest of intentions. When we shoot our enemies, we aim not to kill them unless we cannot help it. The man who brought you knew those other men would wake up soon enough, or their friends would come looking for them. He felt your chances were slim if they found you. What he forgot was that you were a trained American combatant. You would probably have survived better if you were fully conscious and ambulant, on your own."

"Was that all?" Alex asked skeptically.

"If you mean your bruises, you are a very heavy man to carry, Lieutenant Pearson. The men who had to manoeuvre you unto the donkey were considerably shorter than you. We understood two of them had some difficulty achieving the task and then bringing you here. The bruises were inevitable. Those could not be helped."

"I appreciate your explanations" Alex said. "However, if we are to become friends, hadn't we better be completely honest with one another?"

"You are right, Lieutenant Pearson" Nazo now added. "When Siddiq saw you attending to Zohra, he panicked, not knowing what it would be for the identity of Il Dhost to be so revealed, even to a friend."

That was as much as Alex thought. The rest of the story was probably true. However, this was the explanation that made the most sense.

"So now that I know Il Dhost is a woman, what are you going to do about it?" he asked.

"It is more a question of what you are going to do about it" Raziq now said, speaking for the first time.

Alex did not have time to answer him because at that moment Zohra marched into the room, regal in her anger. She addressed her mother in rapid Dari. Alex could not follow everything she said but as close an interpretation as he could fix on it was, "I will thank you Madaar for calling a family meeting behind my back" among other things. Despite her splinted arm, she still seemed very much in command. She now turned to Alex and said, "You, follow me!"

Alex remained where he was, not in defiance, and not so much as out of amazement as out of admiration. Dressed as a woman, and in a towering rage, she could have been an avenging goddess with the white bandage round her forehead like some superhero. Her flaming hair contrasted sharply with her alabaster white skin and those flashing green eyes. He was mesmerized. "I am addressing you" she said, as to an errant schoolboy who was not paying attention in class.

"Excuse me Ma'am, I might be in your realm, but I am not one of your subjects. If I irritate you so much, execute me and have done with it. If not, I demand to be treated at the least politely, and as an honored guest. I am not something the cat dragged in from the sewer. I am not here by my own will. You do owe me an apology!"

He had started out speaking calmly enough but by the end of his impromptu delivery, his own eyes were a blazing blue fire.

It is said that some hawks mate for life, but O what a dance before they finally get to roost together. As one observer put it, "It does not in any way look like any familiar love dance of some other species with alluring songs, seductive moves, and colorful displays." The hawks fly very high up in the sky with frightening screeches and hisses, with terrifying clangs of beaks and talons, slashing and tearing at each other in an unmistakable aim of doing real harm to each other. It is more like a war dance than a courtship. Blood is drawn in no small quantity. The final scene plays out when joined together they plunge straight to earth as in a dead feint, headed for sure destruction. And then, at the last possible moment, they straighten themselves, floating on an air current, supporting each other until they safely land on an inaccessible crag. Thereafter, they never fight again. They jointly build their nests, take turns sitting on the eggs, hunting together, feeding each other, and fighting common enemies jointly for the rest of their lives. It is truly very amazing!

That was how it was for Alex and Zohra. On the first day after Zohra's unmasking, there was so much electrifying antagonism that all the other people around them felt it and watched with fascination. They did not have beaks and talons, but they tore into each other with their eyes, their stances, and then their words. The witnesses did not see any physical blood. However, they cringed inwardly and outwardly as the two faced off.

"I will not be spoken to like that!" Zohra answered. "Out! Come with me now! We shall go out and thrash this out: you and me!"

"Fine" Alex replied hotly, getting to his feet at once.

The spectators who had been watching the drama silently broke into speech all at once.

"You are wounded..."

"You are still weak..."

"You can't go out like this..."

"Remember that when you act in anger you are likely to make mistakes..."

They spoke in both Dari and English. Some even spoke a mixture of both. Zohra was already out of the doors, Alex hot on her heels. "Let them be," Serisha told the men who had risen to follow. "Perhaps our Zohra has finally met her match in this American officer."

They relaxed and continued with their shura.

Alex followed Zohra to the back of what had been shown to him as the bathroom. She opened a concealed door and they found themselves in the desert. They went round one dune, round a rock, and then they were completely hidden from the compound. To the uninitiated, the countryside always appeared like a contiguous flat and open barren land especially at that time of the year. After some time, however, one began to see, not only the landmarks, but also the many hiding places.

About ten minutes later they came to a secluded hollow. Zohra pointed to a rock and said "Sit!"

Alex resented her commanding tone. He pointed at the same rock and said to her, "Sit!"

They glared at one another for a moment and then she said "Fine!" She went to sit on the rock. Alex stood, glaring at her from his superior height.

"Why do we see you all over the countryside? You have your duty to perform but why does it always have to abut ours?"

"And how am I to know you are not the ones tailing me? You admitted to doing so yourself, once!"

"It was necessary at the time but what I am getting now is that whenever I turn around, there you are."

"I can assure you I was only following an intelligence tip. What were you doing there anyway? In any case, no matter what you say now, if we had not arrived when we did, your enemies nearly had you fixed."

Her bosom heaved up and down with effort, whether it was at containing her anger or at speaking, Alex did not care which. Starting with this point, they argued everything from the incompetency in each other's camps which ran interferences with their particular operations and methods of operation; to personal matters like eating habits, bathroom habits, and how dependable their friends and associates were. Some of their arguments were purely meaningless except maybe serving them the purpose of hearing each other's voice, spoken thoughts, and ideas. Alex gave as good as he got, not caring about being a gentleman at all in language or proceedings. After all, he reasoned, she wanted to be treated like a man, so like a man she would be treated! Zohra took a while to calm down but then at last she asked, "Okay, what do you want to know now?"

"Why did your men drug me and bring me here against my will? Why do you go traipsing round the countryside dressed like a man? What kind of outfit are you running, playing tag with the mean Taliban? Who exactly were those men trying to wipe you out?"

"First, you have no right to tell me how to run my life. My men had to drug you because that was the fastest thing which came to their minds. I traipse around the countryside, as you so delicately put it, dressed as a man because I have to defend my territory the best way I know. We are sorry we spared your life. We should have left you there drugged, until the Taliban found you!"

"No, I would have fared better if I was not drugged at all."

"Probably, but you were already drugged so…"

She stood up, intending to make a regal exit but she swayed at that moment. Instinctively, Alex caught her. It felt so good to have her in his arms, O so good. He wound his arms more tightly and held her more closely. She felt warm and soft in all the right places. Inside him, Alex felt so buttery and melted, manly and needed, all at the same time. He did not want to let go, if it were possible.

Zohra relaxed against his tall muscular frame. It was good to be held in strong arms and to let someone else be in charge. She dropped her head against his chest. It lasted for maybe just a second, a minute, an eternity… and then they both came to their senses and remembered they were still supposed to be fighting each other. Zohra twisted herself slightly. Alex let her go so suddenly that she stumbled again. He caught her again, but she suddenly crouched down and held a finger to her lips to signal silence. Instinctively, Alex crouched too. There was the scuttling of some unsettled stones and some movement. About a minute later a wild goat passed. They kept absolutely still but there were no more noises.

"Coming here like this was a mistake" Zohra said relaxing her vigilance. "I have no weapon. I cannot even use my two arms."

"Your men also disarmed me. I have not been treated at all like a friend in your camp."

She looked at him searchingly. "This discussion is not yet over but we shall continue it in a safer place" she said. Turning, she led the way back to where they had come from.

He followed her, taking more interest in the undulating sway of her hips as she walked, than in the path they were going as a good surveillance officer should have. This woman filled him with all manner of contradictions. One moment, he wanted to thrash her and teach her some harsh lessons. The next minute he was imagining what it would be like to really love her, hold her, and kiss her… but none of those happened. They continued to argue in snatches of sentences and phrases as they walked.

When they were within sight of the compound, Zohra sat down again on a rock. This time Alex sat on a nearby rock facing her so that their eyes were almost on the same level. "I probably saved your life yesterday." Alex began.

"In more ways than one, I am told, but then we saved yours before, too."

"So, my supreme crime was that I unmasked you."

"Have you ever thought what that information would be in the hands of an enemy?"

"What about in the hands of a friend? If we are to be helping one another and saving one another's lives, should we not be friends at the least? Your people say that the first day we meet we are friends, and the next time we meet we are brothers. We have met so many times now. Does that not have any significance to you?"

Zohra smiled at his adept use of the proverbs of her people. "That is what it ought to be, and what it is many times. However, these are evil times. These days, brothers betray one another under pressure. Sometimes they do so without even meaning to."

"And my food of last night; was it drugged too?" Alex now asked. "I wouldn't know. I did not prepare it nor order it. You must understand that you are in opium country.

There are many good uses of it, apart from getting stoned on it as your people say. My mother was a research pharmacist before the advent of the Taliban. She has knowledge of how to combine herbs and minerals very usefully. In fact, she does not just have the knowledge, she is gifted in that area. Tell me, did you not feel better when you woke up this morning?"

Alex was miffed. Rather than answer the question which truthfully was that he did feel better, he got up and began to pace. A lot of things made sense. Under different circumstances he would have been satisfied with all the explanations. However, he did not like situations in which he was not in reasonably good control."

"So, what are your plans for me now?" he asked at last.

"I don't know. I will have to think about it. I am not in the best of states myself!"

"What do you mean you have to think about it? Are you intending to keep me as a prisoner within your citadel indefinitely?" Alex was seething with fury again.

"Are you not being selfish Lieutenant? You are a wild card right now. You did not figure at all in our plans. In case you have not noticed, I am also wounded in battle. I have not had time to think about you much less take a decision about you. I want you less in this place than you want yourself to be!" Zohra replied equally furious.

Standing up, she managed a regal exit this time around. Alex stood still and glared at her retreating back. He had fairly determined not to return willingly to the compound but to find his way back to the base unequipped, even as he then was. He was about to turn around and go back the way they had come when Zohra suddenly collapsed to the ground before getting to the door in the wall. Alex found himself sprinting after her.

CHAPTER 6

∞

That afternoon, when Alex returned carrying the unconscious Zohra in his arms like a baby, the first impression the onlookers got was how tenderly he cradled her. Then they wondered why she was almost breathless when she had walked out on her two legs not long before, virtually steaming.

After Zohra fell, two of them had continued fighting over whether Zohra needed to be carried or not. Alex was of the opinion that she might be a seasoned warrior but at the moment she was a critically wounded woman, maybe even concussed. Next, they quarrelled over who should be taking care of the other, and then whether Zohra should not just shut up her mouth to conserve her energy. By the time they reached the others, she had stopped talking altogether. That worried Alex because he was sure it was not merely in obedience to his wishes. She was totally sapped and passed out completely.

The people were still having their shura when he walked in. The ladies jumped up in alarm. Several arms stretched out, willing to relieve him of his burden but he would not let go. "If you will just show me where to put her down, it might be better than transferring her from person to person" he insisted.

Serisha led the way to what Alex now recognized as the women's section of the compound, and into one of the rooms. The room was much the same as the one Alex had slept in except that it had a wider bed, a bigger window, a few other furniture, and throw rugs on the floor. He put her down very carefully on the bed and then turned to her mother. "She must have bled considerably yesterday. I am also sure that she is fairly concussed. What she had was a brief lucid episode. She is very critically wounded and will benefit from hospital care. If you could just arrange for the transport, I will get her there, sooner rather than later."

"Believe me" Serisha replied, "She is much better off here than in any hospital around."

"If it's for security reasons, we could have her treated at the base" Alex argued back. "I am sure my commanding officer will understand."

Serisha took a more careful look at the obviously besotted young man and answered, "We appreciate your concern Lieutenant Pearson. I will certainly keep your offer in mind. For now, let me see how much I can do."

With this she firmly shooed Alex out of the room. He wandered back to where the men were still sitting. They hushed their conversation when he came in. Finally, Raziq said to him, "She really is in the best of hands. There is nothing to worry about at all."

Alex acknowledged him with a brief nod. Eventually, the conversation resumed in rapid Dari. Alex paid no attention to them. He made no effort to follow as he ought to, being an intelligence officer. After an interminable period, food was served. All the men ate communally as was the custom. Alex was still too abstracted to dig in with the others. Someone kindly served him a plateful. He ate it without actually tasting the food.

Eventually Raziq addressed him again. "We lost four men there at the mountain. It would have been worse but for your intervention. We really appreciate that. We buried them that same evening. However, we will hold the funeral service for them today, this evening. Would you want to come?"

Alex had no strong feelings for or against going. What he really wanted was news from the sickroom. Nevertheless, he went with the men for the funeral service at dusk anyway, having nothing else to do. To his surprise, when it was time to go, they just moved aside some rugs on the floor of the room where they had been sitting, went down some rough steps, and emerged at a fairly large cave with a sandy floor. There was the noise of running water close-by. Most of the men had carried lanterns and so the cave was well lighted. There were prayers. People came forward to talk about what good things they remembered about the men who had died. They spoke slowly in Dari but Raziq, seated close to Alex at the back of the gathering, also interpreted for him in a low voice.

Someone preached about Jesus Christ being the resurrection and the life. He reminded everyone present of how fleeting life was, and how unexpectedly death could come. "We shall all die one day but let us live our lives in a worthwhile manner, with the hope that our Father will tell us 'Well-done good and faithful servants!' at the end of it all."

The service ended with their praying for the living. They prayed for all the others still recovering from the skirmish. Alex thought of Zohra. They prayed for God's continued guidance and protection in this ongoing battle, and for their country. They prayed that God would cause those who would know Him to still come to do so in spite of, or because of, all the problems they were facing. They thanked God for the foreigners in their country trying to help them. They asked for God's protection on them, and that these foreigners too will get to know the loving nature of God and become His children. They thanked God for Alex, how He used that vessel to save them. They prayed that God would reward him richly.

Alex actually appreciated the service, especially the prayer bit. Imagine that these poor needy people were praying for them who had good things going, at least far better than the Afghans had it. What they complained about in the States were paltry compared to the life-or-death situations faced by these Afghans on a daily basis. The prayer part of services was generally his least favorite. However, it was different on this occasion. Maybe it was because this was done by different people and in as simple a language as possible. These were heartfelt prayers, not read from books or anything like that. He certainly emerged from the service rather refreshed and less tense. Alex decided to stay for one more night, ask for his weapons early the next morning and then be on his way. He did not know how many days he had been away and could only imagine what they would be thinking at the base, not knowing whether he was dead or alive.

He again slept on the floor of the room allocated to him. They even provided him with basic toiletries. The next morning, he asked for his gear. Raju told him that his friend had been seen taking away his gear from the battlefield. They gave him back his sidearm and knife and offered to escort him to the Farah road from where he could then safely return to the base. He was ready to go but asked to see Zohra one more time.

Serisha came herself to conduct him to Zohra's chamber. She lay pale and drawn on the bed looking lifeless with her white skin contrasting very sharply with the dark sheets. He came nearer, knelt on the floor on one knee and took her hand. "Zohra" he called, "Zohra!"

She did not answer. Her eyelids did not even so much as flutter. He gazed at her steadily and squeezed her hand. Was that a faint answering squeeze? He tried it again but this time there was no response at all. He stayed crouching by her bedside for some time. When he looked up, there was such anguish on his face that Serisha hastened to console him. "She will be all right" Serisha said. I just gave her something to make her sleep very deeply. The body heals itself when we rest but our Zohra never rests except when she is forced to by circumstances like this."

"I cannot leave while she is like this. May I stay a day more?"

"Certainly, Lieutenant Pearson. You can be our guest for as long as you please." Very kindly she slid a chair under him so that he could be more comfortable.

"Thank you," he said in acknowledgement. "I need to get word to the base so they will not worry too much about me."

"I will tell Nazo to see what can be organized."

As Serisha left to make the arrangements Alex continued his vigil at Zohra's bedside. He sighed very deeply trying to gauge his feelings for this captivating woman. She made him ache in places which he did not know he possessed. He felt like punishing her and cuddling her at the same time. He admitted to himself that most of his anger at her was fear for her safety. As he continued to sit there, he found himself actually praying for her, to recover so that he would have occasion to speak to her again, "Even if it's to fight with her Lord, please let her become well again."

Serisha came twice to check on the patient but seeing Alex still there crouching meditatively, she withdrew. At about noon she brought him food, but he did not feel like eating. Towards evening Nazo brought news that a message had been dropped at Farah to say that he was safe. The runner had seen the message picked up by someone returning to the base. Alex merely nodded. Zohra continued to lie unnaturally still in bed. The only sign that she was still alive was the regular rising and falling of her chest as she breathed.

As the night deepened, Serisha brought him tea and rice cakes. "You have not eaten the whole day" she said. "You must eat now. If you do, I will tell you about Zohra and what makes her the way she is."

Alex took the proffered mug. He sipped to pacify her.

"Once" Serisha began, "We lived at Kabul and lived a thriving life. My husband studied engineering at the University where I had also studied pharmacy. I was majorly interested in folk medicine and worked with a research team at the university in that area. Our families had known each other for long. We were all from this area and stuck together in the big city. When it was arranged that me and Hameed should be married, we were still young and rebelling against the traditional ways. However, we had no objections at all to the union. Our families enjoyed the privileges of being connected to the royal family. The connection was not so close that when the revolution happened, we were in any way implicated. Hameed did as well in the new republic as under the old monarchy. We lived happily enough. We had seven children by the time the war with the Russians broke out.

"Hameed volunteered for the Afghan army. He was an excellent organizer and leader. His engineering expertise was considered a bonus. With his war involvement, he thought we would fare better in Qandahar than at Kabul, so we moved. The children got good education despite the country's turmoil. Sometimes, we had to send them to Iran where our families had extended to. At other times we sent them to Pakistan where other relatives had fled but both of us remained here. "The war with Russia ended. It was easier to align oneself with a powerful warlord than to try to survive on one's own. Hameed at first resisted this but eventually he allied himself with a warlord up north. You must permit me to leave out specifics for security reasons. By then our older children were grown. They were full of patriotism. For safety, Hameed felt it was better for me and the younger children to come back here to Farah. It was probably a lucky decision. Not long after we did, the Taliban came to power.

"The Taliban restored some peace and order by invoking religion. War-weary, we were all willing to accede to whatever would give us a breathing space from war and destruction. That peace was at a huge cost, however. They killed and pillaged under any pretexts at all. They set farms on fire and impoverished the people. Professionals like me were forced to give up public jobs and go underground. We bore it in silence. Hameed was more often at Qandahar. He hardly came back to Farah. "We consciously decided it was good for the children to run a bit wild and learn how to survive. They soon came to know most of the nooks and crannies of Farah. The ones who were not in school at Pakistan or Iran were being homeschooled. We learned how to outwit the Taliban even as we had outwitted the Russians before them. Finally, one day, it hit us right at home.

"Nazo is my third child, but my oldest daughter. She used to be a brilliant, lawyer even though she was quite young. She then lived at a suburb of Qandahar with her husband who was her childhood sweetheart. One day, the Taliban accused her of treason, and of consorting with men who were not her relatives. She was giving legal advice to men in her home! "We believe now that she was setup. The Afghan constitution had been suspended by the Taliban. We were to live by the Moslem Sharia. Women were to keep quiet at home and appear in public only if they were suitably encased in Burqa, and in the company of male relatives only. "The mosque police were ordered to give Nazo forty strokes of the cane. When they went to her house, her husband objected. He demanded a fair trial, even in a Sharia court. Right there and then, at their doorstep, they shot him in the head. They took Nazo away and administered the punishment, anyway.

"Zohra was just twelve years old at the time. She had gone to help Nazo care for her newborn baby. When they shot Nazo's husband and took Nazo herself away, Zohra took the baby and went to tell her father what had happened. Hameed got to the marketplace when the punishment had been completed as a deterrent to other rebellious women. He collected the bruised and broken body and spirit which had been his daughter. The next day, the Taliban leader came to see him at the house. "Hameed braced himself for an onslaught about his daughter's offences. He swore to control his anger at her sudden widowhood until he could find a way to remove her from further danger. Hameed was prepared for everything except the man's actual request. He had seen that Hameed had a nubile daughter. He had come to ask for the hand of that daughter in marriage. Zohra!

"Hameed was prepared for anything but this. When threats did not work, he resorted to pleading. He tried to explain that Zohra was already betrothed... There was a recent death in the family, and no one should talk of a wedding... The girl was sick... The mother had to be sent for, and so on. "He had so many other excuses. The Mullah overruled them all. He pointed to the Moslem traditions. 'The prophet himself, peace be upon him, said that women could marry even while mourning their loved ones... The prophet himself, peace be upon him, had caused some betrothals to be broken when he married some of his wives... The prophet himself, peace be upon him...'

"Hameed saw that it was no use. He resolved to send the girls away that night. However, his house had been surrounded. It was being watched by the mosque police. Caring friends and neighbors dared not even visit them. Nobody wanted to tangle with the Taliban by trying to help him. He stayed the whole night awake, and desperate. The girls were frightened but did not know what to do. Between Nazo's bereavement, injuries, and caring for the baby, this new catastrophe had just about drained them.

"In his final letter to me that night, Hameed said that he thought of killing his daughters, granddaughter, and then himself but was unable to do so. Early the next morning, they came for Zohra. "Hameed and his brother put up a stiff resistance, but they were hopelessly outnumbered. Hameed was stabbed in the chest. His brother was shot in the tummy. Zohra was taken away. Nazo called for friends. She buried her husband, her father, and her uncle on the same day. As for her sister, she knew that she faced a fate worse than death. She could do nothing about it. "She gathered the barest essentials, took her baby, and found her way back here to me. It took her many years to begin to heal from that tragedy. Even now, she might not even be fully recovered." Serisha stopped, either sunk in the terrible remembrance of it all or having come to the end of her narrative.

"And Zohra, what happened to Zohra?" Alex prompted.

"I thought you had fallen asleep" Serisha replied slyly. Her voice was surprisingly devoid of anger. Her eyes were sad but dry. She was even smiling! She had overcome the horror and the bitterness of those terrible memories, and not because she was callous or undergone some expensive psychotherapy. She had frankly found a way to deal with it. She had put the energy she would have used for vengeful thoughts to good use in other areas.

She now continued with her tale. "Zohra is a very tough girl. That is why I have every confidence that she will recover from these injuries also. One of her brothers was killed by the Taliban trying to find where she had been taken to. Another one was killed when the men of Farah put up a resistance to fight the Taliban. They were all summarily rounded up and executed. "My third son had settled down in Pakistan. He married another Afghan girl when we sent him there to school. He stopped visiting Afghanistan. After the family tragedy I sent my two youngest sons to him. Two years later they were granted Refugee status to settle in Canada. He asked if he could go with my children. I thought of what we have here. I wanted them to be patriotic but what were they coming back to? "I asked Nazo if she would want to go too. She felt strongly about staying back but she sent her daughter with them. We are hardly ever in contact with them. I know life is also quite tough for them there. Nevertheless, would they have had it any better here? Me and Nazo remained here believing that Zohra would one day return. She has never told anyone all that she suffered in those days. I can only tell you what I have pieced together from what she lets slip from time to time.

"The old Mullah married her that very day even before the corpses of her father, her uncle and her brother-in-law were buried. He got tired of her after a short while and arranged to send her to his son at Jalalabad. "She managed to escape somewhere close to Jalalabad, wandered about the mountainside until a Christian family took her in. The family nearly got into trouble for harboring her. One day she stole some food, dressed up as a boy and went into the cold again. "She joined up with some Kuchis for a while and went with them into Pakistan. She could not remember how to get to any relative in Pakistan. She felt safer remaining with the Kuchi camp anyway. "One day they met another Kuchi group which was coming back towards Farah, and she transferred to their camp. As soon as the landmarks became familiar to her, she made her way back home. It took her about four years. All the while, we did not know whether she was alive or not. We just kept on believing blindly. And then one day, we got up in the morning, opened the doors, and there was Zohra at the doorstep! It was like a dream.

"It was all we could do to contain our joy at her returning. However, we had also been broken in spirit. The young men had all been killed, joined the Taliban or given up. How long could a people endure war and trouble, first with the Russians, then the Mujahedeen, and then the Taliban? Spirits were weak, fleshes were even weaker. "Me and Nazo were frankly just drifting along, with virtually nothing to look forward to, nothing to hold on to except the dream that Zohra would one day return. When she returned, Zohra woke us all up. She did not speak of what she had suffered but she told us of what was happening in other parts of our country: from the north to the south, east to the west, and even across the borders. Zohra had been there and had firsthand experience. "She told us it was about time we stopped sitting down helplessly while the bad men waxed stronger and stronger, unopposed. She was a mere sixteen years then, and female to boot. But she has her father's inherent ability to organize and to direct. She organized the resistance and became its leader. Many of us are way older than her but she woke us up to what we could be. 'You are not any less than you were because you don't have big offices and sophisticated equipment' she said. 'Your knowledge was not taken away too. Fight with what you have got now!'

"She caused us to begin to dream and to hope again. We saw that we did not have to give in to the Taliban without a fight. If your enemy is bigger than you in might, then you have to plan to attack him with wits! That was what we did; what we are still doing."

When Serisha paused this time, Alex did not prompt her. A word, it is said, is often enough for the wise. A good storyteller lets the hearers figure out the morale of the whole story. At last Alex said, "But she was only a girl."

"A mere girl" Serisha agreed.

Alex understood then. To convince more people, she had to dress up as a man and disguise herself so that her youth and her gender would not be held against her. Her voice lacked the necessary timbre, so she spoke through other people. Her turban concealed her beautiful face and her gender. It also kept her from being easily recognized. Only a few people must have been in the know of whom Il Dhost really was. It explained why Alex had become a wild card – he was now in on the secret!

"When did the Christian element come into your group?" Alex asked.

Serisha sighed and then answered, "That is another long story. The truth of the matter is that in a way we have always been Christians. The land we occupy now was Christian before it became Moslem. Our ancestors around here were Coptic Christians. We are all Moslems on the surface but at birth our parents go underground, literally, and baptize us. "When we come of age, we're told the secret as a form of family initiation and a rite of passage into adulthood. We are asked to hold onto it; but it all had no meaning except for a few who chose to explore the faith. It was the coming of the Taliban that forced many of us to take another look at what Islam offered, and to compare it with what Christianity offered. Frankly, after how our family fared with the faith, we would rather be animists than Moslems. The Taliban had the power and the guns, but they were against the people. Any alternative was welcome at that point. Many of the young people, especially the returning refugees were beginning to look at those other alternatives.

"When Zohra returned, she had a lot to share about her own experiences. She is a great organizer. However, she did not need to organize us on this very aspect. We saw the reflections of it in her life and we wanted what she had. It was only a matter of time before we linked up with people of similar convictions. Some of these people were in very key and sensitive positions. Most of them were just ordinary people, living their lives as they could manage, from day to day. "They all want to do something about what they believe in, overtly or covertly. However, they lacked the direction and organization to do so. That is where Zohra's talents come in. I need not tell you the risks we take daily. Our parliament does not call it murder when someone kills a convert from Islam to Christianity. Nevertheless, that very edict becomes a driving force for us. Now we have something, and Someone, not just to live for, but to also die for! Besides, we derive joy from sabotaging the Taliban and offering people an alternative" she ended with a short laugh.

As Serisha spoke, the compound had quietened down. People had gone to sleep all around. It must have been past midnight when Zohra finally stirred and murmured "Madaar". At once Serisha was at her side. Alex made to move away to give her some space but at that moment Zohra's eyes flew open. She focused her gaze on his face. "Lieutenant Pearson" she said.

"At your service, Ma'am."

"Am I dreaming Madaar?"

"No" answered Serisha, "He has been here for quite some time."

Some of the fire returned to her eyes. With all the vehemence she could muster she asked "Why?" making it sound like an expletive. Without waiting for a reply, and without preamble she announced, "I need to go to the bathroom, Madaar."

Serisha leaned down to help her, and Alex slipped away at that instance. By the time Zohra was up and leaning against her mother, she was no longer sure if he had really been there or if it was just a part of her dreams. She slipped right back into sleep afterwards. Alex, now somewhat reassured that she was going to be all right, went back to his allotted room. His mind was so busy with too many things. At last, he went to sleep. He had resolved on what he would do the next day.

CHAPTER 7

―∞―

The morning after his vigil, Alex requested a shura of the leaders of the network, at which he insisted Zohra must be present if she was recovered enough. The shura held that evening in the big room under which was the entrance to the secret passage. Apart from Serisha, Nazo, and Zohra, only four other people were present, all men. Apparently, these constituted the innermost circle. Since Alex had asked for the shura, they looked to him to put forward his point after everyone was served with tea. With every eye on him, he began very cautiously but waxed stronger as he progressed.

"I want to say that I represent the United States as I am standing here but my few short years of living have shown me that everything is not always clear-cut black or white. We must make allowances for the grey areas." The people gathered nodded gravely. He had begun with humility and with proverbs. These were valued attributes in the wise. "I have had the privilege of knowing and working with your outfit for a few weeks now. I can confidently say that we serve the same Cause, or at least we seem to have the same common enemy. You say that the friends of my enemy are my enemies too. In the same way then, the enemies of my enemy must therefore be my friends as well." His listeners continued to pay attention.

"I want to refer to what happened at the mountains a few days ago that brought me to where I am now. We were following some intelligence tips about something rash going to happen. Without pointing out what is in between, if it was not by you, then it must mean that some other factions are keeping an eye on you. They must be very close on your trail. Me and me know that our common enemy is not a fool. Whether they have become smarter over the past few weeks or there is a leak in your network, it shows that you have a need to reorganize. Your enemy did not decimate you this time around because we happened upon them by chance. However, I want you to admit that they were close enough indeed.

"This was my observation. Now tactically, I would advise you to step back, reorganize, recoup, and ask yourselves what you are doing now which you need to change. Perhaps you need to decentralize, relocate, or do some sweeps. Il Dhost came close to being unmasked this last time, and not by me but by an enemy. It could have happened this time, it might happen next time, and we don't know when the next time will be. I want to advise that she drops out of sight for a while, at least until the enemy stops looking for her. In your leadership, you need to do what you did with the organization of your education. Put up other arms so that if one fails or falls, the others would still be waxing strong independently."

With his cards on the table, Alex sat back and listened to what they had to say to one another, and to him. He stole a glance at Zohra and saw that she was also looking at him with something. Was it respect, admiration, or something else?

They discussed what he had just said and agreed that something wrong was happening to their vigilance or their surveillance. They always had one over their enemy. However, the enemy had come too close for comfort. The enemy could have destroyed them in one fell swoop. Yes, Zohra was a good leader and organizer. They had let a lot depend on her. They ought to decentralize, still let her be the leader and consult her on occasional basis but no one was impervious to torture. It would help if they did not all have comprehensive knowledge of the doings of one another so that if one faction was in trouble, the whole network did not have to collapse. They agreed that if Zohra had become a target, she ought to drop out of sight for a while, but they disagreed as to where she ought to go. Someone suggested the mountains, some Iran, Pakistan, or Uzbekistan. Someone even brought in Qandahar. However, they all had objections to each suggestion. It was as if they had reached an impasse.

Alex stepped in again at this juncture and said, "I want to offer her a place of refuge at the army base."

There were various murmurings and rumbles of wonder or disagreement. Some said some phrases in Dari which he could not quite understand but the meanings were plain from the knowing smiles that accompanied the words. He disregarded them all and ploughed on with his idea. "It might seem preposterous, but I think the army base would be the last place the enemy would look for her. I know you think you have even more secure locations but let's face it: if there is a leak among you, such locations would not only be known but also be in danger if she is discovered there. Yes, the American army would delight to have her to pump her for information but what if I were to give those of you seated here my personal word of honor that not only would she not be tortured for information which she does not wish to disclose, but that I alone will personally be in charge of any interrogation, and no one else. "I can also promise that none of what she tells us will get into any official records for the sake of the security of your organization. Yes, we also have leaks, but I appreciate now that your outfit must be protected at all costs."

"And is that all the reason, Lieutenant?" one man asked snidely.

"That is all that I can tell you for now. Can you think of any other reason?" Alex asked almost sweetly, and with a straight face.

Nobody asked him anything anymore after this. Serisha said it would be good for them to adjourn the meeting. They would think about all of these individually, and then meet again to discuss it. They dispersed. Alex decided to take a walk around the compound to give them room to think, but also to be available nearby in case any of them wished to discuss it further with him. At least he now knew with whom he should be dealing.

The first person who came out to him was Raziq. Apparently, he was on sentry duty. He met with Alex at a corner from where one could see the compound and all the approaches to it from the north and the east. He sat on a stone and asked Alex to sit on another one nearby. "You are head over heels in love with Zohra" he stated bluntly.

Alex regarded him stonily, neither confirming nor denying the statement. Raziq continued, "We have all been there, so I know. I even sympathize with what you are feeling now. Me and Zohra are cousins, thrice removed. She was betrothed to my elder brother before she was taken away to marry the Taliban mullah. My brother died defending our village from the Taliban, along with Zohra's brother and other young men. After a long while, when she came back, I fell in love with her all over. I had always held a torch for her since we were children, but I felt she was out of reach because she belonged to my brother. Two years after she returned, with my brother dead and out of the way, I dared to tell her how I felt. Do you know what she did?"

Alex continued to keep quiet because he did not know and could not imagine. Besides, he did not start this conversation. The other man did. Raziq continued. "She did not laugh as some other people surely would. Instead, she smiled very sadly which was more cutting than any laughter would have been. It only made me love her even more. 'Raziq' she said, 'some of us are not made for that kind of love. I am married to the Cause and must give my whole life to it. I must live life like a nun. Consider me a nun on a horseback, and not in a convent.' She then did something even more cutting. She kissed me on the cheek and thanked me for having the consideration to tell her!"

Alex did not know what to make of the story. He too had never wished to marry and give up his chosen way of life. He too, was married to his Cause despite what his parents and his sister hoped for or tried to persuade him to do. That was why he never considered Laura's infatuation an obstacle. Oh, he knew what she felt about him and knew what everybody had hoped on his behalf. He knew the pull of Laura had been different from that of any other ladylove he had encountered in his life. Nevertheless, he knew what he wanted and what he believed, so he had been safe, even from Laura. But this thing he had for Zohra was something else altogether. He could not fully analyze his feelings. He did have some selfish undertones in wanting to take her back to the base. He wanted to protect, but he also wanted to possess. Raziq was right in his perceptions. His feelings for Zohra had so much more running underneath, but he had not yet taken time to analyze, and understand much of it.

Raziq went on, "I am not the only one whose devotion to Zohra is often confused with our devotion to the Cause. It might be good for her to drop out of sight for some time, so that we will see what we believe more clearly. More than that, I want her to be safe, Lieutenant; I want her to be safe."

Alex did not know what to reply so he just grunted. Getting up, he returned to the compound. He had not said a single word to Raziq, only listened. He had said a lot to himself however, and he needed time for reflection.

The next person who came to him was Serisha. She brought him his dinner. Before he began to eat, she bluntly said, "You love my daughter Lieutenant Pearson. What are your intentions towards her?"

Sometimes bluntness has a lot to be said for it for truth's sake. For one it deters reading in between the lines which often led to a lot of misconceptions and wrong conclusions. And so equally bluntly Alex replied, "I love your daughter, Madaar. I have just realized it and I don't know what to do about it. If it were back home, I would have brought her chocolates and flowers. I would then have laid myself out and asked you if I may court and marry her. I am not even sure what rules apply in this situation. However, I know one thing for sure: I love her, and I am willing to give my life for her."

Serisha nodded wisely. "It will never be easy and straightforward with our Zohra. That is for sure. The obstacles are not going to be few, but you have done the first right thing Lieutenant. You have called me Madaar. I hope you mean it. You have also told me the truth. I will always appreciate that." Alex smiled. Calling her by the familiar Dari term for mother had slipped out very naturally, and unbidden. "And please call me Alex, Madaar. Give me your blessing and I will try my best to win Zohra. If I have your support, I will try to surmount all the obstacles."

"I will call you Alex in private, but this must be our little secret. Once it gets out that I call you Alex, it might not be safe for Zohra." Alex understood this too. "I also think your plan of hiding her at the base for some time is good. Loyalties keep changing. We need to sift through our people now to know who is who. I can offer to drug her and have her delivered at the base. However, I think it will be much better for many reasons for you to talk to her directly. Try to persuade her."

"I think so too Madaar. That is what I would prefer myself."

And so, Alex was invited to come to Zohra's chamber later that evening. Nazo and Serisha were there as well. Serisha might have worked on Zohra some more, or Zohra herself had taken time to think about his proposal and arrived at the same conclusion. It might also be that being physically better had made her less cantankerous. In any case, she was surprisingly very agreeable to his earlier proposal. She began, "That was a very wonderful plan you had Lieutenant Pearson. Of course, if you are going to do my debriefing personally, and not leave me to the mercies of your other officers I will greatly appreciate it. I also think it is about time we all started diversifying and spreading out in our organization. There is strength and beauty in diversity."

Alex inclined his head, and said, "Thank you!"

"When the heat is off, I will of course then make plans to return. I will not mind running a more compact or even a totally new outfit by then. I think I have demonstrated to everyone that we are capable of doing whatever we set our minds on doing. I have always felt that my mission was to awaken people to the possibilities, not necessarily to continue heading the outfit forever. I think I have more than achieved this objective, and I am willing to step aside."

"You are wise, and you are right" was all Alex found to say.

"You don't know it, or probably don't remember it Lieutenant, but about ten years ago you saved my life for the first time. I have never thanked you enough for it." At the bemused look on Alex's face, she laughed, and would have clapped her hands but for the sling on her arm. "I told you!" she whooped like a little girl. "You do not remember it! It was probably all in a day's job for you. I had sabotaged a Taliban meeting and gained some information. I was running home to deliver it and they were hot on my tail. I did not see the trap which was stretched across the path. I fell from my horse and was dazed. When I came to, they had tied me up and were planning how to torture information out of me…"

Alex now remembered. The light of that remembrance showed on his face. "You see, you see! You are now remembering" Zohra whooped again. "That was when I learned that grenade trick. There is nothing like an explosion to divert attention or to warn. You set me free at the cost of subverting your own operations that day. The thought of you has never left my heart since then!"

Alex hoped she meant the last sentence in more ways than one. He felt unexpectedly humbled at the reminiscence. From the look on the faces of Nazo and Serisha, this was also the first time they were hearing the story or at least his specific part in it. "But enough of memories" Zohra said briskly "Nazo has a plan for our trip."

"Since everything is all agreed" Nazo began, "The best time to leave is now. There is a truck ride to Anar Darreh. You will go to Musa's house and use the tunnel to Lor Koh. Siddiq will meet you there with donkeys and a change of clothing. You will shelter for the day at Sayed's house and enter Farah in the darkness of night. I have made arrangement for you to go to Mehmet's teashop. From there Alex, you can call the army base to come and pick you up. It might be wise for them to bring along a marine uniform for Zohra to dress in. It would also be wise if several people come so that no one keeps up with the coming and going from the teashop that evening."

It was a good plan, all the more admirable in its simplicity. They left within the hour. Alex did not have much to pack. To his bemusement, neither did Zohra. Serisha hugged Zohra, and then Alex. She whispered to Alex, "Take care of my daughter. She's very special."

"I will Madaar, I will" he whispered back.

She gave them provisions for the journey. Zohra put on the dressing of Il Dhost which hid her beautiful face and her feminine figure until only her eyes were visible and glittering, this time with amusement, and the anticipation of an adventure. Nazo and Raziq went with them as far as Musa's house. Thereafter, they were on their own.

Only Musa was awake to greet them at his house. He was the only person they saw in all of their fifteen-minute stay. Alex removed the battery-powered torches from their pack as directed by Zohra. Handing Zohra their drinking water canteen, he shouldered every other thing in a backpack. Musa led them down the stairs into a secret room and bade them goodbye. Alex took the canteen from Zohra. She took the torch and led the way. They trekked underground through the night, stopping only when they reached a sort of hollowed out place from where they could hear people's voices. Zohra called a halt. Curling up on her good arm, she went to sleep immediately. Alex sat beside her to keep watch. It must have been about two hours later, around midmorning when Siddiq gave a bird call. Zohra came awake immediately like someone accustomed to danger. They stood and listened. When they did not hear any voices, Zohra cautiously ascended some rough steps cut into the hollow. Alex, following her saw that they were at the mountainside. Almost opposite them was a village well from which the voices had been coming from earlier on. It was now deserted. The people had gone about their daily businesses. Alex wondered if the villagers knew about the secret tunnel, and where it led to.

There was not much time to wonder, however. Siddiq was there on the other side of the trail holding three donkeys. He held out a bundle. Alex saw that it was a

Burqa. Zohra donned the Burqa. Immediately she became transformed. She climbed a donkey and sat on it sideways like women were wont to do. She held out the kaffiyeh she had been wearing as Il Dhost to Alex. Alex took it and held it at an arms length, not knowing what to do with it. Siddiq laughed. Taking the kaffiyeh from him, he gestured for Alex to sit down then proceeded to wrap it around his head and lower face until only his eyes were showing. Zohra's slender frame shook with laughter. They dared not make noise or attract unnecessary attention to themselves.

His job done, Siddiq led his donkey off the trail. Alex mounted the remaining donkey and they set off after him. Sayed's house was just about two hours away, on the outskirts of Farah. They were led into a room inside the compound and served with refreshments. Alex fell asleep almost immediately. He did not wake up until Zohra was shaking him by the shoulder. It was dusk. People were streaming in and out of the compound. Nobody paid much attention to them as they left. hey entered Farah just as the call to evening prayers was concluding. Nobody took any notice of them as they went into the designated teashop. It was a place frequented by the Americans. Siddiq produced a cell phone and Alex called the base. He had the base call him back. He gave them detailed instructions about what he wanted.

An hour later, an army jeep drew up to the tea shop jammed with men in uniform who were laughing and talking. Half an hour later another one drew up, spilling out yet another group, also talking and laughing. Two hours later, the second jeep left but not with as many people as had come in it. No one took particular note to count. Thirty minutes later the second jeep left, looking as crammed as when it had come. As the shop was about to close for the night, the remaining soldiers left, still laughing and talking as when they had come in. Apparently, they had decided to take advantage of the balmy gap in the cold weather and walk back to the base. By the time they got there, Zohra had long been installed in Laura's room. Alex was just concluding his report to Major Grafton after being absent from the base for two weeks!

CHAPTER 8

∞

Zohra's presence at the army base was totally different from Laura's but no less engaging. Major Grafton had listened to Alex's reasons for bringing her back to the base. He was a little dubious as to how they were "going to gain information from her and enhance their relationship with local factions also resistant to the Taliban." However, he had always trusted Alex's hunches. They had produced good results in the past. Besides, the proposal followed the current principles being pursued by the Allied forces of empowering the natives who were amenable to peace. He had to leave for a tour of duty the next day but was confident there were enough people on the base to keep an eye on things. By the time he returned two weeks later, Zohra was firmly entrenched at the base, and had carved out her own niche.

Where Laura's presence was quiet and calming as she shed her serenity on the men at the base, Zohra's was anything but that. She meekly kept her sling for about a week more and then firmly discarded it against the advice of the medical team. Even before she discarded it, she appointed herself the game critique for the men on their hand and wrist movements when they played recreational ball games. She pointed out how wasteful of resources they were in their mess, their laundry, and even in their transportation. She listened to them discussing imaginary combat strategies and challenged them by playing the devil's advocate. She even actually proposed excellent ideas on how to achieve the same results with less moves or more covertly.

After she took off her sling, she was not averse to sometimes participating in their games.

Alex's attitude puzzled her, however. He studiously avoided her. If she came out to the courtyard during games, he found a reason to go inside. If she was already at the mess when he arrived, he took a table at the other end of the room or hurriedly ate something standing up, then left again. If they happened to be in close proximity, he kept quiet and hardly looked in her face directly. She confronted him once, "I thought the whole essence of my coming was for you to grill me and find out all I knew. When are we going to begin?"

Alex always replied that he was not yet ready; he was busy elsewhere; he would come round to it soon, and so on. Zohra felt annoyed and relieved by turns. She bantered with the men all the time yet found time to bemoan loss of feminine things with the few women who came to the base. However, the only person she ever had any degree of an intimate and meaningful conversation with was Tim. Tim had a natural gift of drawing people out of themselves. In addition to his counselling training, he was an excellent listener. It was with him that Zohra discussed the weightier things that bothered her like the outfit she founded, her hopes for her people, her aim in agreeing to come to the base in the first place, and most of all her frustrations in how Alex was now avoiding her. "I agreed to come because he promised some heart-to-heart talks. I direly needed to have some meaningful talks with someone without the fear of being spied on or being misunderstood. The problem with being a leader is that everyone looked to me for answers when I did not always have one. I had hoped Alex would allow me to bounce a few ideas off him. I had looked forward to not being in charge for some time. Now he hardly even looks at me, not to mention talk to me."

"Hmm," Tim wondered briefly, "I could swear that I catch him staring at you very often."

"That is news. How come I don't catch him at it?"

"Maybe he does it when he's sure you're not looking. If you were to talk to him, what would you have told him?"

"I don't really know for sure. I was hoping he would ask the questions while I would supply the answers. In talking to him, I would be talking to myself and mulling over my ideas."

"Maybe there's something he's waiting for. He will come round to it eventually."

Zohra had to content herself with that.

It was to Tim she told the fullest version of her ordeal. "That murderer killed my brother-in-law, my uncle, and my father in about a day. For the next one month, every night he would come, expecting me to gratefully take him into bed as a husband. I was just twelve years old. I didn't know much but I was determined that if he was going to rape me, he would not get away without scars. "His older wives talked to me about what a great privilege it was to be his wife. They talked of helping me to bath and prepare but I would have none of it. I refused all the food and water they gave me. I was not my mother's daughter for nothing. I knew there were many compounds of opium that could do things to people's consciousness. I was determined to starve to death if need be. "I also knew I had to eat and drink to keep up my strength so I stole out at night to forage for food when I thought people would be asleep. The compound was well-guarded so that I could not easily escape but I was always able to find someone's left over food or pick something from the kitchen garbage. I avoided all attractive food or drink knowing they could be traps. I drank only the ablution water near the mosque in the compound hoping even that was not spiked.

"After about a month of this I was locked in a room and had nothing to eat or drink for five days. I think they were trying to starve me into submission. The day they opened the door and found me drinking my own urine, they decided I was to be sent away. "I remember the mullah's speech as he sent me away. He said I ought to have known what honor I could have brought to my family but now I was bringing an eternal curse of separation from Allah on them. 'The prophet, peace be upon him, married Aisha when she was merely six years old. He married Hafsat when she less than your age. Look what beautiful unions he had with them and what contributions they made to the Hadith. Not wanting such a privilege shows you are not a good Moslem. A curse will be upon you for I cannot help you. I am sending you to my son Nawab. Hopefully, he can tame you. Whatever happens on the way with my men will be upon your head'.

"I should have taken that as a fair warning. However, I was still too young and still very naïve.

"We left on horses. I was the only female among five men. These men were not like the mullah. Every night as we set up camp, they said their evening prayers, and then took turns raping me. I fought, I really fought very hard but what was I, a thirteen-year-old girl against five men? "Two of them held me down; another covered my mouth while the others took their turns raping me. The more I struggled, the more they laughed and seemed to enjoy it. Not one of them showed the minutest compassion, not one! The next morning, they would rise, say their morning prayers, put me on a horse with my wrists tied together and off we would go again.

"By the third day I stopped struggling. I cursed God. I cursed religion. I cursed my parents. I stopped being afraid. I stopped being angry. My spirit just died within me. When I stopped fighting, I think the novelty wore off for them. "Two nights later, when we had been on the road for about a week, they came back to camp with a young girl. She could not have been up to ten years old. Her breasts were not even developed. Like they did to me, they held her down and raped her, laughing while she struggled. That night, nobody touched me or even approached me. I guess they believed they had totally broken my spirit. They did not even bother to tie my hands and legs as they had done every night till then. When they were done raping the girl, they set up the night watch. Four of the men went to sleep. The girl had fainted from pain and exhaustion. I knew exactly how it was.

"If I had a knife that night, I would have killed them while they slept. As it was, I didn't have a knife then. I acquired one later. While they slept, I crept up to the sentry and hit him over the head with a stone. He fell down, grunting. I would have gone to also hit the others. However, I imagined they could wake up and I would lose the advantage I had gained. I dragged the girl over to where the horses were. She was so slight, but I was not that big myself. I took the knife in the belt of the sentry. I roused her enough and somehow managed to get her unto a horse without waking the men. I mounted behind her. Leading the other horses, I rode out of the camp.

"I had no idea of where we were. We had lived at Kabul when I was very young; and later at Qandahar but I had no clear recollections of these places nor knew people in these places. I did not know anybody or anywhere to go to. We had been heading northeast. I decided it was probably the last direction they would search for us in. One thing I knew for sure was that two girls on a horse leading five other horses were going to attract a lot of attention. "As day dawned, when we found ourselves near a village, I cut the horses loose. The girl was now fully awake and aware. Her name was Yelda. She did not want to go home. The men had killed her father and her brother. She did not know what had become of her mother and her little brother. She knew enough to tell me we were close to Jalalabad, and that the Taliban was not popular where we were.

"We tried to avoid villages, towns and cities. We stayed in caves and holes. We had no plans. As soon as the food we got from the saddles of the horses was gone, we did not know what would happen next. Finally, we plucked up courage and went into a village to beg for food. One of the pillars of Islam is Zakat – giving alms to the poor. We approached a marketplace to beg. For two days we got bread, fruits, and nuts. At night we slept in empty market stalls being careful to wake up and leave as soon as morning prayers were called. "On the third day, there was a commotion. We did not know we were the center of attention until one woman practically snatched us off the street and started yelling. 'They're my daughters! They're my daughters!

What do you want with my daughters? Since when did it become a crime to beg? The prophet allows it.'

"Surprised, I looked up at her. Yelda clung to my arm and peed in her pants. The woman was not even looking at us. From behind her, we watched her confronting four burly mosque policemen. Through her Burqa her eyes glittered at them. They tried to stare her down, but she held out. Her husband came out to ask, 'What is it? What is the problem?'

"We clung to her for life. At last, the policemen left. She dragged us further into the shop, and through it to the room behind. She did not even ask us who we were. She gave us food and water. It was not much but that was the first hot meal we had eaten in a long while. That evening, the couple took us to their home. They lived in an Afghan-style compound with three children of their own. She did not explain who we were. Everyone just took it for granted that we belonged with her. Obviously, she did this kind of thing often.

"We noticed something peculiar about the compound. The early morning call to prayer was unusual. The words were different. It still talked about leaving sleep to come and pray. The men still gathered in the mosque to pray but not by the regular bowing down and standing up which we were used to. The women and children gathered in the inner yard to pray but it was also different. "They talked to Jesus and prayed through Jesus. They read from the Bible or told a Bible story. However, it was so different from what we had been used to. The facts of the stories were totally different. It took me and Yelda some time to understand that this Jesus was actually Prophet Isa. The other people they talked about, Prophets Ibrahim, Musa, Dauda, Maryam, were somehow different from those we had known too, all of them.

"Our family has a secret Bible at Farah, but it is never read. It is shown to us when we reach twelve years. At this time, we are told how our ancestors were really Christians. We are then sworn to secrecy on it as part of an initiation into adulthood. My rite of passage had taken place the previous year, so it was still fresh in my mind.

"Births, marriages, and deaths are also recorded in that Bible; but it was never actually opened or read. In fact, only the oldest male member of the family may touch it as the family head, and that, only to make records. On the other hand, we are forced to memorize the entire Quran in Arabic by age seven, at which time a party is called to celebrate the achievement. Of course, we didn't always understand what we memorized but it's there somewhere in our memories. And then, there we were, being introduced to the actual content of the Bible! It was a novel experience.

"Me and Yelda stayed with that family for about a year, and then the mosque police started asking questions. The Taliban was not so strong in that area, but they had representatives. One day, I recognized one of the men who had raped us along the way. It might have been my imagination but in that moment, I felt he also recognized me. He might reclaim me as a runaway wife, and the mosque police would support him. I told Yelda I thought I would need to go and find my way home. I wanted her to remain with the kind family, but she was adamant. She was coming along with me. Somehow, we had become dependent on each other because of our common ordeal at the hands of those men.

"The Kuchi usually passed through town to sell their goods and buy supplies from our benefactors. One day a large group came. They spent about four days. People from their camp came to the unusual worship gatherings of the compound every day. The last thing we did to that family which had been so kind to us before we moved on was to steal some food and some of their sons' clothes. "When the Kuchi moved on at the end of their four-day stay, we went with them, dressed as boys. I have been to see the kind family often in the past few years. They are an important part of our network so I must not tell you particulars which might give them away. Nevertheless, they were the first part of what I became later in life.

"The Kuchi never questioned our presence. We trudged along with them from the first day. One woman began to send us on errands and reward us with food.

Under the broad sky we could live very much as we pleased. The only law seemed to be 'Never lose sight of the group'.

"It was very much a communal life. Eventually, we discovered there were other orphans like us in the camp, but no one would have guessed it. They were mostly girls. We all belonged to one another. "One day, me and Yelda went to gather cow dung which was the fuel used for fires most of the time. There in an opium field, we came across a man trying to rape another little girl. He was alone and she was twisting and struggling to no avail. As your people will say it, I saw red. In that moment I saw him as the embodiment of all those men who had raped me, the mullah who had ordered the execution of my brother-in-law, my uncle, and my father and then ripped me from my family. I forgot all the other men who had ever been kind to me. All the anger that had smoldered in me burst into flames. "Yelda said later that I gave a blood-curdling cry. I don't remember doing so but I must have done something like that because the man stopped what he was doing. He turned a startled face at me as I lunged at him. I still had the knife I had taken from the man whose head I had bashed.

I found myself plunging it into the man again and again. He tried to parry my attack, but I was too furious. I drew blood with my first stab and his right arm hung limp and mangled at his side. He managed to hold me with his left hand but the fury I had was too great. I was fighting with all that I had, my hands, my feet, my teeth, everything. I was much smaller than him, but he had the use of only one hand. "His victim and Yelda kept screaming. They ran back to the camp yelling. The next thing I knew, the man was on the ground gasping while two of the Kuchi were holding me back, and then handing me over to one of their women.

I kept screaming until my voice became hoarse. The woman took me first to a nearby stream and bathed me like a baby. She then took me back to her tent. My eyes felt dry and hot. I couldn't cry, and I couldn't sleep. I stayed awake the whole night. "Around dawn the next morning, I went out alone. I went to the riverside to think. That was where I had a visitation.

I am convinced it was Jesus Christ himself. I have asked myself over and over what He looked like, what He sounded like. I can't say for sure. I didn't even see His face, only His bare feet. His voice was in my head so I can't say if it was like thunder or like many waters. But I know what His presence was like. It was like a mother's hug or like a soft wool blanket on a very cold night. It was warm and safe, intimate and comforting. I know because I still feel it from time to time. Am I making sense?"

Tim assured her that she was.

"I feel awkward sharing this. However, I know some others who have had similar experiences. Anyway, that early morning, there He was with me at the riverside. Frankly, I was thinking of ending my life. I had no hope, no goal, nothing. I felt dead and empty inside. "When we were with those Christians near Jalalabad, I already hated the God of the Moslems. I wanted nothing to do with the Christians' God. I told myself if I ever met Him, I would ask Him where He was when I was being starved, raped, and denied my family's comfort. Here He was, and all I wanted to do was fall at his feet and remain there forever. I had absolutely nothing to say. I kept weeping in shame for my worthlessness. "He did all the talking. He told me He knew me and had great plans for me. I was to go with the Kuchi to Pakistan and learn all I could about Him. I was to get baptized because He was bringing me back for a specific job among my own people. He told me I would get back to my mother one day, and He had great plans for her too. There were so many other things but as He left, He tucked me into a hollow close by. "I slept the whole day. When I woke up, I was clutching this smooth pebble which was a rarity in that particular area of Afghanistan though very common elsewhere. It was a polished nugget of lapis lazuli. In its center shone a perfect white cross. Without the stone, I still would have believed, but I have treasured it since then. It reminds me that I have a purpose to fulfill.

"To my surprise, the Kuchi did not flee the area as they were reputed to do whenever there was trouble. They located the family of the little girl and stood by them while charges were leveled against the man who had tried to rape her. I don't know how it was all settled. I was never indicted nor called to give witness. I don't know what I would have done. We moved a week later. Just as I had seen in my vision, we crossed the border into Pakistan. There were so many Kuchi camps there holding an annual festival. Afterwards, our own group moved deeper into Pakistan. That was when I was first properly introduced to a Bible. "I read it through twice, and God spoke to me very directly through it. I also had a lot of questions. Thankfully, very willing and knowledgeable teachers were available. They too, had also searched for, and found answers. By the end of a year, I asked to be baptized. Me and Yelda were accepted and baptized the same day. There was a lot to learn. We spent the following year doing so. The original Kuchi group we came with had since left but we now belonged to the family of God. I had blood relatives in Pakistan at the time and even now. However, I didn't know how to go about contacting them or asking for help.

"I told those kind people that I wanted to go and find my own people. I did not mean my brother who was somewhere in Pakistan then, nor other of our relatives there. When I said my people, I meant my mother back at Farah. One day, the person in charge of the compound told me there was a Kuchi group headed towards Farah; would we want to go with them? I jumped at the chance. Yelda did not know where her family was. She did not want to go back to them, anyway. Wherever I went, Yelda went. We joined the Kuchi group. "There were Christians and Moslems in the group but they lived together tolerantly. They did not snitch on one another. Each group practised its own religion as it saw fit. Me and Yelda shared with the camp children what we had been learning. We even made a few converts among them. Their parents objected. Tensions arose. The elders told us to desist. We tried, but we were mere children even though I was all of sixteen years old then. "The Moslem children still asked us questions. We answered them without guile except that we began to communicate in whispers. They too, now knew better than to run to the adults with what we were saying. In less than two months on the road we were at Farah and O what a glorious reunion with my people. The rest, they say, is history."

Intrigued, Tim asked "So what happened to Yelda?"

"She returned home with me. My mother accepted her as her own daughter. She has since acquired several such daughters. Yelda is more of a homebody than me. She felt secure staying with my mother while I go 'traipsing round the countryside' as Alex so colorfully put it. "About five years ago, she married one of my cousins. They live at Farah. She has never found what might have been left of her birth family. I continue to make discreet enquiries, but I have not located any of them. She is my mother's daughter now in every sense of the word."

Zohra shared with Tim her campaign activities in the roughly ten years she had led her group, including the triumphs and the losses. She shared her plans and her frustrations. She told him the reason they had for kidnapping Greta, Laura, and Lil.

"We realized that rescuing the children was not enough. We also had to give them a future, a hope, a focus in life, and a means of supporting themselves. Officially, we would never have been allowed to even consult with UNESCO officials. We needed teachers trained on a large scale, and we could not send out our own teachers covertly for training. It was really a desperate measure. However, we had been watching and praying for such an opportunity. When we saw it, we seized it! I cannot say now that I am sorry or anything like that. We only hope they will come to forgive us and bless us one day."

Unofficially, Tim assured her that the women were already blessing them. Overall, three of them thought that their kidnap and eventual release was the highest point of their stay in Afghanistan. Officially, he told her never to admit to the kidnap, ever!

Zohra also shared the frustrations of living the Christian life in Afghanistan with Tim but added, "Perhaps, it's the challenge of it that keeps us going. We have clear-cut lines and choices. I guess it is not like that in your own part of the world. Here we make decisions knowing we could die for them or lose everything for them. Nevertheless, we choose to follow Christ anyway. It is infinitely easier, and more exciting to be a Christian here" she said.

Tim understood what she was trying to say but obliged her by arguing the point a bit. "It is easier to be a Christian in our own part of the world. You can read your Bible openly; attend church meetings when you want; and openly share your faith with anyone. In fact, in places like London, you have the Hyde Park Corner where you can set up a soap box and shout your faith to all takers. The same thing could happen at the Times Square in New York."

"So how many people actually do those things?" Zohra asked astutely.

Tim answered her with a sad shake of his head, "Not enough, not nearly enough. In fact, most Christians in the so-called Free World do not know enough about their faith. They cannot negotiate their way through the Bible, even though everyone can have as many copies of the Bible as they want. Majority of Christians go to church only for weddings or funerals. A few more also go for occasions like a Christmas service. Some others feel that if they can give God an hour of a church service a week, they have done a lot. Christianity is very watery and meaningless in the West now I am afraid to say."

"You know what will happen" prophesied Zohra. "A vacuum will be created. A new generation of young people will come up seeking for the meaning of life. When they do not find it anywhere, Satan will introduce them to some other alternatives. You know that was how Islam prevailed around here a long time ago. Even now, the Taliban gives meaning to those who had lapsed in their faith. Your countries are in trouble. Your people just don't know it yet."

Tim agreed but did not want to delve more deeply into this area with her.

They talked about killing in battle. "I am sure I have killed my own share of people. However, it is something I try to avoid by all means. My mother compounded something with which we can knock them off for about four to six hours while we make our escape. It doesn't always work because they aim to kill us while we aim to keep them alive. Sometimes too, when they're knocked off some other elements come along to rob or kill them, so indirectly we killed them anyway. "It's not easy for our group but we have learned to live by our wits, and God has been very merciful. So far, we have not had a lot of casualties; but for every casualty I still feel if we had killed those people the last time, they would not have lived to kill one of us the next time. It's really tough but did the Bible not say that the weapons of our warfare are not physical? I feel we are no less than them if we resort to using their own weapons and methods. "Inevitably, I have factions in my own camp who disagree with this view. One cannot always convince all the people, all the time. I do not have much ambition. I settle for carrying along most of the people, most of the time."

When Zohra looked back at her stay at the army base, she always felt God took her there to be trained and polished by Tim. About ten days into her stay, he connected her by Skype to the ladies her outfit had kidnapped. He led in with "We have a very special guest here at the base that is very eager to speak with you."

The ladies proclaimed themselves eager to meet with this guest too. Tim turned the camera on Zohra. Zohra recognized them immediately of course but they did not know who she was.

"Wow" said Greta.

"She's beautiful" crooned Lil.

"Who is she?" asked Laura, and not without a twinge of jealousy.

Zohra clapped her hands and whooped with glee. "Hi ladies" she said in her throaty melodic voice. "It is nice to finally speak to you without trappings."

"Have we met before?" asked Lil.

"How come I don't remember you?" asked Greta.

"Wonderful joke, Tim" said Laura.

Zahra whooped again and taking up her ever-present kaffiyeh, proceeded to expertly wind it round her head until only her green eyes were glittering from within the folds. When she looked up all the three ladies gasped out at once, "Il Dhost!"

"Speak only in whispers, ladies" she whispered theatrically. "This is a secret mission. You never know who might be listening."

She laughed again and took off the kaffiyeh. They had so many questions to ask but Tim told them they were classified information. "However, if you all agree to come out for Easter, I will personally see to it that all your questions are answered!"

"Bribery does not befit you, Preach" Greta said. "Just say you want to see one of us in particular."

"Oh, but I am seeing all of you now. I just wanted you to come, relax, and wind down." Tim parried.

"Speak for yourself Greta. I for one will very much like to go" Lil said assertively. "Laura's vote goes without saying."

"Sorry, Greta" Tim said. "It appears you are outvoted."

"I haven't said anything yet" Laura said petulantly. "I don't like competition."

"Who is competing with whom?" Zohra asked.

"Preach, the beautiful ladies are asking you to declare your leanings" Greta clarified for Tim.

Tim blushed but Lil came to his rescue. "Don't worry Padre. We're very sure of where your heart belongs. Laura knows there's no competition or she would have stopped talking a long time ago and become stony." Laura feigned a punch at her. Lil feigned a collapse, panting, "Il Dhost, beware! Beware!"

Thereafter they talked and laughed freely like old friends. Everyone avoided mention of the postponed wedding. The ladies understood it had to do with Zohra now being at the Marine base, however. The bride and groom to be had felt it was a divine intervention and were still ostensibly praying about it.

They met on Skype one more time before Zohra left the base. "No" she told them, "I do not hope to be here at the base when you come at Easter. How about I arrange for us to meet at Asmaa's place for Easter? I understand you enjoyed your stay there very much. I know that Zohra would really like to get to know you all. Il Dhost has his impediments!"

They promised to discuss it among themselves and get back to her with an answer.

Uncharacteristically, Alex was not around for these two meetings. The ladies just assumed he had become very busy. That was not unusual.

CHAPTER 9

∞

When Major Grafton returned, he observed the happenings at his command. For the first two days, he was busy with paperwork and catching up with what had gone on in his absence. By the third day, he observed Zohra playing basketball with the men through the window of his office. He saw her again at the mess holding court and laughing with the young men. He reserved his comments. The next morning, he sent for Alex to report on his progress.

"Frankly" Alex admitted, "I have not interviewed her at all."

Major Grafton was silent, indicating that he was waiting for further explanations. Alex began to crack his knuckles nervously. "I have found neither the right time nor the right atmosphere to interview her, sir."

"The truth, Officer, I want the truth! Me and You do not have the time to bandy words" Major Grafton was getting angry.

"The truth sir is that I have not felt comfortable interviewing her. I have tried to create the right mood and atmosphere but have found myself incapable of total objectivity."

"She has been here for over two weeks."

"Yes, Sir."

"I see" Major Grafton said, and he really did see. There were undertones and currents here which with hindsight, and having seen the lady in question, were not totally unexpected. "You do realize this is totally unacceptable from an officer of the United States army. You know what the rules are."

"I am aware of those, Sir" Alex replied looking as miserable as Major Grafton had ever seen him look.

"I see," the C.O said again. "And can you not assign some other officer to debrief her?"

"One of the conditions for her agreeing to come was that I would personally do the debriefing, Sir."

"In that case, I suggest you find time. Create the right atmosphere as soon as possible. Finish the job."

"Yes, Sir" replied Alex.

As he turned to go, Major Grafton added, "Another thing... please watch your backside. I would not want to institute disciplinary actions against you. Is that clear?"

"I understand sir." Alex saluted and left.

The interview had not gone well at all. When in a pleasant mood, His commanding officer called him "Alex". In official mode, he addressed him as "Lieutenant". "Officer" was reserved for when the C.O was very angry with him. Alex admitted there was every justifiable reason for this. He would try to redeem himself, do a good job, and make a report to his commanding officer. He would try to get Zohra away from the base as quickly as possible. He admitted to himself that he was in a quandary as far as the lady was concerned. She managed to twist his life into knots without even making any effort to do so. He avoided her as much as he could because he found himself wanting to do things to her, and with her which were totally inappropriate for an officer of the United States army. He found himself getting angry and jealous at her easy interaction with the other men. He had to restrain himself so many times from just going to snatch her away and give her a thorough shaking or a proper kiss. He caught himself wishing for this more and more often. He even got jealous of the cup she used to drink, and the food going into her mouth. It was insane. He gave himself a mental shake.

Fraternizing too intimately with locals was forbidden. Romantic attachments were even more forbidden. The men in the ranks had been known to circumvent this. They had gone as far as secretly, or even overtly marrying the native women, and then making their cases with the public afterwards. Human rights activism was a natural American culture. Every cause always found supporters. However, an officer of the United States army had the trust of the president. He was expected to brutally cut off anything personal which would in any way impinge upon or compromise this loyalty to president and country. Fraternizing with or marrying the natives, especially in an enemy territory during an ongoing conflict was definitely one of such things. Perhaps bringing her back to the base had not been the smartest idea after all.

The next day, late in the morning when Major Grafton was thinking of taking a lunch break, there was a firm knock on the door of his office, the kind of knocking that had character. The aide who should have been at the outer office had gone on an errand for him. Thinking it must be one of his men, Major Grafton grunted "Come in". He was immediately surprised to see Zohra in his office. She paused at the threshold and said, "I really want to see you but if now is not a convenient time, I could come back some other time."

Major Grafton had to hand it to her for guts and poise. He honestly was not doing anything serious at the time but felt ill-prepared for her at that moment. However, considering there was never going to be a better time, and curious as to whatever she had come for, he asked her to come in and take a seat.

Without preamble she went straight to the point. "I'd like to thank you very much Sir, for having me over here at your base. It has been a quiet period of healing and recuperation. I want you to know that I am very grateful for it." She took a breath. Since Major Grafton made no comments other than to slightly incline his head, she went on. "I however need to get back to my own people. I have an organization to run. I know I have not in any way paid for the hospitality I have received here but I will ever be in your debt. I will oblige you with my services whenever you need it."

"And what would those services be?" Major Grafton asked suggestively, leaning back in his chair.

Zohra did not even have the shame to flush. Maybe she did, but the lighting in the room was too dim for Major Grafton to notice it. "I mean of course that I could put people and intelligence at your disposal if you ever needed such, seeing as we have a superior knowledge of the terrain and of people's moods and loyalties around here."

Major Grafton decided that it would not hurt to also be straightforward. "I see. Do you have designs on any of my officers?"

Zohra frowned, not understanding him at first. Slowly and tentatively, she answered, "I have no designs at all on any of your officers. I like pitting my strength and intelligence against theirs. We also like competitions as you do in your own country, and I have had nothing else to occupy my time."

Major Grafton decided he had not been straightforward enough, so he launched a full-frontal attack. "What is going on between you and Lieutenant Pearson?"

Zohra's frown deepened. Her eyebrows went up, making her even more beautiful. Slowly, speculatively she answered, "Nothing is going on between Lieutenant Pearson and me; which I find all the more puzzling. I accepted his invitation to come here to be interrogated but he has been avoiding me, as your people would say, like the plague! I have tried confronting him, but he avoids me very studiously."

"And why do you think that is so? What could be frightening him?"

She shook her head. And then the light of understanding dawned on her mind, reflecting on her face. "You think I frighten him because he has some romantic attraction to me?" Zohra laughed shortly. And then in a surprisingly bitter voice she said, "You don't know enough about me. If you did, you would understand how far this could be from the truth. You are a wise man Major, but some things are too far from plausible."

Major Grafton did not think he was too far from plausible as she put it. However, this was a course he did not wish to progress, so he did not pursue it. He said now, "Please enjoy our hospitality for a few more days. Within that period, I hope Lieutenant Pearson will do what he had set out to do originally. "Of course, you are not confined here against your will. You may leave whenever you wish to. We are grateful that you agreed to ally yourself with us. We hope to find many occasions to call on this alliance in the future. May our two organizations be of mutual benefit to each other."

Zohra nodded. Getting up, she said, "Thank you very much for seeing me."

She left the room, her mind very full of half-formed thoughts.

Alex was away on an assignment for a few days. Coming back, he saw what he assumed was the shadow of Zohra on the curtain of Laura's room. Tim was getting ready for dinner when Alex walked in and asked if he could tell Zohra to meet him, Alex, at The Rose Balcony an hour after dinner.

The Rose Balcony faced a small ornate garden with an ornamental fountain of a cherubic child perpetually pouring water into a basin. A smile called an observer's mind to the great pleasure the child derived from this mundane activity. Someone had started a rose garden round the fountain. Every succeeding group at the base usually had at least one person fanatically devoted to keeping up the beauty of the garden. Two park benches had been put there so that people could enjoy it on sun-soaked days or on balmy evenings. Some windows faced onto the balcony, but it was secluded enough that even when craning fully out, only the furthest parts of the garden could be seen from the house. It was a place to come to be alone and meditate. Because it was so small, it favored individuals rather than groups. Tim and Laura had loved coming there a lot on those evenings when they had plenty to say to each other.

On this particular evening, no one was in the garden. It was a bit cold because winter was still in the air, even though there was the occasional warm draft from the plains.

Zohra arrived a full half hour early, but Alex was already there. He was walking down the far end of the garden with his hands in his pockets, seemingly examining the dried-out plants. When Zohra caught sight of him, she paused, her heart racing. A gasp escaped from her throat. Alex turned. Without planning it, he just opened his arms and Zohra ran into them sobbing.

She was just comfortably a head shorter than him. She fit into the circle of his arms and against his body as if it were made just for her. He held her with one arm and stroked her hair and her back softly, murmuring into her ears. "Oh Darling, don't cry. Don't cry my sweetheart. I love you so much. Oh Honey…"

He did not know so much endearment was in him, yet he felt that he lacked all the words to express all of it. Zohra clung to him weeping with love, dragging air into her lungs with difficulty, but enjoying the sheer pleasure of being held by him. She inhaled the smell of him, his soap, his aftershave, his lotion, and just that smell that was so peculiarly him. It felt so familiar, so him. It was as if she had known that smell all her life. At last, she lifted her face. With his thumb he wiped away some of her tears. Bending lower, he kissed her lips. It was everything he had imagined it would be, and more. Her lips were soft, sweet, yielding, and kissing him right back. They held each other and swayed, almost falling. At last, when they surfaced for breath she asked, "Oh Alex, what are we going to do? What on earth are we going to do?"

He led her to a park bench and sat down still cuddling her. He stroked those glorious tresses he had been longing to touch. "I have been thinking and going round and round it but first things first. I don't apologise for loving you. It is the most wonderful thing that has ever happened to me."

"To me too" Zohra said. "I love you Alex, with my whole heart. I think I began to love you since that day you cut my bonds and rubbed life into my hands and feet again. I just didn't realize I did, or how much until Major Grafton pointed it out to me."

"You spoke with my commanding officer? Aren't you something?"

"You bet! We had quite a conversation too."

"I think you captivated me that first time too. I always felt so inappropriately drawn to the glittering green eyes of the Il Dhost. However, it took your mother's confrontation for me to put my feelings into perspective and then into words."

"My mother knows? How come my mother knows you love me before I did?" she asked playfully chagrined.

"I am telling you she knew even before I did. That was mostly why she allowed me to carry you away."

"What mother would do something like that, I ask you?"

"The wisest and best of mothers, I assure you. But this brings us to the real problem. I would have liked to take you out there and proclaim it to the whole world that I love, and I am loved by the most beautiful and the bravest of all women."

"But you dare not!"

I have been asking myself why not? What would it cost me? I want you to be in every part of my life. I cannot imagine living without you Zohra."

"Nor can I imagine living without you now that I have found you. O Alex there is so much about me that you don't know. You might not think me the same person when you do know!"

"You mean things like your forced marriage at twelve, and your eventual return; or the consequences of your crusades around the countryside?"

Startled Zohra looked at him. "How did you know all that?"

"I would have liked to dazzle and impress you by telling you that it is my work to gather intelligence, but your mother told me part of it. However, after unmasking you, I have learned quite a lot about your recent activities. Wherever I go, I find myself wanting to talk about you, needing to hear about you."

"My mother must like you a lot. That is not a story that she shares easily. But even she does not know it all."

"I agree. There are even a lot more attributed to you that even you yourself probably do not know, like mystical powers. For instance, do you know that three days ago Il Dhost put some Taliban men to flight by causing their horses to bolt in a village twenty miles from here while rescuing some girls on their way back from the well? And all along I thought you were here at the base recovering from a dislocated shoulder!" Zohra laughed. "Do you think there is anything that I can uncover about you that would make me stop loving you Zohra?"

She could not think of any. She kissed him soundly to let him know. But there were still obstacles. "There is nothing I am likely to hear about you, or that you can do to make me stop loving you too, Alex but you know there are obstacles."

"Which are...?"

"Your commanding officer told me more or less to keep my tentacles off you. That was before I even knew I had any. Ssh" she said as Alex was about to say something. "I have spent the last few days finding out what your laws and rules say about a situation like ours. I would have run away a few days ago but I tried to keep my word to Major Grafton to wait and be debriefed by you. Alex you must not be dishonorably discharged from the army. Think of what it would mean to you, to me, to your parents... "Sssh" she hushed as Alex tried to interrupt again. "I know I could never live with myself knowing I came between you and what you love to do most. And then there is me. I have a work to do among my own people too. Yes, I am trying to decentralize and disburse power. Nevertheless, I know this work to me is a lifetime commitment. I will always be here as long as my people need me. I can never leave this land. I received it as a commission from God, and I want to think I owe Him allegiance more than I owe you."

She could feel Alex emotionally withdraw even though he still continued to hold her. "Are you saying this thing we have between us is not of God? Why then would He allow it if we are never meant to be together?"

"I am not saying it is not of God. In fact, I am saying that because I am sure it is of God, He is going to make a way. However, we need to give Him time."

Alex continued to hold her and to stroke her hair, but He was thinking deeply. At last, he said "How much time do you suggest we give to God? Should we give Him ten minutes, an hour, a day, or two?" Zohra laughed but Alex continued with a very serious tone. "I want to marry you Zohra. I want to make a home with you, and that, as soon as possible."

"I know" Zohra said in a very subdued voice, "I know. That is what I want too!"

They both fell silent again until at last Alex said, "You know what just happened here and there were no fireworks, no ringing of bells and no blaring of trumpets?"

"What?" Zohra raised her head from his shoulder and looked into his face.

He gazed down at her with shining eyes "We just got engaged. This was not how I imagined engagements should happen. I should get down on one knee and offer you an expensive ring which has been in my family for generations. Bells would then ring, people will cheer, and you know, the works..."

Zohra silenced him with a kiss. "Of course, I will be glad to marry you, Alex, as soon as we find a way."

He kissed her again and held her as if he was planning never to let her go. It was some time before they surfaced. He said, "We should begin your debriefing tomorrow. That was what I originally wanted to tell you."

"Is there anything which you don't already know?" She asked.

"A lot, probably. You have quite a reputation out there. Instead of the usual questionings and prodding, why don't I write up what I have? We will then sit together to decide what goes into the final report?"

"That sounds okay to me. However, I suspect it's going to be very hard working with you. "

Alex laughed. They spent over four hours of the night doing what lovebirds all over the world do. They talked of sweet meaningless nothings, as well as shared deep philosophies which had ruled their lives. They discovered they had a lot in common notwithstanding their widely different backgrounds. They deliberately avoided talking about the future but felt their common faith in Christ would find them a way over every obstacle. They talked about those who were dear to them. They talked about the troubles of the country they found themselves in at the moment, and the military strategies for defending it because they had it most in common at the moment. They talked and cuddled until Zohra pointed out how inappropriate it would seem if someone saw them there. Alex looked at his watch. Realizing it would soon be daylight he jumped up and made to escort her to her room. Before they got into the building again, they paused and shared one more embrace. "I'm so glad I found you, Zohra." Alex sighed.

"And I am glad I found you too. I love you so much Alex."

Reluctantly they parted and went their separate ways with springy steps despite all the odds they knew were stacked against them.

Chapter 10

---∞---

Just as Zohra had predicted, working with Alex proved to be very difficult. They had agreed that their love should be secret but how secretive could one get? If either entered a room where the other already was, their eyes would be drawn irresistibly to each other. As much as they tried, a smile of pleasure always escaped. Alex tried to keep avoiding her as he had been doing but it was becoming more and more difficult. He yearned to be with her every minute of the day. He realized that Major Grafton's fears, or the fears of whoever instituted those rules, were not unfounded.

Two of them had agreed that Alex would write out his impressions the following day, and then they would meet two days afterwards to start going through them. However, the very next night at dinner, Alex could not bear it anymore. He approached the table that Zohra was sharing with Tim and two other men. He said to her, "I need to see you again today, same time, and same venue."

She nodded. One of the men remarked, "Geez! He looks as if he could bite off someone's head. Better you than me, Zohra."

Tim, observing them shrewdly said, "I beg to differ on the biting off of heads. Nevertheless, I agree he means business though."

"As I said again Zohra, better you than me. Good luck!"

Later when they met, Alex and Zohra had a lot to chuckle about. Again, they spent most of the night talking, kissing, and embracing. Their parting would have been harder than the last time except for the prospect of meeting the next morning to begin their debriefing.

Alex had worked the whole day to type up his notes. However, he kept getting interrupted by images of Zohra across the pages. He saw how she smiled, her teeth gleaming like smooth white pearls. He saw the way her brows rose and arched when she was thinking something over. He saw the little dimples at the sides of her mouth that came and went as she talked. He saw the glittering of her green eyes with anger or with amusement. He saw the smooth sweep of her neck; the silky smoothness of her skin; and her hair… ah her hair like a glorious sunset… Alex did not know he was such a romantic with so much poetry inside him. Many times, he had to call himself to order. However, working away the rest of the night, he finally had something to at least begin with.

The next day they met at ten o'clock sharp. Alex had commandeered one of the interrogation rooms. At the door he had left a notice which said, "Do not Disturb, Interview in Progress."

They started soberly enough but were soon in gales of laughter over Alex's attempt at formality. They soon found themselves in each other's arms until Zohra said, "Drunk with love! That is what we are. We are drunk with love."

They separated and went to sit at opposite ends of the long table but a few minutes later Alex had to show Zohra something he had written. There he was at her own end of the table. When she frowned into his eyes trying to find the right words to explain something else, they found themselves tangled together again until one of them surfaced and they tried to sober up again. When it was time for dinner, Alex called a halt. They had not accomplished a lot. "Shall we meet at The Rose Balcony again after dinner?" He asked.

"You bet!" Zohra said, trying to sound American. This caused both of them to break down again in laughter. Oh! to be able to laugh with someone with whom one was in love, totally unfettered and unburdened! Even if this was the only thing they had in common, it was priceless. Their third night at The Rose Balcony was interrupted by another person who came out to enjoy some solitude. Fortunately for them they were not caught in a compromising position. They were just sitting on the bench talking. They left early promising to do a lot of work the next day. "Tell you what" Zohra suggested, "Why don't you give me what you have written? I will go through it tonight so that when we meet, I will already know where to make alterations and corrections."

It was a sound idea but… Alex realized that his reluctance was in the amount of time it would take away from their being together. At the end, he reasoned that their love might just be like that. They would maximally enjoy what they had whenever they had it!

When he went to get the sheaf of papers from his room, he met Tim on the way. "Where have you been?" Tim asked. "I have hardly had the time to talk to you since you came back."

"Hang onto that thought," Alex answered. "I will be right back. I want to talk to you as well." He zoomed past, found the papers, took them to Zohra, and kissed her a quick "Goodnight". They were not in a secluded place. And then he went to see Tim in his room.

"Preach, I am in a really bad situation. I could use a friend right now!" he began.

"It's about Zohra" Tim said. It was a statement, not a question.

"Yes" Alex acknowledged, surprised. "How did you know?"

"It's written all over you. I know because I am still in it myself. Maybe when you are the one involved you are often the last person to see it."

"It's that obvious huh?"

"Maybe it's that obvious to me because I am close enough to it. I can't say any other person has noticed it or maybe they have just not commented on what they noticed."

"Except maybe for the C.O?" Alex said somberly

"Major Grafton! What did he say?" Tim asked, surprised. "Zohra said he was the one who opened her eyes to her true feelings. Apparently, he chewed her out for trying to divert me from my duties."

"Wow! That introduces other elements, very serious elements. But you know the rules, Alex."

"Don't I just? I might not have been the one who wrote them, but I certainly put my signature to my own bit. I had even helped to implement them on at least two occasions in the past few years. What am I going to do Tim? What am I going to do? This is nothing at all like you and Laura."

"It certainly isn't. Nevertheless, that does not make it any less beautiful. Zohra is a very special girl, Alex."

"Yeah, I'm so lucky. But tell that to the bureaucrats! I don't see any way-out Tim. I have thought of resigning my commission or even simply deserting."

"And smearing your name? Disgracing your family and your calling? Are these what Zohra wants for you?"

"She's firmly discouraging me from doing anything like that but where is the way forward Tim? What should we do?"

For a moment both men kept silent. Finally, Tim said, "I have no trite answers. However, this is what I know: if the hand of God is in this, and I sense that it is, He will surely show you a way forward."

"That is exactly what Zohra keeps saying. Have you been doing my girl behind my back, Preach?" Alex asked with mock seriousness.

Tim laughed. "She's too fiery for me, I can assure you. I much prefer my serene Laura. I will never have enough of her. She's peerless! I just commiserate with you, in love."

Alex laughed for the first time. "That is the poet in you talking, Preach. I just discovered I am a poet too. I don't know what it is about love that does that to a man; but each to his own taste Preach, each to his own. I feel better already. Can we pray about this right now?"

And they did. Alex had a childlike way of praying which Tim never failed to find refreshing and sometimes entertaining. He always "Let God have it" whether "it" was praises or petitions. In a way he felt the burden his friend must be under. Nevertheless, he was tremendously happy that Alex had found the kind of happiness with Zohra which he himself had found with Laura. It was once-in-a-lifetime occurrence.

Prayers over, Tim told Alex about Zohra's conversation with the girls about spending Easter in the Afghan countryside. Very soon they were talking about the planned wedding which Alex's adventure had ruined. Alex did not feel bitter at all towards his friend for having such easy luck when he himself still had a lot to plough through, and almost no hope. Life seemed too good to him at the moment, and Tim was such a dear friend. A man in love could afford to be generous.

Zohra's debriefing the next day went much faster than the previous day even though they sat together. They yielded to their impulse of maintaining contact by playing footsie under the table. After lunch, a signal came in that required Alex to leave the base in two days' time. He had to be away for about a week. "I'll be gone before you return" Zohra told him quietly.

Alex smiled sadly and bravely. "I know" he said. "I talked and prayed with Tim yesterday. I have no definite resolutions. However, I know I had this feeling that we should maximally enjoy any time we get to be together, not knowing when next we will meet. At least whenever we are together, we should create enough memories to live on for the times we would be apart."

It made a lot of sense to Zohra. "So, The Rose Balcony this evening?"

"You bet," Alex said, and they laughed.

That night when they met, there was another person already at The Rose Balcony. They sat at the further bench. They dared not share even a hug. Alex opened his hand and in his palm was an old British penny with a hole in the center. It was on a chain with one of his dog tags. "I don't have an engagement ring to give you now" he said in a low tone "but these are things which have a lot of meaning to me. My grandfather gave me this coin from his collection a long time ago and I have cherished it. Always be mine, Zohra. One day we will make it more concrete."

Zohra also had something to give him. She brought out the lapis lazuli with the white cross at its center which had been on a locket round her neck. She gave it to Alex and then told him the story about it. When she finished, they clung to each other and wept, not caring who was looking. But the other occupant of the garden had long since turned in.

The next day when they met in the interrogation room, it was to put finishing touches to Alex's report. They then talked about how to meet and drop messages for each other, secret signals, and modes of contact. She hugged him tight, and he held her no less tightly. If it was possible, they would have become physically absorbed into each other.

The next day, feigning indifference to each other, Alex and his team gave a ride to Zohra on their way to their mission. They each nevertheless wept inside but clung onto the hope which they had bred the previous night. They let her off at the entrance of the Namaksar police station. They did not even wait to see her emerge approximately one hour later as Il Dhost.

Just round the corner Siddiq waited with donkeys. Into the mountainside, through some secret passages, two and a half hours later, she was reunited with her favorite horse which whinnied in pleasure and recognition. Il Dhost had returned.

CHAPTER 11

∞

On a few occasions that month, the American marines based at Farah had cause to meet with the Il Dhost outfit. As always, Il Dhost spoke through another person. Always however, as soon as the meeting was over, the leaders of both teams found time to go riding off together into the mountains or plains.

It was becoming harder and harder to restrict their physical contact to just hugs and kisses. Both Alex and Zohra were becoming more and more miserable and frustrated. "Sometimes being a Christian and maintaining chastity outside of marriage can be so hard. Let's elope" Alex suggested. "Surely you know where we can go and get married secretly."

"Are you willing to do that for me?" Zohra asked.

"Not for you" Alex corrected, "with you! Can't you guess that goes without saying Shirineman?" he asked, using the Afghan term of endearment. In their Dari lessons he had laughed at his men trying to learn such phrases. Now, not only was he familiarly using them, but he was having them used about him too. Love can change a man in more ways than one.

"That is good of you to say Joonam," Zohra replied, "because I can come up with something." An idea was already crystallizing in her mind.

Alex looked at her narrowly. She refused to divulge what she had in mind until she was good and ready.

The next time they met, Zohra told him, "Greta, Laura, and Lil talked of coming for Easter to the countryside on my invitation. Can you and Tim also get away to Qandahar at about the same time? Of course, you cannot all travel together. I can arrange for some of you to come through Kabul, and some through Tarin Kowt. Don't tell anyone but if you don't change your mind, we should be able to get married at that occasion."

Alex believed her. He loved this woman so much that he could trust her with more than his life. He did not tell anyone except Tim. He suggested to him that both of them go with the ladies for the Easter getaway to one of Zohra's hideaways. "It will be a unique opportunity to get to see the countryside, and to do those baptisms very secretly."

Tim thought it was a splendid idea. He and Laura had finally decided to wait until her term with UNESCO was over in August before they got wedded, there at Farah. This did not stop his wanting to be with Laura. Springtime in the Afghan countryside with no thought of duty was something to look forward to.

Inasmuch as he did not want to deceive his parents, Alex knew what he was doing was going to be very difficult to explain in a few words over the internet. He wanted above all things to tell his mother about Zohra and to introduce them to each other. For the meantime, their courtship was classified information. He began a series of letters which he never posted, telling Libby all about Zohra. He described how he saw her, how he felt about her, what his hopes and fears about a future with her were. And because he was hoping never to post those letters, he really poured out his innermost thoughts in them, holding back nothing, editing nothing, not even his language as he would have, so as not to shock her.

In his emails and Skype sessions with them however he told his parents that with his next leave, he would not be coming home unless there was a dire emergency. "Some of our colleagues, Laura, and me will be taking a tour of the countryside at that time instead. This will be our last opportunity to do this kind of thing before Laura's time is up."

"Is it safe?" asked Roy. "We hear about all the things going on in Afghanistan and what they do to foreigners."

"I can assure you that it is safe, Dad. I wouldn't dream of putting Laura in danger."

Libby purred like a satisfied cat. The time away must be softening Alex up towards women in general, and Laura in particular. She had known about Laura in captivity, and prayed right along. It was natural that Alex should take the lead in trying to find her. She had spoken with Laura by Skype over the Christmas period after they had been found and came to recuperate at the base. In Libby's mind, there was nothing like getting a stallion in heat by constantly throwing a filly before it. Libby felt she was that much closer to having Laura as a daughter-in-law than ever. Consequently, she fully sanctioned the Easter get-together in lieu of Alex coming home on leave. She encouraged them to go. "Don't worry" she told her husband. "Laura is a very sensible girl. Alex will not let anything go wrong. You kids have a good time" she told Alex. "We shall look forward to the next time you can come."

The major obstacle was Major Grafton. He was skeptical about his two Lieutenants deciding to go to Qandahar for their vacations, especially Alex who would ordinarily have gone to see his parents back home under these circumstances. The fact that Alex's mood had become chipper after his talk with Zohra was not lost on his commander. Major Grafton concluded that Alex must be keeping the lady as a mistress somewhere. The law frowned on officers having foreign wives but accepted their keeping foreign mistresses. Apparently, mistresses required less commitment and demanded less loyalty. At the end though, the C.O could not keep the men from their merited vacations, especially since it was not hampering their duties. Tim was supposed to hold Easter services with the men. However, he knew better how to do that job. Besides, if he went with the group, he was more likely to keep them all in line. And so Major Grafton sanctioned the getaway for Tim too.

Greta, Laura, and Lil were excited about the visit to Asmaa. They were even more excited when they learned that Tim and Alex were coming as well. When they learned about the opportunity for baptism, they nearly touched heaven. A phone call later, Bjorn was included in the party. Easter coincided with the Nimruz break. Their understudies insisted on taking time off for the break. Ayesha did not mind having them out of the house. The story was that they were going to Qandahar for the break and meeting up with Tim, Alex, and Bjorn. Ayesha sensed that Romance was in the air. She urged them to take lots of pictures.

They met at the army base at Qandahar and set off early the next morning to Tarin Kowt. From Tarin Kowt, Raju appeared with a truck to take the ladies, dressed in their Burqas; while the men continued to Kabul along Highway 1. This time around Greta and Laura were not drugged. They endured every minute of the hair-raising ride to Sayghan. They cast down their eyes at the checkpoints but made excited noises at every other time. If they had thought the countryside beautiful in autumn, it was breathtaking in spring. The mountainsides were covered with even carpets of green grass relieved by beautiful wild spring flowers growing prolifically and colorfully at the roadside. At Sayghan, they were met by Siddiq with his donkeys. They went into a house, through a tunnel, and emerged at the other side of the tunnel about two hours later. There stood Asmaa, looking as Jasmine-like as ever, waiting to welcome them back into her fairy tale castle. By her side was Zohra, looking even more beautiful in the flesh than they had imagined, dressed in native feminine Pashtun attire. The men arrived an hour later. By then Khalid, Asmaa's husband, was there to welcome them all.

Khalid was taking some time off from his official duties at Kabul because of the Nimruz holidays. He looked very distinguished with his twirled moustache, full head of black hair touched with white at the temples, and twinkling grey eyes. His beard was clipped, and shorter than the popularly accepted Taliban bush. He was such a fitting husband for Asmaa-Jasmine, and they looked as if they were still very much in love.

They all settled in. Greta enjoyed seeing the awe in Lil's eyes as they introduced her to the lush domain. There was a cave meeting two days after they came. The Afghan pastor, along with Tim baptised everyone in their party. Doing it the native way, with Asmaa as an interpreter, they bore testimony to the congregation of how they had come to meet with the Lord, and what they hoped to do with their newfound faith in serving Him. There were tears. There was laughter. There were lots of hugs and kisses. Afterwards, they had a picnic at the riverside. When they finally meandered their way back to Asmaa's formal dining room, Alex and Zohra announced their wedding plans.

There was all manner of surprises expressed which were mostly of the pleasant kind.

"I had no idea you had gone that far," said Laura.

"Zohra, this is extremely feminine! It is not at all what I would expect of Il Dhost!" cried Greta.

"We get to have another Afghan wedding! We get to have another Afghan wedding" chanted Lil happily.

Bjorn clapped Alex on the back and said "Way to go, man! Way to go!"

Only Tim remained glumly silent. Nobody really noticed it in the midst of all the chatter and congratulations.

The wedding would take place in two days' time. Zohra's mother, sister, and their party were to arrive the next day. Although Asmaa had taken the liberty to order clothes for everyone, final fittings would be done the next day. They talked and laughed in merriment. It was long after midnight when the party finally broke up. Alex, Tim and Bjorn returned to the room they were sharing. As Bjorn wearily threw himself down on the bed, Tim invited Alex to come and examine the sentry posts. They went out into the grounds through the French windows.

"I don't know, Alex" Tim began. "A secret wedding appears to me very underhanded and a breaking of the rules.

"That is true, but can you see any other way around it? The rules permit me to keep a mistress under these circumstances but not a wife. The Bible on the other hand says if I find myself behaving inappropriately towards the lady I am engaged to, I had better marry her. Believe me, it's becoming more and more difficult to behave very properly with Zohra, Preach. I am mere flesh and blood. She is so exquisite, so delectable. What do you say? Should I obey man, or should I obey God, Preach?" He could not be accused of being flippant because his tone was deadly earnest.

"The army will never grant you a licence to marry her" Tim said.

"I know. I am not asking the army for one seeing that I really want to keep the marriage a secret from them. I have thought this matter over a lot. I have also prayed a lot concerning it. I feel it is better this way than to openly flaunt the rules, setting a bad example and precedence for everyone else. I know I could get court-martialed or even shot because of it. Let the army keep believing that I am keeping a mistress but before God, and some of His men who matter to me and Zohra, we will be legitimately married."

"You know it will create all manner of problems. You are planning to have children, aren't you?" Tim asked.

"I wouldn't say that is at the top of our list of priorities, but yeah, why not?" Alex replied gravely.

Tim continued equally gravely, "If the army does not recognize your marriage as legitimate, the children you have together will also not be recognized as legitimate. Zohra will never get the perks that the army gives to legitimate relatives. If on a future date she wishes to migrate to the United States, it will be near impossible for her."

"Zohra has no ambitions to ever leave this land. I see with her that this is her life's calling. As for raising my children in this unstable land, I certainly don't cherish the idea. Nevertheless, we shall cross that bridge when we get to it. Those are the least of our problems now. "The major and the most immediate ones I envisage is that I might be transferred to the other end of the world any day soon, seeing the interest our C.O has also taken in this matter. He will tell himself he is doing it for my good. What happens to this marriage then? I also brought this to the Lord. The reassurance He keeps giving me is to take one day at a time, and to always use every opportunity maximally. This is not a rash decision Preach. It's just that I have had to make it without really consulting anyone. I didn't want to bring you into it except to ask you to be my best man, and a signatory on our marriage certificate."

Tim did not honestly know what to say or do. He stood there with his hands thrust deep into his pocket. He was torn between conflicting emotions and loyalties. Being a man often required taking tough decisions. This was a grand example of such an occasion. Alex, sensing his friend's need to be alone turned and went back into the house. It took a few hours, but by the time Tim came in later, he had made up his mind what to do.

The next morning, he discussed these decisions with Laura and discovered that the ally he needed was Nazo. As soon as Nazo arrived by midmorning therefore, Tim took off with her. Both of them were not around for the final dress fittings. Serisha already knew what would fit Nazo, and Alex had to find some clothes of Tim's for the tailors to make estimates. He did not know what his friend was up to. Nevertheless, he was determined to go on with the wedding even if a bomb went off under them. The only comfort he had was that Tim had not completely deserted or he would have taken his bag and kit with him. The day they had spent at Qandahar awaiting the ladies, both of them had gone to buy and engrave wedding rings. Whereas Tim had been full of talk about his August wedding as they bought the rings, Alex had merely remarked, "It never hurts to dream". Tim had not known those dreams were closer to being fulfilled than his own. The sight of the ring Tim bought was what also reassured Alex that his friend would be coming back.

Tim and Nazo returned late. By the time they did, everyone was already at dinner. In lieu of all the pre-wedding festivities, Asmaa and Khalid hosted an informal dinner in the dining room. Two of their teenage daughters were also around. Those who came with Serisha included Raziq, Yelda and her husband with their two children, and Soraya! There were also the sentries and the household staff. They were all getting to know one other. It was a noisy reunion. Everyone wanted to know about everyone else, and to catch up. Compared to the number that had been there during the teacher training sessions, a mere forty people was nothing. At last, Asmaa called a halt and told people to try to get some sleep. There was a lot to be done the next day. This wedding was to start by noon, earlier than Afghan weddings which usually started in the evening. She told them that the segregation of the house was very strictly male and female. They were not to see one another until it was time for the wedding.

They all laughed good-naturedly, and obediently went to their rooms but not to sleep. "Don't worry" Soraya assured the ladies. "I will brew us something better than coffee in the morning."

And so, they spent much of the night chatting and laughing, despite Asmaa's warning.

It is doubtful if anyone slept much. The very next morning, the ladies all congregated in the big room where Zohra was dressing up. It was not to be a large wedding by Afghan standards. Nevertheless, Asmaa had a henna artist come. She enjoyed dressing the ladies up. They bathed, scented, and bejewelled everyone until they could hardly breathe. Soraya caught it on pictures and tapes. She had also become proficient in motion pictures. Laura did her own bit. Some of them would be edited later and doctored for showing to people like Ayesha and other people who had been interested in their Easter getaway vacation. For the moment, they just had fun.

Zohra had chosen to dress in a long white satin gown, Western fashion. Her rich coloring contrasted very vividly with her off-the-shoulder dress. Her piled up and bejewelled hair caused her graceful long neck to stand out. The full lace sleeves of the gown puffed up at the shoulders gave her the look of a young Queen Victoria. She was regal. She was beautiful. There were tears in everyone's eyes. Greta appointed herself as the advocate. She asked the ladies present to advise Zohra on how to have a successful marriage. They recollected some of the ones which they had heard at that other wedding and burst into gales of laughter. They made up a few of others just for her.

"Don't take a weapon to bed" ... "You might be inviting your husband to bring missiles."

"Don't let people know you married an American" ... "Just pretend he is a language-deprived Uzbek!"

"Teach your children to gonna wanna" ... "But make them say it with an Afghan accent..."

"Remember to dream as Zohra when with your husband, and as Il Dhost when not with him" ... "Otherwise, wake up, go back to sleep and wake as with the right persona..."

And so on.

Finally, they took their places opposite the men at the right side of the long corridor leading to the formal dining room. The wedding and reception were to take place there. They almost did not recognize the men. They all looked like Persian warriors. When Alex entered, he looked like Aladdin himself. His full head of hair had been swept back and gelled. His blue eyes shone more brilliantly: with love, happiness, and anticipation. Zohra, veiled with a thin white sheet of delicate lace, was escorted in by her mother, Nazo, and Yelda.

The bride and groom sat at their designated thrones and recited passages they had chosen from the Bible. Asmaa passed them a decorated mirror and they grinned at each other under the veil. "We've done it!" Zohra said, "We've done it!"

"So we have, My Heart, so we have" Alex replied.

The Cave-Meeting pastor came to officiate. He put them through the steps of their vows Western-style. When it came to asking if anyone had any reason why they should not be married, both of them held their breaths. However, there were no objections at all. They said their vows, exchanged rings, and then they were married in every sense of the word, and according to their respective cultures.

Even as the buffet started, the magistrate brought their marriage certificate for them to sign. It proclaimed that Lieutenant Alexander Dennis Pearson, a bachelor of the United States Marine at Farah was that day married to Miss Zohra Aminat Hameed, a spinster from Anar Darreh, Farah Province, Afghanistan; in the presence of the magistrate there in Bamiyan, Bamian Province, Afghanistan. There was room for four witnesses to sign. Tim, Laura, Raziq, and Nazo put in their signatures, and their respective statuses. And then with a flourish, Tim brought out a New York State Marriage License and certificate. He had gone to download and print it with Nazo the previous day. This one proclaimed that Alex and Zohra were married before Tim, a United States Marine Chaplain. Alex and Zohra put their signatures to these documents as well. Laura, Greta, Lil, and Bjorn signed as witnesses. Tim gave them to Alex and said, "That's my gift to you, Mate."

Alex knew then that Tim would never betray his secret. His friend was tacitly telling him that he felt he was doing the right thing. He had his support and ongoing friendship, always.

Both documents were signed in triplicates. Raziq wanted a copy for the family archives at Anar Darreh. The couple held onto a copy. Alex gave a copy to Laura saying, "Keep it safe for me. You will know what to do with it one day." Asmaa and Khalid asked for a photocopy for their own records, and to refer to the local registry if the need ever arose. Who knew pieces of paper could ever have such significance?

There was no live band but Khalid turned on their sophisticated music equipment so the natives could teach the foreigners how to properly dance Attan. The party would have gone on. However, Raziq called a break to again congratulate the couple, and to tell them their escort was waiting. There was a secret route to Uzbekistan where they were to honeymoon for a week, staying with some friends. He said the party in their honor could go on without them but if they were to make their rendezvous, the couple had to leave immediately.

For the week they were away, the people they left behind had their own honeymoons of a sort. Bjorn and Lil benefitted a lot from Tim's teaching and counselling. Tim and Laura spent hours walking round the grounds, making plans for their own future. Greta finally achieved her ambition of jogging to the gate even though it took her the whole day and a picnic basket on the way. Khalid returned to his duties after a few more days. Asmaa and their daughters went with him. Serisha and her party went out daily to visit friends and relatives around the area.

When Alex and Zohra returned, they looked flushed, happy, and very satisfied with each other. If anything, they seemed more in love than even before they left. Zohra showed them Alex's wedding present to her. It was a bushy red beard with a matching moustache, to go with the Il Dhost outfit. "So that she will be thinking of only disguising her voice since she insists on running around the countryside as a man instead of sitting down in the kitchen to fix my meals" he told them. They all teased him that if he had wanted that kind of a wife then he was less than a wise man.

"You know" Zohra said to Laura and Lil, "you should have taken the opportunity to also get married since your grooms were right here."

"What?" exclaimed Laura, "and steal your thunder?"

"You didn't inform me on time to bring my mother along" Lil said. "She will never forgive me if I got married without her."

Zohra understood what she was saying. It was just that she was so happy, and she wanted everyone else to be as happy as she was. They had spent their time away very well. They had developed what they considered their word from God into a motto, "Maximally use every opportunity, and be happy!"

Right there in their midst another romance seemed to be blooming. With Zohra inexorably out of his reach, Raziq finally noticed what had been under his nose all along. Years later, when people asked him how he and Nazo decided to get married, he would answer, "We were both on the rebound from loving the same person."

By the next day when they dispersed and returned to Qandahar on the first leg of their trip back to their respective posts, there were lots of tears. There were also a lot of promises, and a lot of beautiful memories. It had been a wonderful time.

However, rose bushes have thorns as well as flowers; and even in paradise, the serpent was present.

SHORT STORIES BY IJEOMA OZED-WILLIAMS

Definitions of Love

Running to Win

He answered! He answers!!

Kingdom Tales

Kingdom life tales

These Messengers of God

The Battle of Ten Women

The Burdens of Ten Women

The Tales of Ten Women

IN PARABLES – DRAMA SKITS BY IJEOMA OZED-WILLIAMS

At Your Service

Daddy is coming

Follow your leader

Triplets!!!

The Trial of the Saints

Chapter 12

∞

The weeks after the wedding, life went back more or less to normal. Alex still went about his duties of gathering intelligence and executing special duties for the army. If his colleagues found it odd that he sometimes went off by himself, and that his hitherto unclaimed off-duty days were now claimed in full, and often not spent at the base, nobody mentioned it. Many of them were wont to do the same. Lieutenant Pearson was known to be prudish. However, this was often attributed to his close association with the chaplain. Therefore, nobody took any real notice of this his change to "normal" behavior except for Tim who knew and understood what was happening. Major Grafton had his own suspicions. He was surer than ever that Alex was keeping a mistress, but he could not confirm it. He could do nothing about it except put in his recommendations that it might do his men a world of good to be relocated as soon as possible.

In the countryside, a new legend was growing. This one was known as Il Komak, the helper. Il Komak was known to be every bit as wily as Il Dhost. He had the same interest in helping the people against their oppressors. Although Il Dhost had been famed to have the ability to be in more than one place at a time, Il Komak could be in even more places at the same time. When one understood fully, this was not so surprising. Zohra had made good her hope of decentralizing the organization so that it could operate independent of her. The strongest of the splinter groups that emerged was headed by Nazo and Raziq. Nazo was not as tomboyish as Zohra. She was much older and more dignified, but she had also inherited from their father her own fair share of the ability to organize and direct. Added to the fact that Raziq had no need to speak through a transmitter, they had a very strong network going, and could be in several places or do several things at once.

Serisha continued to develop means of knocking out their enemies. Knocking them out was often more effective than killing them because whereas it humiliated some of them into a greater fury, it positively humbled others into philosophically rethinking what they believed, and for which they had nearly died. Some of this latter group actually emerged to organize resistance movements against the Taliban. They sought alliance with this different faction. It was a fifty-fifty chance what their preys emerged with. However, Serisha's groups reasoned that even one person won over was worth something to heaven, especially if that person also eventually became a Christian. According to her, "A wise man once said that an eye for an eye will not get us anything except more blind people. Kindness, however, often breaks even the stoniest of hearts."

Sadly, not everyone agreed with this philosophy. Some of their splinter groups actually finished off their enemies. In the long run, they also became the enemies of the other resistance groups. It was a vicious cycle.

In the midst of these, Zohra became sick! It began with weakness which she took absolutely no notice of. And then she began vomiting profusely. She totally lost appetite for all food. Ever slender, she almost vanished altogether. She was not feverish or sick in any other way. Serisha did a quick calculation and informed the worried husband that Zohra was probably pregnant.

Alex and Zohra were surprised. They had not taken any precautions against starting a family so soon because neither of them had really thought about it. He felt both happy and confused. To be a dad! Of course, there were issues. Zohra would never be persuaded to leave her native land. His transfer could happen anytime soon.

Even if he was posted at the other end of the world, he had long since made up his mind that every spare moment would be spent in Afghanistan, no matter what the United States Army thought about his movements and behavior. But the child to be born… what were the chances of the child having the best advantages in Afghanistan? He had no doubt that his in-laws would do a great job raising the child, but was that all he wanted for his child? This was one of those moments he would have loved to share with his own parents. However, he had still not even told them he was married. He still felt strongly constrained in his mind. Back in his room he put it all in his letters to Libby. He told her about his doubts and fears, his hopes and elation at becoming a dad. A pregnancy could go in any direction. Who knows, with the kind of strenuous lifestyle which Zohra chose, she might even have a miscarriage, but Alex did not want this! Suddenly, his mind was cleared of all doubts. Of course, he wanted this baby. He wanted the baby by all means. He told Zohra as such. "Now you have yourself and our baby to think about, should you not reduce your activities?"

    This was the right thing to say. Zohra wanted an indication from him that he wanted the baby as much as she did. She tried to slow down and curtail her activities. Obediently, she agreed to everything Serisha suggested or administered to her. Nevertheless, she grew worse rather than better. Some days would pass and the only thing she could take without vomiting would be some sugared tea. She chaffed under the inactivity. "Don't worry," Serisha told her. "It's a passing phase. In a few weeks' you will actually start enjoying the pregnancy. You will start eating to make up for this lost time."

    Zohra was dubious. She found out that physical activity seemed to improve her symptoms and made her less listless. A week of physical activity actually did a world of good to her. It improved her appetite. And then one day she noticed blood spots on her underwear. She panicked. For the first time, even the unflappable Serisha also panicked. They decided to wait and see. If the bleeding continued or she started having pains, then they would do something about it. Alex was due to come in about two days. They decided to set that as a time limit.

By the time Alex came, everything was back to normal or as near normal as it could be. Zohra still lacked appetite and seemed to vomit everything she ate or drank. He wanted her to see a doctor, have a scan… he had been doing some research on the internet. Zohra would have none of it. "Believe me, it's too dangerous for me to be seen in any Afghan hospital now. I know somewhere I could go to across the border at Iran but think about not seeing you for the next two weeks, and not being able to get word across."

Alex suggested the army base at Qandahar, "And blast whatever the consequences."

"No" Zohra objected. "I am not ready to blow my cover yet, nor your own for that matter, over what might be of little consequence. Let us leave it for a bigger purpose. The bleeding as it was, was not much, and was only for one day. I have not had any pain or any unusual discomfort except for this vomiting. I wonder if I will ever find food attractive again. What was it that God told us, Alex? We shall maximally use every opportunity and be happy! Let us enjoy the moment. If any real obstacles arise, we shall tackle it. I promise to be reasonable."

Alex saw the sense in her words, and he backed down. For the two days he spent with them, there was no more bleeding, and no pain. Zohra actually seemed to improve. She ate a bit and kept it down. She was no longer so weak and lethargic. Alex filed it away in his mind. If anything uncomfortable happened, he would have her flown to Pakistan rather than Iran. He had more contacts at Pakistan than at Iran.

That was really the turning point though. Zohra improved slowly but steadily. Her aversion to food became narrowed to only a few things. She stopped riding, and deliberately played down her role as Il Dhost. Most of her contribution was now advisory. It was just as well because by late 2009 there were suddenly more militant activities in southwest Afghanistan which demanded more and more of

Alex's time. The contract which Greta, Laura, and Lil had with UNESCO was due to end in July. Tim and Laura were planning their wedding for the end of July. They would take a late honeymoon at the end of September so they could travel to attend Lil's wedding at Sweden. Alex had his hands full.

Laura's wedding was beautiful and gay. It was more solemn and less colorful than the Afghan weddings they had attended but what was a wedding if not the gathering of one's friends and well-wishers? Some of the friends whom Laura had made in Afghanistan could not be there, but they made their presence felt. Zohra did not come. She sent Laura her wedding dress as the "Something borrowed". She added, "So I will know for sure we are really in the same family."

It fit beautifully since both of them were the same size. Asmaa sent an expensive set of pearl earrings, necklace, and bracelets which went with the wedding gown, through Soraya. Soraya was to also do the informal video and picture recording of the ceremony. The Marine base was to do the formal recording, since part of it was to be used as army propaganda. Shamir and Ayesha came with a party made up of their two cleaning women, and their sons. Aziz and the other driver brought some of their families as well as the people Greta, Laura, and Lil had been mentoring. Other people from the UN offices at Lashkar Gah and Qandahar came also. Courtesy of Greta, even Katie, who was still afraid of flying to Afghanistan, attended the wedding by Skype. She made them go through the session of giving advice to the bride before the wedding.

Alex served the dual offices of giving the bride away and being the groom's best man. Greta and Lil were bridesmaids, dressed in matching Pashtun attires. Major Grafton officiated at the wedding. The marines did the romantic crossing of swords for the new couple and all the tradition of cutting the cake with a sword. They also catered the food for the wedding reception and really did a great job of it. They served both Western and Afghan cuisine. The multicultural guests pronounced themselves very delighted with it all. The gathered guests did not know how to dance the "Attan" but there was music and dancing anyway, until the couple left by helicopter for a pre-honeymoon honeymoon at Kabul. The real honeymoon, they hoped to incorporate into their visit to Sweden two months later.

During the reception, Major Grafton gave a toast to the couple, "To the land that brought you both together, may there soon be lasting peace! And to the land you shall soon be returning to, strength and glory"! And then he added, "Ladies and gentlemen, I got a signal this morning that we shall all be returning to the States by this time next year!"

The announcement was met by loud cheering. The men had been at this post for three years, some for longer. Major Grafton had been there for almost six years! It was welcome news to the majority of those gathered there. The next evening though, when Alex told Zohra about it, he was definitely not ecstatic.

"Remember God's word to us" she reminded him again. "We shall maximally use every opportunity to be happy! Do you know the story of the King and the Thief?"

Alex reminded himself that he was in the land of "A thousand tales". He had learned to enjoy their storytelling, more so since his venture into Serisha's family. He was just as eager as that Persian monarch of old to hear whatever story this wise woman had to tell. He cocked his head and paid attention.

Zohra laughed. Her laughter was always like a balm to his battered soul. "It is said that luck once ran out on a very clever thief. He was arrested and brought to the king. After he had exhausted all his defenses, the king ruled that he had to be executed. 'Please have mercy on me for one more year, Your Majesty' the thief pleaded. 'Within this time, I shall teach your favorite horse how to converse with you.'

"Amused, the king agreed. Later the thief's friend asked him what kind of foolishness he had let himself into. 'You have just postponed the evil day. You will live the next one year apprehensively awaiting your execution.'

"'Far from it' replied the vagabond. 'A lot can happen in one year! I could die; the king could die, or who knows, the horse might even teach itself how to talk. Until then, I intend to go out every day and have me some fresh air while I ride that wonderful stallion.'"

Alex laughed. He had heard a version of the tale somewhere before, even though it had not been told in such a succulent manner. Zohra had not finished yet. "That is not the end of the tale" she said.

"There's more?" asked Alex.

Zohra nodded and then continued. "Before the one year was up, the king died. His son became the new king. He had seen the vagabond come out every day to exercise the king's favorite horse whatever the weather. 'I admire such consistency in a citizen' he told his grand vizier, 'Get that man as my head groom.' That was his first edict.

"Remember, at God's command, we shall maximally use every opportunity and be happy! A year is a long time. A lot could happen in one year. I don't know what, you don't know what, but God does." Alex laughed again but now he was also very thoughtful. Zohra had given him many gifts but her insight and devotion to God never failed to amaze Him. Surely, when God was in a matter, one should have no cause to worry for what the future would bring.

But the future is not always what we hope it would be.

Chapter 13

∞

Laura settled into the base and immediately became its functional hostess. Major Grafton wondered how they had ever managed without her. She did have a way of putting a feminine touch into everything they did. Where Zohra pointed out how things could have been done more economically and efficiently, Laura actually set about arranging things so that not only did they run more smoothly, but she also even saved the army a lot of money. Major Grafton insisted on including her on the staff list and paying her a regular salary. She tried to resist this until he let her know that confirming her as a member of staff was the only way of getting her access into some necessary official documents. Since she needed this access for what she was already doing, she finally agreed to it.

One day Laura asked Alex about Zohra. Offhandedly he replied, "She is feeling much better now."

"Much better?" Laura asked. "Was she ill?"

"Oh! she was, but she is much better now" Alex replied sheepishly.

Laura had so many questions about the illness. In the end Alex agreed that it was probably better for her to see Zohra and hear from the horse's mouth. It was one thing for Alex to go to see her alone. He would usually go through torturous routes to protect the secrets of the outfit. It was going to be more awkward with three of them together. Eventually, they arranged a Saturday picnic on the mountainside.

"Accidentally", they bumped into a friendly Kuchi camp, and there was Zohra in one of the tents! She was looking even more beautiful than the last time Laura and Tim had seen her. She looked somewhat softer, sweeter, and rounder. And when she stood up to embrace them, Laura remarked on how plump she had also become. And then light dawned. "You're going to have a baby!" she exclaimed.

"Yes" Zohra agreed grinning very broadly.

Tim and Laura fussed over her, but Zohra only laughed. "This is part of what I enjoy about being pregnant," she said. "You always get to be the center of attention. Everybody indulges you!"

"How far along are you now?" asked Laura.

"My mother thinks I am due in late December."

"Oh Wow. That is barely in about two months. How are you holding up?"

And while the women talked shop and babies, the men talked about the practical implications.

"I know" Alex said when Tim brought up the issues that troubled him. "I definitely would have loved my children to grow up in the good old U.S. of A. They still might, but for now I am playing this by the ear. The more immediate thing is that Zohra refuses every kind of help. I know Serisha is good and has the knowhow. However, I wish things could be done where I can at least have some measure of control. I have been reading all kinds of horror stories about childbirth, maternal, and infant mortalities. "Did you know Afghanistan has the highest maternal mortality rate in the world? Very scary! I tell you Tim, it's not very encouraging. Sometimes, it is only my faith in God that sustains me. And then I tell myself all this is too good to be true. Maybe it really is too good to last. I keep waiting for the other shoe to drop."

He did not know how prophetic he was being.

Their daylong visit ended. Alex lingered with Zohra in the Kuchi camp. Tim and Laura returned to the base. "It's so wonderful" Laura gushed. "Oh Tim, let's start our own family. Let's start now!"

"I know how you feel Darling, but won't it be less complicated if we wait till we return to the States next year?"

"To the States" Laura echoed, only now realizing. "What will happen to Alex and his young family when that happens?"

And then Tim had to tell her the other side of this wonderful new development.

Life went on with no big changes. Alex was due a two-week leave by mid December, and he was still trying to determine how to spend it. The days became quite cold and the nights even colder. Once in a while however, a warm pleasant day would emerge, inviting people to come out into the fresh air. On one such day, Tim was very busy ministering to the sick. On the spur of the moment, Alex invited Laura to go to Anar Darreh with him. Halfway there, they took to the hills, following a tortuous route which was not familiar to Laura but all too familiar to Alex now. They finally arrived at the enclosed compound that Zohra's people had called home for generations.

Very earnestly Alex begged Laura, "I want you to talk to Zohra. Talk to her about the advantages of having this baby in a hospital. Her mother has been a great help. So far, nothing has gone amiss. However, I am so scared of losing the baby or the mother. Please Laura, tell her whatever it is that women tell one another. She should not be a fool and lose everything. I know I cannot bear it if anything unpleasant happened to them!"

Laura was totally in agreement. However, she barely had time to acknowledge what he said because Serisha came out to the courtyard as soon as they entered. It was as if she had been watching out for their approach. "Oh good. You are here," she said to Alex. "Where did Siddiq find you?"

"Siddiq did not find me" Alex answered with a puzzled frown. "I just came on my own."

"Never mind," Serisha said almost impatiently. "You are here now. I sent him to fetch you. Zohra's water broke and she went into labor early this morning. I know you would have wanted her to deliver at the base or something but she's as stubborn as a mule. She's in there now."

Serisha could have been talking to empty air except for Laura who was still there looking at her with surprise. Alex had vanished to find Zohra as soon as he got the gist of the matter. Laura now said to Serisha, "Show me where she is. Perhaps I can talk some sense into her."

Serisha showed her to the room where Zohra lay groaning and sweating, holding fiercely onto her husband's hands. Nazo was there in the shadows. As Laura and Serisha came in she was saying to Alex, "I think the baby is close to coming. Moving her now will not make sense at all." When she saw Serisha she added, "Madaar just bring the instruments. I will lay out the sheets."

Laura also saw that delivery was imminent. There was no more time to persuade Zohra about anything. Serisha and Nazo were galvanized into action. They had done this several times before. They prayed there would be no complications. They wanted Alex out of the way, but Zohra clung to him very fiercely. She would not let go, so they let him be. Back home, he would have been there anyway. In less than an hour everything was set. Laura felt like a spare tyre but on the spur of the moment she decided to turn on the video of her ever-present camera and capture the moment. She was just on time too because Zohra bit out through clenched teeth, "I think the baby is coming."

Serisha bent and encouraged her to bear down. Zohra did, still holding tightly to Alex's hands. The next minute, the baby was born! It was a boy. He announced his entrance with a very authoritative cry. Everybody present: Alex, Zohra, Serisha, Nazo, and Laura, the erstwhile video operator cried with him. The baby was in good company. Back in the States, Alex would have been asked to cut the umbilical cord. There was no such ceremony here. Serisha tied off and cut the cord in a no-

nonsense manner. She gave the baby to Nazo to dress up. Turning to Zohra she said, "Time to deliver the placenta. Are you up to it?"

Zohra nodded. At Serisha's command she bore down, but instead of the placenta, another baby literally erupted into the world in its bag of water. The water sac burst, bathing everyone in the room with the warm fluid. This one was a girl. Whereas her brother had entered the world crying authoritatively, she entered the world demanding angrily! This one was going to be a warrior princess like her mother!

Everyone was surprised. "What is happening?" asked Nazo who was still trying to clean and dress the baby in her arms. "What is happening?"

"Where did this one come from?" Serisha asked. "Your tummy did not look that big!"

"Twins!" Alex exclaimed, "A boy and a girl! Azizam, you have outdone yourself! You are so full of wonderful surprises!"

"Wow!" Laura said over and over. "Wow!"

Zohra was too exhausted to talk. She only kept smiling beatifically. "I feel like bearing down Madder" she said weakly.

"Another one?" Serisha asked teasingly.

But it was really the placentas this time around. A push, a slide, and they were both out. Alex bent and gently kissed his wife. Laura caught it all on tape.

With her arms busy and full of the first baby, Nazo asked Laura to suspend her duties as video-master and attend to the second baby. It was a good place to pause. When she reviewed it later on, it was all so beautifully orchestrated. Everyone's comments could not have been better if the whole thing was professionally scripted. If this was not God in action, what else was it?

Zohra lay languidly, sweetly tired, and exhausted. With the babies nicely dressed, Serisha and Nazo went to clean up. Laura turned on her video again to capture the first moments of parenthood for the new parents. "We shall name the boy

Dennis after his father and grandfather, and Hameed after my father. We shall simply call him DH" Zohra said.

"And we shall name the girl after the two grandmothers, Dawn Elizabeth" Alex said.

"How does Dawn come into it?" asked Laura.

"That is the English interpretation of my name" Serisha said huskily coming in at that moment. She rushed out again so nobody would see the tears that had sprung to her eyes.

"So, the next one shall be Allison?" Laura prodded.

"Not on your life" Alex laughed. "That name is reserved for your own first daughter, I was seriously warned."

Now it was Laura's turn to flush with pleasure. If Alex and Zohra could do this with all the difficulties they faced, she saw no reason why she and Tim should not. She resolved to broach the subject with Tim again as soon as possible. There was nothing like holding a newborn baby to stimulate or enhance the longing for one.

It would all have been the sweet end to a beautiful story but about an hour later, as Zohra got up to go to the bathroom she suddenly swooned and collapsed. Alex and Laura shouted. They reached for her at the same time, butting each other at the head as they bent down to her. As Alex scooped her unto the bed he said, "Quick, get Serisha!"

Laura ran out calling for Serisha. When they returned, most of the floor was covered in blood. Zohra was on the bed. She was still conscious but very weak. "I put a thick towel expecting this kind of thing" Serisha said bending to check the pad. She straightened immediately. "That too, is totally soaked, and she's still bleeding!" She looked into Zohra's eyes. They were looking very pale. By now she was barely conscious. "Alex," said Serisha very solemnly, "I think we need to get her to the hospital."

Alex did not even wait for her to finish. He was already outside talking to Nazo about logistics. It so happened that Raju had been standing by with the truck. She sent for him at once. Everyone was busy doing something. Laura, not knowing what else to do, remembered she had read somewhere about a way of stopping bleeding after childbirth. It was to massage the womb which should still be felt like a football just below the belly button, until it became hard. She started doing this now while she prayed and begged God to intervene. Zohra's womb certainly felt soft and flabby but as Laura massaged, it seemed to grow firmer. Under Laura's kneading fingers it became quite hard. Zohra tried to still Laura's fingers but she was too weak. Laura felt encouraged by her success to continue. Weakly Zohra said, "Makes me want to pee!"

Hardly were the words out of her mouth when her bladder suddenly emptied onto the bed. She strained as if she was about to do number two as well. Out popped a big clot of blood. Panicked, Laura snatched her hand away and jumped up. She had also read that when people were about to die they suddenly lost control of their bladder and bowels. She now stood uncertainly by the bedside, not knowing what to do next.

Serisha came in at that moment with a basin of water and saw what looked like more blood all over the bed. Her heart hammered within her chest. Briskly, efficiently, she cleaned Zohra up and tried to put her into clean clothes as best as she could. She had seen death at close quarters often enough to know what this all meant. Her only comfort was that she believed in miracles. Besides, Zohra still responded to commands to lift her hands, her legs, or to turn over, albeit very weakly. Just as she finished, Nazo and Alex came back. Gently cradling her in his arms with all his love in his eyes, and begging her to hang on, Alex took her out to the truck. He laid her on the back seat and made Laura get in to ride shotgun with the driver. Nazo came out and handed the twins into Laura's arms. It was not the least bit easy to hold both of them at once. Nevertheless, she managed the best she could. Alex himself jumped onto the bed of the truck. Throwing all caution to the winds, the odd party headed straight to the US Marine base by the shortest, quickest route! There was no time for camouflage or innuendoes.

CHAPTER 14

Alex had to get down before they reached the gate to make the sentry allow the strange vehicle through. Even if Alex was not there, the sight of the weakened Zohra, and Laura covered in blood was enough to galvanize the medical team into action. Zohra was barely conscious. She was just hanging on by sheer willpower. The medical team decreed she needed to be transfused immediately. Fortunately, Alex and Tim had compatible blood. More people would be found later. There was nothing to feed the babies with at the base. Nazo had had the presence of mind to throw in spare clothing for them. However, the U.S. army is nothing, if not very resourceful especially under dire situations. At first the babies were spoon-fed with dilute dextrose which was meant for intravenous usage. They were diapered with paper towels until Major Grafton himself sent for baby formula, and proper diapers to be delivered from Qandahar with supplies coming in that very week.

Alex came clean. He told his C.O everything. There was no time to chastise him when Zohra was fighting for dear life. There would be time for that later on. Besides, he was not telling the C.O anything the older man did not already suspect.

To Laura's surprise, the medical team told her that she had probably saved Zohra's life. "By rubbing her womb and causing her to pee, you singlehandedly stopped the bleeding." Again, Laura felt this was God moving in His mysterious ways. She certainly had not done any of those things intentionally. Whatever the case, Zohra did not bleed again after that large clot came out. She improved so much with the initial blood transfusion that she had the energy to resolutely refuse all further transfusions. All said and done though, she remained at the sick bay for a whole week before she was deemed movable. With Laura now sharing Tim's quarters despite the fact that there were no special provisions for married officers at the base, the room which had been called Laura's room was now made over to Zohra and her babies. Alex's room was too small for them in the first instance, and Major Grafton had not yet decided what his final stance on the matter should be. For now, he told Alex he must not in any way allow this new development to hinder his official duties.

Alex was due a two-week official leave. He wrote his parents explaining that since they were coming back soon anyway, he would not be coming home in December. He spent all of it looking after Zohra at the sick bay. By the time his leave was spent, the festive season was upon the base. By the time Zohra was moved out of the sick bay, Alex was ready to throw himself back into as near normal a life as possible. His duties still took him away from the base for days at a time, but whenever he was at the base, he spent as much time as he could with his family. It was known to Major Grafton that his officer slept more in the room that was called Laura's room, than in his own bed but he chose to ignore this irregularity.

By mid-February, Zohra began to chafe under the inactivity. Laura, between her administrative and social duties at the base tried to help her out with the babies as much as she could but Zohra wanted her mother. Caring for a new baby was one thing. Caring for twins when one had not even so much as learned the art of motherhood beforehand was too much. She felt that she had no talent for it in the first place. She cajoled and begged Alex. At last, when he got a request from Serisha through one of the drop boxes for them to come home, he relented. By the end of February, therefore, they left the base, much to the comfort of Major Grafton who was beginning to feel he was exhibiting a double standard to his men. "This," he told

Alex, "never happened. However, if you put in a request for birth certificates, I will see that they are processed."

Alex understood. He was very grateful and moved by this small but very meaningful concession on the part of his commanding officer. Of course, Raziq had also had their names entered into the old family Bible. Nevertheless, Alex wanted his children to also be registered as Americans citizens.

Zohra left just on time. Barely a month later, Laura herself became too sick to take care of anyone. She vomited incessantly and was very weak. They transferred her to Qandahar when the medical team at Farah came to its wit's end. At Qandahar she was no better. They talked of flying her back home until someone had the presence of mind to suggest they did a pregnancy test. The results came out positive. Laura was going to have a baby too! The news seemed to make her better. Four weeks afterwards she was back to the base at Farah. Soon after she left, Qandahar and the areas around it began to experience a rise in insurgency.

The year 2010 in Afghanistan was a year full of controversies. It began with Peace Talks. There were talks of the Allied soldiers and peacekeeping forces leaving Afghanistan. A few weeks into the year, there was a rise in insurgency and militancy. And then the Allied forces began to make mistakes. Whether through faulty intelligence or outright deceptions there were increasing incidents of civilian casualties. On a few occasions, the Taliban would carry out a deliberate raid and try to pin it on the allied forces; or unlike themselves totally deny their involvement in the matter. Sometimes, they hid behind women and children. If the allied forces tried to flush them out with resultant casualties, they quickly announced to the world how the allies were killing helpless women and babies.

There was also a rise in the persecution of Christians. Some foreign workers were killed because the Taliban said they were proselytizing and converting indigenous Afghans. Some native Afghan Christians were publicly executed or if the international community intervened, exiled from their native land. Some secret

Christians in top Government positions were exposed and executed. Khalid, Asmaa's husband left the country for some weeks. When he returned, he resigned his post at Kabul to contest for a local position closer to home. At least this was the official stance. Apart from the Taliban, the constituted government declared there was freedom of religion but killing a Moslem that had converted to Christianity was not a crime. Even some Kuchi groups were targeted and summarily decimated for being different.

Christianity went even deeper underground in Afghanistan. Zohra and groups like theirs worked harder but were now in more danger than ever. However, in areas where they were strong, things seemed a bit better than in other parts of the country. Zohra was glad they decentralized when they did. As things became tougher however, she still found herself having to put on her Il Dhost outfit and riding out to help once in a while.

The month of May that year, they made a major conquest. Their old enemy and erstwhile hunter, Neem Omatullah, with his fort near Zaranj was caught in a fight with another rival group. Believing themselves to be fighting against Il Dhost, the two groups had laid ambush and nearly decimated each other. Coming upon them later, the real Il Dhost group waited in the bushes watching the battle play out. Omatullah was among those left wounded and dying in the field of poppies. Il Dhost and her people walked among the bodies, trying to tend the wounded enough to keep them alive until they were found by those to whom they belonged. When they came to Omatullah, his eyes flew open. He focused on Zohra's face. "You are the one they call Il Dhost."

It was a statement not a question. Zohra nodded in answer.

"You will kill me now?"

Zohra shook her head. The man had some bad lacerations, and what looked like a gunshot wound to the shoulder. She tended to him, and they dragged him into the shade of a tree.

That was all it took: a little kindness! Nevertheless, it made a deep impression on Omatullah. Sometime in the dim, distant past, someone had told him the story of the Good Samaritan. He had pooh-poohed the story, despising the sucker do-gooder Samaritan. His admiration was for strong men who fished out advantages and knew how to use them. In fact, he saw the bandits in the story as the true heroes. Now the story came back to haunt him. He did not know it, but he had just had what evangelical Christians call a touch from God, and a change of heart. He was never the same again after this occasion. His enemy had bent down to help him instead of finishing him off at a very vulnerable moment. He became very introspective and never organized any more campaigns after this. His associates attributed this change to wounds he had sustained that afternoon during the skirmish. In his own heart however, he knew it went much deeper than the wounds.

Zohra was now more engrossed with motherhood than fighting insurgents. She was a surprisingly good mother. The twins were a constant source of delight to her. Alex went about his duties, but he begrudged every moment he could not be with them. He started a video diary. He started with the video Laura made during the delivery of the twins. He added subsequent videos that he, Zohra, and sometimes even Serisha made. They were of what the twins did. There were the twins beginning to smile socially, the twins learning to sit up, the twins learning to roll over, the twins reaching out to be carried, the twins grabbing at things, the twins beginning to crawl, and so on. Once, Soraya saw it and borrowed it.

She worked on it: splicing, cutting, editing, and even annotating in English and in Arabic. After a week she presented it to him. It was a masterpiece, complete with music in the background. There were clips from the wedding; clips of Zohra at a shura holding court; Zohra on her stallion on the mountainside dressed as Il Dhost. There were clips of Zohra the woman, dancing Attan at the wedding, Zohra proudly outlining her tummy big with babies. There was Zohra caring for her babies, chatting with "The girls", or just gazing adoringly at her husband. There were also clips of Alex.

There was Alex with his men on a scouting operation; Alex with his friends at the base; Alex in a teashop and so on. There were even clips of Greta, Laura, and Lil at different times of their captivity, and at Laura's wedding. She even discreetly included Nazo, Raziq, Serisha, Yelda, Asmaa, and Soraya herself. The whole video was about six hours long. She captioned it, "Afghanistan with love."

When Laura saw it, she insisted on making copies for herself, Greta, and Lil. She assumed Alex had sent copies to his parents, but he never did. They were part of things Laura gave to them later on, together with his journal of letters to Libby.

The month of June brought a lot of changes to the base at Farah. It became obvious that the promises made to Major Grafton that he and his men would soon move were not empty. Key officials came to understudy those they would be taking over from. Major Oliver Sandwell came to understudy Major Grafton. Lieutenant John Brixton came to understudy Alex, among others.

Alex and John Brixton did not get along well. At first Alex chided himself for an undercurrent of resentment over his having to leave his family. However, it was more than just that. Their philosophies and methods did not agree. Whereas Alex tried to make friends with the Afghans who were likely to give them information and cooperate with them in crisis, John hated what he called "Blurring the lines". He wanted a clear demarcation between the Afghans and the Allies. "I believe every Afghan would pretend to be your friend until they steal your technology from you" he said.

Whereas Alex believed in going out to the fields to gather his intelligence, John believed that if intelligent sources were brought to the base and "properly interrogated", they were more likely to yield "better quality" information. He told Alex, "We are not here to coddle them. I believe we should do our best to end this war very quickly so we can all go home. Our men have been away for too long. The sooner this is over, the sooner we can face the domestic problems we have at home."

Many of the men at the base did not like Brixton that much either. Although no one confided in him about Alex's secret family, he found out soon enough. He was not an intelligence officer for nothing. He took note of Alex's habit of always disappearing when off-duty. He tracked Alex. Although he did not get any definite incriminating evidence, he put two and two together and concluded Alex was keeping a significant Afghan mistress. He began to compile a dossier on Alex which he titled, "The betrayals of an American Marine Officer". In it he claimed that Alex and people like him were hobnobbing with the warlords whom the Taliban had displaced. "This kind of behaviour" he insinuated, "would bring the Afghanistan problem back to square one."

Major Sandwell and Major Grafton did not get along much better. They were more diplomatic about their own disagreements as men in leadership should be. The former had a lot of reservations on how competent his colleague was. He felt that he lacked a good control over his men; and showed favoritism to his Chaplain by allowing him to have a wife on the base. This was until he found out that the said wife was also a legitimate employee of the Ministry of Defense. Her work was not only impeccable but extremely necessary. He grudgingly acknowledged that her competencies helped a lot in planning and operations at the base. "But you should not have allowed her get pregnant and be parading herself all over the base like that" he complained. It was as if Major Grafton could have had a hand in the matter.

Laura's baby bump was beginning to show on her slender frame. She was justifiably very proud of it. Even if she did not want to talk about it, the men always asked her how the baby was doing. Expecting the baby was just one more thing that bound the unit together. Besides, they all had an especially soft spot for Laura. They had shipped out with her, searched for her when she was missing, and more or less taken responsibility for her wedding. Some of them proudly wrote home about her, "Sometimes she is the most normal thing around here. Her presence helps anchor our souls and maintain our sanity in this place."

Somehow, Major Sandwell sensed their devotion to her and was unaccountably jealous of it. Unlike John Brixton however, he did not feel this was treason. He compiled his own dossier titled, "Necessary Changes that must be Instituted at the Base to Maintain Normalcy."

The areas around Farah had remained relatively free of insurgent activity even as the whole country was rocked by one disaster after another. With the increasing mistakes of Allies killing civilians, the loyalty of the natives shifted back and forth between the Allies and the Taliban. They had seen the Allies as their liberators but with these new problems, they now saw them more as their destroyers. At one time, a drone mistakenly targeted and destroyed a hospital. Hospital workers, patients and their relatives were killed. In retaliation perhaps, or for some other innocuous reasons, the villagers withheld information about Taliban movement around their villages. Allied forces walked into ambushes more often. The mortality rate among soldiers climbed. Back home, people pressured the politicians to end this senseless war and "Let our boys come home!"

On ground, people like John Brixton blamed people like Alex more bitterly. "It's your mishandling of the situation which has brought us to this. You should have ended this war a long time ago."

Alex learned how to ignore Brixton. The methods he used had worked for him so far. If Brixton waited a bit more, he would soon get a free hand to use his own methods. He too prepared his own dossier on his impression, and projections about the officer replacing him. He discussed these with Zohra because she was interested and because she understood. She told him, "I know you're disappointed in his philosophy but that is how many foreigners think. Console yourself Joonam. There are many more like you, even though there are uncomfortably some others who are like him. We are used to all sorts. We are also prepared for whatever we get. We shall miss the alliance we had with your group. It will be a lonelier battle after you're gone.

Nevertheless, they are likely to play more into the hands of the Taliban with their thinking and methods."

They did not often talk about Alex's imminent departure. Perhaps, like the proverbial ostrich, they hid their heads in the sand. They clung to their motto of maximally enjoying their stolen moments together and with their babies whenever they could, and for as long as they could.

CHAPTER 15

―――――∞―――――

Zohra did not know how soon her "Prophecy" would happen. One day, a piece of intelligence report was brought to the base that there was an activity planned near Herat. Alex was suspicious about how the intelligence was obtained and how it was delivered. He wished to look into it in a roundabout manner. However, short of accusing him of treachery, Brixton said so many uncouth things. As a last resort, he took two of Alex's men and headed for the hills around Herat.

Alex requested a consultation with Major Grafton and Major Sandwell. He listed his own misgivings about the news, as well as the approach and the methods Brixton had chosen to deal with it. He gave the two commanders a summary of their altercation. Major Grafton asked him to put his report in writing including how he intended to deal with it. Alex did so; and then taking two men with him, he went after Brixton. They were fully three hours behind. As they approached the rendezvous, they noticed an abnormal quiet.

His suspicions aroused, Alex quickly drew up a plan with his men. Instinctively dodging behind a rocky outcrop, he saw his three colleagues trussed and gagged sitting before eight members of the Taliban. The captives did not appear obviously hurt or incapacitated in any other way. In a minute more their torture would begin. Very often, the Taliban began by shooting out the enemy's knees in order to prevent escape. Alex could not follow their conversation because it was in rapid Dari. Nevertheless, he had no doubt as to what their intentions were. One of his men came up behind him. Alex quickly gave him instructions. "Remember, head to Namaksar. It is farther and the road is more difficult but that might be our only hope. Mention Il Dhost and you will get all the help you need. Do not, repeat, do not head back to the vehicles. We shall rendezvous at the base."

He took a quick run past the gathered men but not as far as where they were likely to have posted a sentry. He repeated the trick of lobbing a grenade to detonate almost immediately. He did not wait to see the results of his action but headed right back to where the captives were. The other men who had come with him were creating diversionary shooting, hopefully hitting some targets like shooting out tires or incapacitating sentries. The Taliban guarding the men were fully distracted, and not within sight. Alex deftly cut the bonds which held the captives. There was no time for pleasantries. "Rendezvous at Namaksar. Head north now. Even if everyone doesn't gather, get back to the base by evening, report and get help!"

The men did not need to be told twice. They nodded, merged into the crags, and limped away northwards. They had a better chance with their enemies while unbound than trussed up as they were. They all headed to the northern slopes except for Brixton. Brixton headed to the western slope, towards where they had parked their vehicle. Already on the northern slope himself, Alex heard some thrashing some way far to his left. He looked over the rocks to see Brixton headed that way. He restrained himself from uttering a curse. Even as he looked, he could see some of the Taliban returning from the same direction. In the next minute or so they would meet Brixton face to face.

Alex looked around. He could not see any of his men but sensed them moving steadily north. He paused, on the edge of a moral decision. Should he leave the fool to his fate, or chance going back and suffering the same fate himself? Brixton did not understand the Afghans as well as he did. Besides, he was one stubborn and offensive fellow. At last, he chose the middle ground. He would stay and watch out for an opportunity. No one deserved to die the horrible death that the Taliban meted out to captives. All said and done, he was still a Brother Officer. Alex did not ask himself if Brixton would have done the same thing if the circumstances were reversed. He only prayed help would somehow reach them on time.

First of all, he found a shallow hole and stowed all of his equipment except for his water canteen and the knife in his sock. If he was captured, the less he had to give up to the enemy, the better. A fleeting thought of Zohra and the twins crossed his mind but he firmly put the thought away so he could concentrate on what was at hand. He circled the mountain. About two hours later he crept back to where he had stumbled on the men before. Sure enough, there were now twelve angry men surrounding a barely conscious Brixton. They had given him a thorough beating in their frustration, and were now trying to question him in Dari, and then in Pashto, of which the man understood not a word. Someone tried in broken and disjointed English but by then Brixton could not have answered them even if he understood. They had thrashed him so much that his face was just a pulpy mass. His eyes were swollen shut. Blood ran from his ears, nose, and mouth. He looked as if his jaw was dislocated. He was propped up in such a way that Alex was sure more than one of his bones was broken. The merciful thing would have been to just put a bullet into him and end it quickly. However, Alex had neither the wish nor the bullet to do so. He prayed the Taliban would do the poor man that favor.

After what seemed like an hour, the captors moved away a short distance from their captive and started their ablutions in preparation for Afternoon Prayers. Alex felt this could also be a trap. He kept watching. Sure enough, he felt someone behind him. He had the presence of mind to roll over before the person landed on him with a drawn knife. He managed to stab Alex in the shoulder before the latter rolled away. They struggled but Alex was bulkier and unencumbered while the other man had to also grapple with the gun slung at his back. Alex prayed the gun would not discharge. At last, with an uppercut to the man's jaw, he was able to knock him out. As he rolled over with a grunt, Alex got up, crouching close to the ground, he sprinted for the crags. There was nothing he could do for Brixton now. He hoped his men had escaped and could send some help soon. However, that hope was a long shot. It would take them at least two hours to get to Namaksar on foot from where they had started. They would spend some more time trying to enlist any type of help, and to mobilize men and supplies.

After some time, Alex slowed down to a walk. He patched his wound the best he could. He became aware of how intensely thirsty he was. He had lost his water canteen during the skirmish and was thankful that was all he had lost. He had no idea how long he had been on his present course but knew he was now totally lost. He felt very dizzy and could not get his bearings anymore. There was nothing as terrible as wandering in the dry desert climate without water, and a bleeding wound to boot. He plodded on, one step at a time; one foot after the other; the next foot and the next foot. He thought he saw a fountain of water, ran to it and saw it was just a jagged rock. Swell! He was now beginning to hallucinate. He resisted the urge to just lie down and sleep. He knew men were after him. It was not yet safe enough to just stop and rest. He was past being stealthy or tactical. He was probably blundering round in circles, making so much noise and alerting all the enemies around to his position.

At a time, he thought he saw Zohra astride a horse. He ran to her crying "I'm saved, I'm saved!"

The image vanished before he got to it. He fell down a slope spraining his right ankle. He got up again, settled his weight gingerly on the hurt foot and moved forward. The going now became very hard. He did not know if he could make it. He found himself praying, "God please look after my kids… Please God comfort Zohra… Lord please comfort my parents… Make sense of this to the army…" It never occurred to him to pray for his own deliverance. He concluded the enemy would get him. He had made enough unpardonable mistakes in this outing.

And then he caught his boot in a hole and fell again. This time he stayed down, too tired to get up. He decided to rest for a while before trying again. When he opened his eyes, he saw a circle of faces surrounding him. He knew most of them were the Taliban but some of them looked familiar. Zohra's men? He closed his eyes again and listened to what sounded like a skirmish. He felt himself picked up and tossed on a horse for an uncomfortable ride during which he passed out. He did not know how long he was out but when he opened his eyes next, he was sure he was in the enemy's camp. He was lying on a rug on the floor in a narrow room. Against the other wall was a pulpy mass he recognized as Brixton. Alex knew Brixton was alive because he was breathing very noisily, the way people did when their nasal passages were terribly blocked, or the way they did on the television just before they died.

Alex propped himself up on his elbow and rolled over. A quick mental survey told him his kneecaps were still intact. He crawled over to Brixton and gently turned his head to the side. The breathing became better. Alex looked around and saw a rubber water bottle kept there for them, or by mistake. He did not particularly care. He still felt very thirsty. He would have loved to empty the water into his own mouth. He actually took a gulp, but human compassion again made him move over to the prostate figure on the floor. Holding him up he commanded, and then forced him to swallow some of the water. He thought Brixton must have passed out because he did not groan from pain as one who had so many injuries would. And then Alex distinctly heard him say "Thank you."

"You're welcome" responded Alex. "Sorry I can't do more, Mate."

"I need to apologise," Brixton rasped out. "You were right. I was wrong."

"That's large of you" said Alex without bitterness. He tried to stand up but collapsed with a suppressed gasp of pain. That was when he discovered that both of his unshod feet were swollen. They were probably sprained, dislocated, or broken but he was out of action for now as it was. No wonder they had not busted his kneecaps. Whoever had taken away his boots had also taken away his knife, his shirt, and his belt. Brixton was also in a similar state of undress. They had not bothered to dress their wounds or to kill them yet. This meant they had another purpose for keeping them, maybe for ransom or for exchange of prisoners. Most certainly, they would first be tortured for information. Alex knew what was coming. He only wished he had some water to drink to brace himself.

CHAPTER 16

Zohra was playing with her babies like every normal, proud young mother. She was looking forward to an afternoon with the girls. Laura was coming over from the base, Yelda from Zaranj, and what with Nazo also pregnant, she looked forward to an afternoon of talking babies and diapers. They had done this before. Zohra admitted to herself that she loved being a woman and a mother. Serisha bustled about putting finishing touches to things which already looked perfect. The twins had learned to crawl and were now experts at it. They made a grab for her whenever she was within their reach. Once in a while she bent down to pick up one or the other just to hear them chortle and squeal with laughter. Oh, the joy of being a grandmother! It was much more thrilling than being a mother. She knew because she had so many surrogate grandchildren around. Nevertheless, Zohra's children were very special. They were such unexpected blessings.

Laura arrived first but Yelda was not far behind. She had come with her two boisterous children who immediately followed Serisha chanting "Madaar Bozorg! Madaar Bozorg!" They were determined to fill her in with all their important news while hopefully charming some goodies out of her. They knew they would not be disappointed. Yelda was glad to see them go while she immediately focused on the twins. "They're so sweet at this age" she gushed, hugging and kissing them by turn.

Nazo came to the door and signalled for Zohra. Seeing the look on her face, Zohra quickly got up and followed her. They had a quick consultation. Zohra came back to the room looking very grim. Laura immediately knew there was bad news. "What is it Zohra? What is it?" she asked in alarm.

Zohra gazed at her for some time and then gravely announced, "The Taliban has Alex and Brixton at a place near Karokh. I'm sorry ladies but I have to leave immediately."

Laura wanted to ask if no one else could go but who else could possibly go? Raziq was already far away at the Uzbekistan border. Nazo was heavily pregnant. Besides, this was something very personal to Zohra. Of course, she had to go.

Even as she donned the attire which transformed her to Il Dhost, Zohra was spitting out instructions. She was telling her mother how to care for the twins in her absence. She was telling Nazo about gathering intelligence and mobilizing help. She was telling Yelda about reinforcement and spreading the word in their ranks. For Laura, she wanted her to take a message back to the army base. "I'm sure the news has not reached the base yet. Tell Major Grafton that they are being held in a compound at Karokh. The intelligence we have so far is that both men are wounded but alive. There are about twelve men in the compound but about three hundred around the town. They appear to be fairly well-organized. "We don't yet know who is in charge. I am going to try to extract Alex and Brixton in the next twenty-four hours. Beg Major Grafton to withhold a full-frontal attack before then. After that time, they probably won't be alive anyway. He can then storm the compound. I will have someone meet anyone he will dispatch outside of Herat to the north. Ask him to send Randy. Randy knows our signals and we can work very easily with him. Now go. Someone is waiting to take you back to the base now."

Even before she finished her instructions to Laura, she was already on her way out of the compound: a warrior princess on a tough mission of love. Within ninety minutes, Laura was reporting to Major Grafton and Major Sandwell. She was still with them when the four men who had gone out with Alex and Brixton separately the previous day came back to tell almost the same tale all round. Their news was garbled. They gave an account of how the first set of Marines had been ambushed at the rendezvous and how the other three had come to their rescue. They talked of how Brixton had headed west instead of north as Alex had instructed them. They concluded that Alex must have gone back for Brixton but of that last fact, they were not really sure. "He told us we should rendezvous at Namaksar, but we should head back to the base even if we were not all together. We waited for some time and then headed back as he ordered. We did not go back to look for them. Following orders, sir!"

Major Grafton in his turn filled them in on what Laura had just told him. "We will send out a contingent to Karokh to keep an eye on the compound where they are being held. Keep an eye on any other movements around there as well. Il Dhost has asked that we make a move after twenty-four hours unless we receive a signal otherwise. We will humor Il Dhost as an ally. Nevertheless, we shall send for men from the fort and Qandahar just in case. Is that clear?"

The men saluted and answered, "Yes sir!"

Major Grafton dismissed three of them but asked Randy to wait behind. "Il Dhost has asked that you be part of this operation since you understand their signals. They feel they can work with you. Are you clear on what is expected of you?"

"Yes sir" he answered, really understanding.

"Okay. Handpick the men for this assignment. Report here to me in the next one hour."

Randy saluted and left. Major Grafton felt suddenly old and weary. He went to sit behind his desk carrying his head in his hands as if he was supporting the weight of the world. He dismissed Laura with, "We have done what we can for now. Just go and tell your husband that we need prayers for a miracle pronto."

Laura left to do just that. Major Sandwell had not said a single word. This was as good a lesson as any on what he was to expect when he came fully into his command. It had now become a matter of just a few weeks.

There was no reason to expect any mercy from the Taliban, nor for help to arrive soon. Alex only hoped his men all got away safely. He also hoped that he and Brixton would die sooner rather than later. As time passed, Brixton's breathing became more labored. Sometimes it was as if he had stopped breathing altogether. There was no more water to give him, and he had apparently become unconscious since his last exchange with Alex. Alex crawled to the door to see if he could get some help. It was locked. The room grew chillier in the night cold. He was grateful for little things like the articles of his clothing which were not taken away. His army socks kept his feet warm at least. He was also grateful for the moonlight which crept through the high narrow window from time to time.

Weak from thirst and loss of blood, he slipped in and out of consciousness throughout the night. When the first fingers of dawn lightened the sky, he came fully awake and was briefly disoriented. And then he remembered. Two of them were prisoners of the Taliban! He did not hear Brixton's tortured breathing anymore. He glanced across the room and saw that the hulk of his colleague's form was still there. He crawled over and confirmed that he was indeed dead and grown stiff. "Poor chap" Alex said out loud, "What a way to go! Your own battle in Afghanistan is over even before it has begun."

Alex knew that his own death would soon follow. He went back to his own side of the room, lay back down and thought of all those who were dear to him and would miss him when he was gone. "All said and done Lord, I have had it good in this life. I know I have a welcoming committee in the world to come and I am thankful." He began to think of how it would be to reunite with those who had died before him: his sister, his grandparents, some of his army buddies, Jesus Christ Himself… Maybe dying was not such a bad bargain after all.

He tested his ankles again by gingerly rising to his feet. They were still very painful and stiff but seemed better than the previous day. He rubbed himself all over trying to get rid of some of the cold. Gingerly he tried to lift his wounded shoulder. It was still very sore and painful. He would have liked to do some exercises just to keep himself warm but the only mercy he could pray for was that they would kill him very quickly and very soon. He tried to think of what he would have done if he was in his enemy's shoes. It was not practicable. The American army tried to follow the stipulations of the Geneva Convention. He would have to think like the Taliban. If they left him as he was, in a few more hours he would become delirious. He would start spitting out solicited and unsolicited information. And Alex was a real repository of information. He was United States Marine intelligence. He was privy to the workings of the Il Dhost group and other such internal allies. He even knew enough that could really damage the network of the underground church in Afghanistan. He found a new focus for his prayers, "Lord, please protect all the intelligence I'm carrying."

He was still praying along such lines when they came for him. The door opened abruptly. Two men came in. They first glanced at Brixton and surmised that he was long dead. They came to Alex and told him in precise Dari to stand up and put on his boots. He tried to stand but he collapsed again in pain. Sitting, he tried to pull on his boots, but his ankles were too swollen. He could not force them into the boots. The men yanked off his army socks and tried to pull on the boots for him. It did not work. Someone yelled from outside for them to hurry up. Suddenly abandoning the boots, they grabbed Alex between them and hurried out. Alex had just the presence of mind to grab his socks as they left. They went into another room in the compound; descended some stairs and went into an underground tunnel.

Over their heads, Il Dhost held a quick consultation with Randy. "I think they spotted you. They will try to flee. That house has a secret tunnel, but my advice is that you should not try to follow them through it. Your men might try to storm the compound. Maybe you will find some clues and evidence. However, I think they are gone. Me and My people will try to find out where they will surface. Lateef here will let me know what you find but we must leave now. Godspeed." She turned and rode away.

The Marines stormed the compound. They found no one in it except the corpse of Lieutenant John Brixton. Here was one of those heroes whose careers ended at Afghanistan, another war statistic. They also found Alex's boots but did not find Alex himself. They searched the compound but did not discover the secret passage. Lateef knew where it was, but he had not gone in with them. He would not have shown it to them even if he had. He knew that to follow men retreating through such a tunnel was to court death. As the people carrying Brixton's body back to the base were just arriving at Farah, Lateef was just catching up with, and reporting to Il Dhost that Alex was probably still alive but in the clutches of the Taliban.

Zohra nodded grimly. It would appear so. They were watching one of the known exits from the secret passage. They seemed to be in luck. There were men there, apparently celebrating some sort of victory. Alex was not visible among them but that could have any number of connotations. If he was still alive, he might not be so for much longer. Any sudden moves to rescue him might cause the Taliban to kill him sooner. They had had him long enough. If they had been pumping him for information, there was probably little they did not know already. There was no hurry therefore if this was what his rescuers were trying to prevent. Her heart told her to storm the camp, get her husband and go as fast and as far away as possible but she let her head rule. Depending on how much he had told them, they might have to totally reorganize their network but that could wait until later. For the moment, "Patience" was the name of the game. Runners brought reports from other possible exits from the secret tunnel. Zohra became totally convinced they were watching the right one.

Alex held. They gave him sugared tea and tried to make him talk but he was too weak. He showed them his wounded shoulder and ankles. They were not sympathetic. However, someone spiked his tea with opium. He slept off, and he slept for too long. This had not been part of their plans.

If they had moved that day, Il Dhost might have got them. However, because Alex was too sick to move, they delayed for two whole days more. When they finally moved, it was by truck. Zohra saw Alex brought out by two men and loaded onto the truck. By sheer will alone, she made her men hold back from attacking. They were still at a big disadvantage and on unfamiliar grounds. Instead, she sent heralds along the way to find out where the truck was headed.

The Americans had been thrown off track. They were searching for their quarry far to the northwest of where he really was. They had lost all contact with Il Dhost and did not know how to reconnect. Il Dhost had also made no efforts to contact them. Major Grafton tried to get Laura to physically go to their base, but she was not sure of how to reach them without a guide. They used a drop box in a teashop at Farah but there was no answer for one whole week. Eventually Nazo sent a message to Laura which said, "The camel is still in heat. It has not been received by the merchant." Laura understood this to mean that Alex was alive but still with the Taliban. Major Grafton agreed. From the message he could only conclude that Il Dhost knew where Alex was being held but was not willing to share the information.

Zohra and her group followed patiently. They sent out spies among the Taliban. Alex was apparently too sick to talk and therefore had not yet been interrogated. If he was that sick, he might be nearly dead. Zohra's heart bled for him, yet she and her people patiently waited. The right opportunity had not presented itself.

And then the Taliban made their first mistake. They moved Alex to Qandahar! Their thinking was along the line that the best way to hide a needle was in a haystack! Besides, they reasoned, if the army knew that Alex was nearby, all the Taliban had to do was watch out for the movements of the army. They had this covered also. In a manner of speaking, they relaxed their vigilance and grew careless.

What they had not covered was the movement of other insurgents. They had reckoned without Il Dhost.

One day, a man went into the Taliban stronghold at Qandahar. "I hear I am to take a look at the pig's wound." He spoke in conversational Dari to the guards, denigrating Alex as an unbelieving Moslem.

They let him in to see the prisoner. Inasmuch as they were not suspicious of him, two guards still went along to keep an eye on the proceedings. He casually noted the number of people in the compound and their dispositions. He saw those who were on guard; and those who were currently not on active duty. He took note of the serving women. Alex was in a locked room off the main courtyard where some men were gathered. The portion of the compound where the women lived and worked was secluded. There was a four-story tenement building overlooking this area. Its windows were supposed to be tightly closed at all times. He perched his doctor's bag on the ledge of the narrow window of Alex's room facing these shut windows. He then arranged some vials and bandages. From the fourth storey of the tenement building, another man with binoculars read off the number and disposition of the people between the entrance, Alex, and where they were currently located.

Under the watchful eyes of the two guards, the "doctor" unwound the rough bandage at Alex's shoulder to check the suppurating wound, going "Tsk! Tsk! Tsk!" As he cleaned and re-bandaged it, three men entered the room, blowing darts into the necks of the guards who simply collapsed to the floor. They blew a dart at Alex too even though he was not conscious. They formed a rough sling with some cotton sheets they had brought with them, and carried him out to the women's section. They lowered him from the wall into the next compound where other hands received him. Within minutes of being visited by the doctor, Alex was in a truck headed to Zaranj. His wife bathed his fevered brow and kissed him over and over.

The next decision was where to get him medical help. At this time, the Taliban was watching all the major hospitals and the approach to all the army bases.

Soon enough they would discover what had happened and would start doing house to house searches for Alex. Unlike the Allied Forces, Zohra did not underestimate her enemies. She preferred to overestimate them.

Alex was too sick to move at one go. Zohra had the truck move along Highway 1, praying no one would stop them. They headed for Kadesh, and got as far as a safe house just north of the town. There, they rested for the day. She sent for her mother. Serisha was the best medical help she knew. She asked her to come with the twins, from whom she had been separated for almost a month. That same night Nazo sent a message to Laura, "It is a very sick camel which the merchant received!"

At the base they rejoiced. Alex was at least among friends.

CHAPTER 17

∞

Alex did not become better. In fact, he seemed to grow worse. Serisha asked for the paraphernalia to set up dextrose in saline drips even though she hated anything to do with needles. Alex was not conscious enough to even be force-fed or to get anything down his throat. They had no idea how long he had been that sick. However, even a layman could see that he was certainly going to die without expert help. Their network had connections with some Afghan doctors who had connections with a foreign Aid organization. These doctors helped them out in difficulties. However, with the recent attack of the Taliban on such foreign personnel, the help of such doctors was more difficult to come by. They had gone even deeper underground, knowing that they were being watched more closely, even as they performed their official duties.

Zohra considered the options that were available to her. She could have him moved to Iran where help was more easily accessible to them. However, there were chances that he would be betrayed as an American soldier. Besides, this particular border was the most difficult to cross illegally. Besides, time was of essence. They could break out a way into one of the army bases, the closest then being the large British base at Lashkar Gah. But the Taliban was very alert and closely watching all the bases. They could also get a message to the army to break through and pick Alex up at a prearranged location if they could safely get him to the said location. This would be bloody and not foolproof, based on the intelligence they had. The final option was to kidnap a good doctor and make him work for them under duress.

Zohra was favoring this last option. They were settling on picking up a particularly good one they knew. He lived close to Farah and worked at the Farah hospital. As they were making arrangements on how to pick up the man, Mansur, one of Zohra's trustees entered the sick room. He requested an urgent consultation. "There's a man here who wishes to let the Il Dhost know that the hounds of war have smelt blood."

"Hmmm" said Zohra. "Are we sure it's a friend?"

"He says he is a friend but that you don't know him. He says he can help us."

"Can we verify his claims?"

"Well, we have seen a few curious faces about. In addition, the villagers say that questions are being asked about this compound."

"I will meet with this friend. You know what to do in case of an invasion?"

Mansur knew the drill. Zohra went to don her Il Dhost costume. She granted a five-minute audience to the friend in a semi-dark room. At the end of that time, she concluded the warning was legitimate.

"So how can you help us?" she asked.

"You have less than hour. I can provide a truck and men. Your own trucks are marked. I might get you as far as Farah. The rest will be up to you."

"I will not be going with you. However, I will entrust the wounded man into your care. You will do well to remember that I do not like to be crossed" she said.

Zohra had a cell phone which she rarely used except for emergencies. She dismissed the man and made use of the phone now. Afterwards, she went in to brief her mother on what to do. Mansur was already on the move. The twins had been taken to another compound by an underground tunnel. She told her mother to go with the twins to Anar Darreh. We shall meet at Farah, God willing."

True to his word, in fifteen minutes flat, the man had a truck in front of the compound. Four men, dressed as Afghan militants and could pass as Taliban soldiers came down. They loaded Alex onto the bed of the truck and drove off. Zohra watched from the shadows while she made a call to Raziq and gave him directions.

She was still there at her observation post about thirty minutes later when another truck with the real Taliban soldiers drove up. They broke into their Kadesh compound. Fifteen minutes later when they came out to report to their leader that the nest was empty, Zohra was still there. They would have discovered the secret passage but would not dare to follow, knowing there could be booby traps. They also did not burn down the compound.

"Did someone warn them?" the leader asked.

"Either that, or another of our units got here first. The villagers dare not betray us, so it was probably the latter. The American army officer may still be in our hands."

They did a half-hearted search of the fields around the compound and then they left. So, their informant had been right. They had got out just in the nick of time. Zohra could only pray that her husband would have a fair chance of survival. She used the cell phone again and then rode off into the dark, headed for Farah.

Life at the base had gone on as near normal as it could with the pall of Alex's continued disappearance still hanging over them. With him gone, his work was severely hampered. Nevertheless, his men continued the best they could. It was now definitely confirmed that the whole squad would be moving in August. Major Grafton would fully hand over by September and then also leave. In the meantime, he still continued to run the base jointly with Major Sandwell. They still entertained the few civilians that came their way. This particular day, Laura had been mandated to prepare the room known as her room. A visiting member of the British nobility had a fancy to see "A bit of the Afghan countryside" before returning to Britain. The

Americans had undertaken to host him at the base. Laura was just airing out the room and putting finishing touches to the decor.

She had almost finished when she looked out of the window and had an immediate Déjà-vu! It was just like in her first week in Afghanistan. Riding furiously towards the gate was a lone horseman. Hard on the heels of that first horseman was another one. He did not seem to be in pursuit of the first. However, soon after the first two horsemen turned the bend riding hard for the gate, six more horsemen came into view, obviously hard in pursuit.

Just like that other time too, the sentries at the gate shouted at the horsemen in four different languages to stop. First, they did so with their voices, and then a bullhorn. The horsemen were shouting something back which the gatemen were not hearing nor responding to. In the next minute the gate mechanism would be activated. Laura knew the drill very well by now.

But there were differences from the last time too. There was that second horse. It rode in a zigzag fashion as if trying to cover the back of the first horseman. The lead horseman had something loaded onto the horse in front of him which hampered his speed. Having been in Afghanistan long enough, even Laura knew that this could be a bomb. As they came round the last bend and rode hard for the gate, the lead horseman took a hold of his turban and started yanking while still managing to hold onto the reins of the horse and the tottering form in front. As he yanked, it suddenly became obvious that this was not a horseman but a horsewoman. Her brownish red hair tumbled free and flew behind her like a banner. Immediately the sentries recognized Zohra. Il Dhost had become fully unmasked to both friends and foes at the same moment. Fortunately, she was not wearing the beard disguise which Alex had given her as a wedding present that day or her unmasking. That would have been more terrible, given the circumstances.

The sentries at the gate stopped trying to stop her. They moved to help her instead. At the same time they also worked to stop the already descending gate.

The six horsemen behind kept firing at them. The sentries on top of the ramparts returned fire. As the last time, Laura dashed down the stairs, determined to do something to help, not even thinking of her baby bump. By the time she got there, Tim was again already there. Zohra had managed to dash in with her load which turned out to be the unconscious form of Alex. Tim reached out to pull the second horseman who had fallen from his dying horse. He had just succeeded in pulling him into the compound when the gate went home with a crunch. Tim's left leg, from just below the knee, was left on the other side of the gate.

Laura saw it all. There was no time to even scream. Blood was everywhere. All eight horses lay dead or dying. All the six pursuers were dead. It would probably have counted as yet another Allied Forces military overkill. The difference was that those who had died all had guns, and had actively been shooting them. The second horseman had received several gunshot wounds. He was bleeding from all of them. Zohra had taken two shots to her back and was also bleeding profusely. Alex had taken two to his legs. The stump of Tim's severed leg was also bleeding.

The base medical team arrived on the double. Laura followed them to the medical centre. The Protector died almost immediately. He had turned to Zohra and said, "My debts are repaid. I thank you. I go to the Christian God now." He had then simply closed his eyes and died.

With the limited equipment they had, they labored over Zohra, Alex, and Tim. The team was amazing. Major Grafton signalled for a helicopter that could take them out, but Qandahar was in turmoil from a Taliban uprising. Kabul was in turmoil from the aftermath of an earthquake. Nothing could be sent to Farah, not helicopter, not equipment, not personnel. They bandaged Tim's stump and put the severed leg on ice. Forty-eight hours later, they were told they might as well bury it since it would not take if reattached. Later, he would tell Laura, "A part of me will always literally remain in Afghanistan. Nevertheless, I thank God it was not the whole of me."

Alex and Zohra had lost so much blood but the men at the base were ready to donate as much as would be needed to keep them alive. The medical team did as much limited surgery as they could to save Zohra. Both of her lungs were punctured but they put tubes into her chest. After two days, she was able to breathe on her own again. She lived but she had other very severe injuries. Her left kidney was shot to pieces. Patchwork on her intestines meant she would be on liquid diet for some time. The most serious injuries were to her spine. They shook their heads sadly. If she lived, she might never be able to stand on her feet nor walk again. She would never be able to ever ride a horse, ever again! She would be paralysed from the chest down.

When she had recovered enough, Majors Grafton and Sandwell debriefed her themselves in the presence of Laura as a witness. Zohra told them that the dead man was Neem Omatullah. He was a former Taliban leader with his stronghold near Zaranj. "He believed I spared his life once and therefore he owed that life to me. As a consequence of this event, he became a Christian secretly. He became a double agent, as your people would say. He found out that the Taliban had located our safe house at Kadesh. He came to warn me just about half an hour before they came for us. "He volunteered his men and his truck to transport Alex to Farah. All of our own trucks were already marked as targets by the Taliban. We tried to get a message to any of your drops, but they are all being watched by the Taliban. What was I to do? Alex was getting worse. The noose was tightening about us. Omatullah came up with this idea of a Death Ride. This was the only way to minimize bloodshed. "Now that I am unmasked, perhaps they will leave my outfit alone and give us some breathing space."

The two Commanding Officers reviewed their outfit's reaction to the situation at hand, and the intelligence they had gathered from her. They agreed that even using a sniper team would not have had much advantage. Other means were already being severely criticized by human rights groups all over the world, especially back home. Again, this was Afghanistan. They did not know for sure where Alex was.

Amidst other factors, any other action on their part was very much like flying blind in a storm. Higher authorities could not have taken a better decision.

Major Sandwell was charmed by the brave young woman, even before he heard the legends of Il Dhost being noised about by the men. They were all genuinely surprised that Il Dhost was not only a woman, but their very own Zohra! They were all very proud of being associated with her. It can also safely be said that Major Sandwell's philosophies about warfare in general, and Afghanistan's in particular were positively changed by this situation., He was duly amazed by the singular event of that Death Ride.

As soon as Zohra became well enough, she longed for her babies. There was no way to get them to her or her to them. News of what had happened at the gate that morning had gone far and wide in no time at all. There were many garbled versions of it which reached the Taliban camps, the Il Dhost camps, and as far away as many remote Afghan hamlets. Some claimed that Il Dhost was dead. Some claimed he had mystically vanished. One particular version said that he had suddenly been spared death by transforming into a woman. Even the Allied forces never heard the plain truth as it was. They too got what must be admitted was an embellished version of the real events from the reports sent in by the Farah base.

With the loss of six expert gunfighters, and the apparent betrayal by a top gun like Omatullah, the Taliban was lying low for some time. There was relative peace as they tried to reorganize. Anxious for real news, Serisha uncharacteristically came to the base eight days after the Death Ride to see what was going on for herself. She was accompanied by Siddiq and the twins in a sedate donkey ride. It was totally different from the mad and desperate dash of their parents a few days before. She announced that she could stay for only two hours. She said, "Nazo might go into labor any time now and I need to be there".

Flat on her back, Zohra opened her arms, hugging her mother and babies at the same time. She kissed and cried over them. She was too weak for the boisterous eight-month-olds however. After a while, she indicated they should be taken away. Laura was only too glad to comply. She took them to their quarters to help cheer Tim up.

Alone with her mother, Zohra said, "I'm dying Madaar."

"Why do you say that?" asked Serisha.

"Last night in a dream, I saw Father and Alex. Three of us were all very happy together."

"Your father is dead, but Alex is still alive. It was just a dream. It could mean anything."

"I know what it means Madaar. You know it too. I don't mind dying Madaar. It has been a good life. Imagine, if I live, I may never walk or ride again. Who will then be carrying me about?" she asked lightly, trying to lighten the mood.

"You don't know that, for sure" Serisha answered. She was not amused at all. "They don't know for sure yet that you will never walk nor ride again. Besides, new treatments are coming up every day. Even if it comes to that, many of us are willing to have the honor of carrying you around. I will be there for you, Zohra."

"I know Madaar, I know but I don't think dying at this time would be that bad an idea. Me and Alex always said we would maximally enjoy every moment God gave us. He has given us so many joyful moments, and so much more besides. These last months of my life have been glorious. God has been good to me Madaar." She paused for some time and then said, "Please Madaar, if I die, let the twins be taken to their father's people. Alex's parents have nobody else left."

By now Serisha was weeping softly. In her heart, she knew Zohra was stating the bare facts. To acknowledge it would mean to give up, but to give up what? Like Zohra said, she had lived such a good life. She had made such an impact that people five times her age had not come close to making. Legend has it that people like her never lived for long anyway. They passed through the earth hurriedly, dabbing it with blessings as they passed. Her less than two years' marriage to Alex had been like icing on what had been the cake of her life. It would not be like the last time when she had gone missing. This death would be final but also peaceful because those she would leave behind would have closure. Come to think of it, she might have died during one of her campaigns and they might not have known where her corpse was. At last, Serisha sighed and said, "I will miss you so much Zohra."

"Yes, but I will be looking at you from heaven. I will still be with you Madaar and you will know where I am. Be happy for me that I am going this way." She paused to take some water. She had remained weak and feverish despite all the medical team was doing. I know you will look after Yelda. Tell Nazo and Raziq that the work must go on. God is counting on us." She kept quiet for a long time. Serisha thought she had fallen asleep, but she stirred again. "You must send our treasure box to Laura", she said. "She will keep it for the twins."

The treasure box was a collection of odds and ends Zohra and Alex had been keeping. They were memorabilia they planned to share with their children when they grew up. It did not weigh up to five pounds but everything inside that box had a special meaning. Alex and Zohra had told stories about each of them in the video diary. By the time Serisha's stipulated two hours were up, Zohra was rambling about the happy times she had growing up, and afterwards. She made her mother cry and laugh by turns. Hours passed. Serisha forgot all about leaving. When Zohra eventually fell asleep, Serisha kept holding onto her hands. She stayed this way through the night. She refused all the refreshments which Laura and every other concerned person pressed on her. Nobody saw her getting up, even to stretch or go to the bathroom.

The next morning, when the medical orderlies came to check on her, Zohra was dead. She had been dead for a few hours. They disentangled her fingers from Serisha's and tried to tell her so. Serisha simply nodded. She had probably known the moment it happened. Other than her swollen eyes, she was totally composed. She asked for help so that Zohra's corpse could be transported to Anar Darreh and buried in her ancestral home. Major Grafton was only too glad to comply.

Before she left, she went to the still unconscious form of Alex. She bent over and kissed him on the lips. "Khoda Hafiz (Farewell) from Zohra to you, my son. You have been a very good son to me. God keep you in His love" she said. She asked to see the twins one more time. They were still asleep in Tim and Laura's quarters. She kissed them lightly so she would not waken them. When Laura asked if she should get them ready to go with her, Serisha replied "Zohra wants them to grow up with their father's people. I will miss them terribly. I will miss them all. However, they must have what is best for them. If you ever find a way, please send me pictures of them as they grow." Laura promised. "Zohra asked me to send their box of treasures for you to keep for the twins until they have grown. I know you will tell them all the stories there are to tell."

"I will," Laura promised. On an impulse she asked, "Please also include the last address you had for your other children in Canada. They are family too."

"That is very kind of you. I also thank God you came into my life" Serisha answered. She embraced Laura tightly, and then prayed for her and Tim. She asked for God's blessings upon them.

Finally, she left the army base to go to bury her valiant warrior daughter.

CHAPTER 18

―― ∞ ――

The return of Alex had caused some elation and an air of celebration at the base despite the attendant incidents. Zohra's death cast a pall on everyone again. The visiting nobleman could not have known this, not having known the base any other way. He did remark afterwards though, that this group of Americans was less ebullient than any others he had ever known.

Alex was not showing any signs of improvement. Worried, the medical team sent again for help. A helicopter could not be sent to move him. Instead three medical personnel came from Qandahar by jeep to assess him. "I don't know how he has hung unto life" the main man said after assessing him. "His kidneys have failed. His liver has failed. It is only a matter of time before his heart fails too. This is practically a dead man. He will never wake up from this coma." The man was not being callous, only stating the facts. "The only help we can give him now is an opportunity to die at home. However, I would not call this an emergency which requires calling a red alert. We'd like to make evacuating him a priority but there are so many other priorities ahead of him."

What he said made total sense. The friends of the sick man nodded grimly. They knew that much, being seasoned and practical. Nevertheless, this did not mean they could not hope. They clung onto hope anyway. It costs nothing to hope. They kept supporting him the best way they knew how. They continued to give him intravenous fluids, did parenteral feeding, gave him oxygen by facemask, and so on. Nonetheless, Alex surprised everyone! The night of the verdict, there was a sudden shout of "Zohra!" from his bed. Startled, the orderly on night shift went closer to see. Alex's eyes were wide open and clear. The oxygen mask had slipped from his face. In its place he was wearing a grin. "I'm very sorry" Alex said. "I did not mean to say that aloud. It was just part of a dream."

The orderly was not listening anymore. He had run to get his superiors. The team from Qandahar was still around. "I never!" exclaimed the man who had been spitting out terrible prognoses the day before. "Miracles happen. This is certainly one of them. We will see how he is by morning."

The next morning, Alex was not only still awake but was fully lucid. He was well oriented in person and place, if not in time. He asked what happened and was filled in on the details. He on his part filled in the missing parts, especially regarding Lieutenant Brixton's death. He was told about Zohra. Alex nodded gravely and said nothing else. It was as if the news was not unexpected.

"He's still in shock" pronounced Major Sandwell. "He's yet to take it in fully."

The whole base went into a celebratory mode. Although he was still very weak and confined to bed with broken legs and other factors, he seemed to abhor sleep. He would sleep for a short period and then wake up wanting to talk. He asked constantly for Tim, who was still trying to get used to walking with crutches. The chaplain asked for a room close to the medical ward so he would not have to keep negotiating the stairs. Tim told him that his twins were there at the base being cared for by Laura. Alex asked to see them at once. The twins were glad to see him too but they kept pulling at the wires and tubes which still sustained him. The medical team thought it best not to bring them for prolonged periods anymore.

The third morning after his miraculous awakening, he sent for Laura. "You will soon be going back home" he began.

"Oh yes," Laura agreed laughing, "in just a matter of two weeks. Aren't you looking forward to it?"

"I will not be going with you Laura, at least not like this."

"Of course, you will go in the ambulance plane while the rest of us will come with the regular transport. You lucky man! Maybe I will hitch a ride with you."

"No Laura, I will be going back in a box. I will be dead!"

"If you were going to die Alex, you should have done so a month, two weeks, or even three days ago. Now that you are improving, why do you say you will die? We are all so hopeful."

"Dear Laura. You never found it easy to lose an argument but listen to me now. I know I will die soon. It is probably better this way. When we sing that God moves in mysterious ways to perform His wonders, we never consider that death and dying could actually be wonderful blessings. I've been thinking about it, so you know I am qualified to speak of these things. "Take me and Zohra for instance, is it not better to die and be together than the long separations which would have been occasioned by my postings or by her calling? Think of all the different aspects of our dilemma including where our children should grow up if we were both alive and living. God had a perfectly good plan. I am so glad it includes my dying now. I now understand what Allison was trying to tell me. That seems like only yesterday now."

Laura began to weep. "Oh Laura, weep a bit but listen, you should be glad for me if you can really see it. I have a favor to ask of you though... our babies, please make sure they get to my parents."

"I already promised Zohra that. She asked it specifically of Serisha."

"Good. Serisha is a wonderful saint. You must tell her so for me. There is a box of treasures which we kept."

"I have it too. Serisha sent it for me to keep in trust for the twins."

"Ah, all seems settled then. Please go through my personal belongings with Tim. I would rather you did that than anyone else. You will decide what to keep for my parents, and what to keep for DH and Dawn. Now, if you can compose yourself, I will want you to write to my parents on my behalf."

"I know" said Laura, brightening "why don't we do a video? Roy and Libby will like that very much. I know you wouldn't want to speak with them on Skype as you are now but if they got a video, I know it will greatly comfort them."

Alex agreed. Laura set it all up. The twins were brought to be part of it. However, they became restless a few minutes into the first session and had to be taken away again. Alex talked to his parents about his love for his job and his country. He talked of his love for the Afghans, and of a particular Afghan. He talked about his relationship with God, and the fact that he was not afraid, but rather glad to be dying. "I know I am living on this earth on borrowed time right now. Nevertheless, God must have granted me this chance for a purpose. If this message brings you comfort after I am gone, then I have not wasted this unique opportunity."

About the twins he said, "Please accept them as a gift. They are not meant to be burdens in your old age but blessings. I know by firsthand experience what wonderful parents they will be getting. I was there before them. I know only one other person on this earth who could possibly love them as much as you would. Please also accept her great sacrifice as another big gift from their other Grandma."

Taping it, Laura wept and laughed by turns. They took breaks in between sections whenever Alex proclaimed himself too tired to continue. He also made a short video for Serisha. He thanked her for having been a wonderful mother, and for letting his parents have the children. "…Life is so large, and the world has become so small, Madaar. Please find a way to still be in their lives for my sake and for Zohra's. I know it is never easy for parents to bury their children. I watched mine bury their daughter. I know God is your strength. Thank God for the life we lived and the death we are dying. Just hang in there."

Four nights after he began the video, he slipped into coma again. Two days later, he was dead. The base was not as sad as it would have been. Those ten days of borrowed life he had, he spent saying goodbye properly. Giving everyone a proper closure was so worthwhile. If only all deaths were like this.

Laura and Tim went through his personal effects as he had requested. They found the letters he had been writing to Libby, the video diary he had been keeping, and a lot of other effects which would make meaning to his parents, and later on to his children. They saved them all and added them to their special charge.

Under normal circumstances, the army would have sent a telegram informing his next of kin about his dying on active duty. Laura begged Major Grafton to allow her to personally carry the news to his parents, and he agreed. They had begun to wind down the base and to evacuate to the army fort at Farah even before Alex died. Laura, pregnant; and Tim, an amputee; were allowed to go in the ambulance plane with other such medically incapacitated people. Their parting from the rest of the men was very emotional. "We might never meet together again like this", Major Grafton said. "However, you have touched all our lives, Tim and Laura." The big, strong American marines all wept unashamedly. They asked her to be sure to post baby pictures on their website.

Three days after they left, all the others also left in trucks in what was like a victory parade through the town. They had made many friends among the natives. This was the end of an era for them. Major Grafton went on to Qandahar to complete his reports before going home for a well-deserved vacation. Major Sandwell decided he would need a little more organization before taking over the base and moving in his own men.

The base became an empty shell, a ghost town which missed her inhabitants. That night, the Taliban, having reorganized, decided it was time to exact revenge for all their recent humiliations. In a well-coordinated attack, they set off three bombs to go off simultaneously at the base. The soldiers were far away but a gang of village boys, seeing them go had gone into the compound to see if there were any leftovers to scavenge. They dared themselves to stay and sleep in the compound. They were just boys being innocently mischievous as boys are wont to be all over the world. Later, when it was discovered that those boys had died in the bombing, the Taliban blamed it on the allies. The Allied soldiers blamed themselves for not having locked the compound more securely. It was noted as yet another civilian casualty of that momentous year in Afghanistan.

EPILOGUE

From her phone call, Laura knew the Pearsons would be home. Of course, they would be. For one, they had rarely gone out since Allison died about five years before. They were wonderful people. Nevertheless, grief left a lot of wonderful people irretrievably broken. Their friends, although well-meaning, hardly knew how to break through the fragile shell they built around themselves. Many times, rather than endure the awkwardness around them, many dropped them altogether and let them cope the best they could. The problem was not with Libby and Roy; it was with how people felt around them.

Laura had debated hard and long over whether to let them know they were coming or just to drop in on them unannounced. At last, she felt it was only fair that she gave them fair warning. There was the fact that her even contacting them would awaken nostalgia of the days when they had all been younger, the children playing together. It would remind them of the last days and weeks she had come to spend with Allison. Frankly, she had not really kept in touch with them except by proxy through Alex while at Afghanistan. They knew she had started working at the same place as Alex in the past one year but that was about all. Coming to them suddenly with the news she bore was enough to put anyone to the test. It could break them all over again, maybe even kill them. Nevertheless, she had promised Major Grafton, and a promise was a promise even, or perhaps especially when, it was hard to keep.

Laura drove. Tim had not yet had time to get used to the special disability vehicle which the army provided for him. He was getting better at it every day, nonetheless. They left New York City at the crack of dawn, hoping not to arrive too early. So far, they were making good time. Between 9.30 and 10.00 a.m. had been their target. At the backseat, DH and Dawn slept like only nine-month-old babies could. Fed, dry, and lulled by the motion of the car, they looked nothing like the very active babies they really were. They did not seem to mind the different caregivers who had nursed them over the past few weeks. They were content to smile at friendly faces, assert their rights when necessary, and enjoy the spotlight whenever it was focused on them.

As she drove through town and approached the familiar suburbs, memories assailed Laura. There was the apartment complex which had been under construction so many years ago, now fully developed, occupied, and looking very much lived in. There was the Starbucks and the Subway facing each other across the street like angry competitors. They rounded the Junior High school where she had attended with Allison while worshipping Allison's older brother from afar. At the sizeable park, families still came to play with their babies and their pets on a sunny day like this. Finally, they came to the older single unit family homes. Her heartbeat quickened. Her palms became clammy on the steering wheel. She trembled a bit. Reaching over, Tim squeezed her left shoulder. He draped his arm across her shoulder comfortingly. He had an uncanny way of knowing when she needed reassurance and he always knew the right things to do or say. "They will be thrilled and comforted" he said.

That was just Tim. Some other person might have said something about her being okay or the situation being okay. What bothered her most now was not about her being okay. What bothered her was how Libby and Roy would receive her dual duties and responsibilities at that moment. Of course, she knew she was doing the right thing, but would they be okay with it?

There at the corner was the house where her family had lived for twelve of her formative years. A small boy, of preschool age played on the lawn while his mother or caregiver raked the lawn. Was that the mother, the sister, the aunt or even a non-relative, maybe a hired nanny or even just a neighbor? Who knows? It could be any of those or none of those. However, she was someone who cared very much for the little boy, and was looking out for his wellbeing. Suddenly the thought strangely cheered Laura. What a child really needed in order to thrive well was a concerned adult who cared very much for his or her wellbeing, whether in the United States, in Afghanistan, or in any part of the world for that matter. It was a cheering thought. It came just on time. In the next minute, they rounded the bend and there was the Pearsons' house. Laura drove up the driveway. Before the car came to a complete stop, the door burst open. Libby and Roy spilled onto the lawn as if they had been waiting at the windows as indeed, they had, for the last half hour.

Laura stepped out, her big belly preceding her. Immediately, Libby wrapped her in a big hug, tears running down her face. "You came! You came!" she exclaimed over and over.

Roy managed to get in a hug at last. "Of course, she came. I told you she would come."

Laura returned the hugs. Tears were running unchecked down her own face too but with a puzzled look she asked, "Did you think I wasn't coming? I promised you I would."

"Libby had this crazy feeling something would happen to prevent your coming" Roy replied. "Truthfully, so did I. We've had this terrible feeling of gloom over the past few days. Suddenly it was as if everything was not all right."

"It was just like in the few days before Allison was diagnosed" Libby elaborated, "But you're here now, you came."

She beamed at Laura through her tears. Unashamedly she ran her right hand over Laura's big tummy even as she continued to hug her with her left. "Tell me Alex is responsible for this," she said, smiling. "His letters had so much about you in it. He kept hinting at things in his letters which were not very clear. Tell me he sent you home for us to look after."

Laura cleared her throat in embarrassment. By now Tim had managed to get out of the car. He was leaning on his cane unacknowledged. He now hobbled round to the side where the others had been standing. Laura linked her arm through his. "Roy, Libby, please meet Tim Oswald. Tim is my husband. He is responsible for this." She gestured at her protuberant abdomen. "Tim, Roy and Libby Pearson, Alex's parents, you've met them on Skype."

The smile slipped from Libby's face but ever the polite and well-bred hostess, she extended her hand to shake Tim's. "How do you do Tim?" she said. "Alex talked a lot about you. We have met on Skype so many times. Congratulations."

Roy said "How do you do" as he shook Tim's hand too. He added how glad they were to finally meet him in the flesh. Laura then opened the back of the car, saying, "But, Alex was responsible for these."

First, she unstrapped DH and handed him over to Libby who was nearer, and then Dawn to Roy. This set an enduring precedence. DH always stuck by Libby, and Dawn stuck by Roy. As if on cue, the twins woke up. They stared at their grandparents with fearless blue eyes, so like their dad's. Libby started weeping again. Roy had tears in his eyes which he was manfully struggling not to let go. Laura was still openly in tears. Even Tim caught a sob. He swallowed hard. Only the twins did not weep. They did not smile either. They solemnly studied their grandparents as if to say, "Where have you been all this time?" It was a picture fixed in eternity and there was not even anyone to record it, not even a curious neighbor, not even a passerby. O for Soraya!

"And Alex? What of Alex himself?" Libby finally asked after what seemed like an eternity.

"Alex died in action Libby. He will be brought back next week" Laura answered simply.

It was so plainly put. All her rehearsals of a flowery speech went to the winds. Her delivery sounded just right for the moment. If Libby cried fresh tears, it was not noticeable. She just nodded. Roy nodded too as if they had been anticipating what Laura just confirmed. They had been through a lot already and seemed immune to further distress. This good part of it was so unexpected. They did not even feel they deserved it.

"We felt something like that might have happened" Roy said. "There must be a story behind it."

"Yes, there is" Tim agreed, "or rather there are. It would be nice to tell them sitting down. They are all very long stories."

That was when they realized they had all been standing on the lawn. Laughing with embarrassment, Libby turned and led the way into the house. "We have stuff to be brought out from the car but I guess it could wait till later on" Laura said.

The stuff waited till the babies needed to be changed and fed. The plan was for Tim and Laura to spend the next few days at the Holiday Inn. They would attend Alex's funeral and posthumous decoration, before heading back to Memphis. Roy and Libby would not hear of it. "We have so much room here," she insisted, "besides, we have to hear all the stories so we can tell the twins when they grow up. In any case, we have to plan and decorate the nursery together" she told Laura.

Roy himself had found a son in Tim. They had a lot in common. There was so much to talk about and to plan. There were also reminisces of Alex, what had gone on at the frontlines, what they had faced together, and so on. If only the army had this kind of resource for everyone who was lost at the battlefield, it would have been much easier for bereaved families. The men took their own turns babysitting DH and Dawn when the ladies went on their expeditions. There was almost no time to mourn because there was so much to do. The army had been generous in their allowance to the fallen hero. However, in DH and Dawn, Roy and Libby found a reason to live again. There was no healing balm better than them. Suddenly, they had something to talk to their friends about. They had reason to belong to the society of other parents and grandparents again. It was exhilarating to say the least.

Finally, one day, the thought broke through. "Why don't you both just live here? This is a good town to settle in as any. There are job opportunities. You will watch the twins grow with us. Laura already knows this is a great town for raising a young family."

For Laura, this would be a homecoming, and for Tim? Well, for Tim, this would be like putting down roots. From Afghanistan, they had returned with even much more love than they had invested.

GLOSSARY OF UNFAMILIAR WORDS

Alekheim salaam	Reply to "Salaam Alekheim" Peace be to you too
Attan	A traditional dance done in a circle
Azizam	Darling: a term of endearment
Ba koda	Part of a wedding song (Baada baada elahee mubarak baada; man bat u dada am tawakol ba koda...) meaning: I give you my heart happily; now I leave it to Destiny...
Ben	Co-wives
Bollywood	Indian movie and film industry
Burqa	Body encasement for women
Dhost	Friend
Dhoti	Piece of native dressing worn like a loincloth
Hadith	Islamic traditions that supplement the Quran
Hijab	Truncated body encasement for women
Iddat	Mandatory period of abstinence from sex after divorce, to ensure a woman is not pregnant
Joonam	My love - a term of endearment
Kaffiyeh	Checkered headscarf
Kafir	Islamic unbeliever
Kebob	Skewered meat

Khan	Chief, leader
Khoda Hafiz	Farewell, goodbye
Khoob	Good
Komak	Help
Koh	Mountain
Kuchis	A nomadic tribe that roams the Middle East
Lungee	Headgear, part of Pashtun male traditional dressing
Madaar	Mum, mummy
Madaar Bozorg	Grandmother
Misyar	A contractual marriage (of convenience)
Mujahedeen	Guerilla fighters
Mullah	A Moslem cleric
Mut'ah	A temporary marriage in Islam almost similar to, yet distinct from Misyar
Nowruz	Festival that marks the end of winter/ beginning of spring
Paan	Bread
Pashtun	Major tribe extending from Afghanistan to Pakistan and parts of Iran
Pashtunwali	Tribal Pashtun laws
Salaam	Peace be to you (a greeting much as "Hi")
Sharafat	Honor
Sharia	Islamic laws
Shirineman	Sweetheart, a term of endearment
Shura	Meeting, conference
Zakat	Islamic alms giving

SUGGESTED TOPICS FOR READING GROUPS

There are some interesting concepts mentioned in this book that a Christian should find challenging. Consider:

    A.   These concepts

    B.   The context in which they occurred

    C.   Do you agree with them?

    D.   Why or why not?

    E.   What does the Bible say about it?

    F.   What could have been alternative outcomes given other circumstances.

PEOPLE AND CULTURE

1. Who could argue against God? "Let us live according to the dictates of God" they said. "Let us precisely follow the Holy Book!" (Prologue)

2. What was it Katie had said? Sometimes one needed to take care of another person's needs in order to snap out of one's ruts! (Part 1, Chapter 1)

3. Many times, the allied forces are hard put to draw a line between upholding the native culture of the people, and imposing their own imported western culture.

(Part 1, Chapter 2)

5. We must also aim to go beyond giving them fish, and actually teach them how to fish for themselves. (Part 1, Chapter 2) How can Christians go beyond these mere acts of kindness?

6. Someone asked why the Afghan women were so "Stupidly powerless". (Part 1, Chapter 2) At the end of this book, do you think Afghan women are "stupidly powerless"?

7. What do you think of the place of women in Islam on earth and in the hereafter? Do you think Moslem women also wonder about this?

8. People often have the mistaken belief that the Taliban was a bunch of ignorant, laidback mountain men frozen in the Middle Ages, going about shouting Moslem slogans.

Nothing is farther from the truth than this picture. (Part 2, Chapter 4)

9. "The friends of my enemies are my enemies". (Several places in the book)

PRACTICE OF THE CHRISTIAN FAITH

1. There are times in the army one asks, 'God, where are you?' If one listens, God really answers. (Part 1, Chapter 3)

2. Maybe this was why God sent me to Afghanistan after all. We might be in a position to do the best we ever could in Afghanistan. (Part 2, Chapter 3)

3. What do you think of these expressed views about Christianity?

a) Tim said: "Christianity in the West is so very watered down nowadays it almost makes no sense. Who is to blame for this really? Many young men feel that Islam has more to offer now in terms of giving quality to what one should believe, live for, and even die for. Islam preaches, 'if you really believe, take up your arms and fight a jihad'. Many young people when they come to that spiritual point of seeking who they are and why they are here in this life, weigh between what so-called Christianity allows and what Islam preaches. Whereas Christianity now is a lot of fables like Santa Claus and Halloween, Islam preaches arise, fight, and die for the faith... Serious-minded young people choose the one which gives them a deeper purpose in life. They choose something worth living and dying for. And yet true Christianity is really a call to 'Take up your cross daily, and follow me', for those who really want to believe. It's really a religion of 'live for Christ and die for Christ'." (Part 1, Chapter 3)

b) Greta said: "I never gave much thought to Christianity until we were about to come to Afghanistan, and they started all that brouhaha about not proselytizing, during our briefings. Even then, I didn't think much about it until we were kidnapped... with Christianity being outlawed and everything, I took time to search the internet and read it up." (Part 2, Chapter 8)

c) Zohra said: "Perhaps, it's the challenge of it which keeps us going. We have clear-cut lines and choices. I guess it is not like that in your own part of the world. Here we make decisions knowing we could die for them, or lose everything for them, but we choose to follow Christ anyway. It is infinitely easier, and more exciting to be a Christian here" she said. (Part 3, Chapter 8)

4. Tim understood what she was trying to say but obliged her by arguing the point a bit. "It is easier to be a Christian in our own part of the world. You can read your Bible openly; attend church meetings when you want; and openly share your faith with anyone. In fact, in places like London, you have the Hyde Park Corner where you can set up a soap box and shout your faith to all takers. The same thing could happen at the Times Square in New York..." (Part 3, Chapter 8)

5. The truth of the matter is that in a way we have always been Christians... (Serisha) (Part 3, Chapter 6); Our family has a secret Bible at Farah but it is never read. It is shown to us when we reach twelve years. At this time, we are told how our ancestors were really Christians. We are then sworn to secrecy on it as part of an initiation into adulthood. My rite of passage had taken place the previous year so it was still fresh in my mind. (Zohra). (Part 3, Chapter 8).

What do you think of these secret Christian rites and their implied effectiveness? What do you think of the expression of Moslem faith in the same set of people?

RELATIONSHIPS

1. She had told them once that having one's mate chosen for her was much less tedious than sifting through life to find "The One" (Part 1, Chapter 9)

2. It is said that some hawks mate for life, but O what a dance before they finally get to roost together. (Part 3, Chapter 5)

3. That is the poet in you talking, Preach. I just discovered I am a poet too. I don't know what it is about love that does that to a man. (Part 3, Chapter 10)

4. There was nothing like getting a stallion in heat by constantly throwing a filly before it. (Part 3, Chapter 11)

5. Alex flouted the rules. Do you sympathize with his reasons? The rules permit me to keep a mistress under these circumstances but not a wife. The Bible on the other hand says if I find myself behaving inappropriately towards the lady I am engaged to, I had better marry her. Believe me, it's becoming more and more difficult to behave very properly with Zohra, Preach. I am mere flesh and blood. She is so exquisite, so delectable. What do you say? Should I obey man, or should I obey God, Preach?" (Part 3, Chapter 11)

6. They had developed what they considered their word from God into a motto, "Maximally use every opportunity, and be happy!" (Part 3, Chapter 11)

DEATH AND DYING

1. The Afghan women they had as students had seen enough tragedy and learned to live with it.

They sympathized with Laura and Greta over their grief but knew life had to go on. (Part 2, Chapter 6)

2. That whole family would never be the same again. They had experienced firsthand the dark horrors of all they had been hearing about and thought would never happen

to them. They had lost practically all they held dear up until that very day: materially, morally, and emotionally. In that one night, they had all aged at least twenty years. It would take some time, but they eventually would realize they had not lost everything. Some other more important things were spared them. With time, they gained other things that were even more important yet. (Part 2, Chapter 7)

3. I am sure I have killed my own share of people. However, it is something I try to avoid by all means. My mother compounded something with which we can knock them off for about four to six hours while we make our escape. It doesn't always work because they aim to kill us while we aim to keep them alive. Sometimes too, when they're knocked off some other elements come along to rob or kill them. So, indirectly we killed them anyway. (Part 3, Chapter 8)

4. That was all it took, a little kindness, but it made a deep impression on Omatullah. Sometime in the dim, distant past, someone had told him the story of the Good Samaritan. He had pooh-poohed the story, despising the sucker do-gooder Samaritan. His admiration was for strong men who fished out advantages and knew how to use them. (Part 3, Chapter 14)

5. Maybe dying was not such a bad bargain after all. (Part 3, Chapter 16)

6. When we sing that God moves in mysterious ways to perform His wonders, we never consider that death and dying could actually be wonderful blessings. (Part 3, Chapter 18)

ALSO BY THE SAME AUTHOR

COCKROACHES FOR SALE

The earth is in search of other planets to expand into and calls down a plague on itself which could wipe out the whole world except for a few people, and a few factors…

DUST AND ASHES

What starts as an everyday walk to school turns into a nightmare of kidnap for a group of schoolgirls including some bona fide Christians. Where is God when the righteous suffer anyway?

BEAUTY FOR ASHES

This continues the story begun in Dust and Ashes and also looks at the intrigues of a society which thinks itself safe and untouchable until intimately confronted with what else is out there.

DISGUISED TREASURES

Somewhat concluding the story begun in Dust and Ashes and continued in Beauty for Ashes; this story is also a stand-alone. It illustrates how even though violence is louder than mercy, mercy still triumphs at the end.

Printed by Libri Plureos GmbH in Hamburg, Germany